OSHA and the Politics of Health Regulation

ENVIRONMENT, DEVELOPMENT, AND PUBLIC POLICY

A series of volumes under the general editorship of
Lawrence Susskind, *Massachusetts Institute of Technology, Cambridge, Massachusetts*

PUBLIC POLICY AND SOCIAL SERVICES

Series Editor:
Gary Marx, *Massachusetts Institute of Technology, Cambridge, Massachusetts*

STABILITY AND CHANGE: Innovation in an Educational Context
Sheila Rosenblum and Karen Seashore Louis

FATAL REMEDIES: The Ironies of Social Intervention
Sam D. Sieber

OSHA AND THE POLITICS OF HEALTH REGULATION
David P. McCaffrey

Other subseries:

ENVIRONMENTAL POLICY AND PLANNING
Series Editor:
Lawrence Susskind, *Massachusetts Institute of Technology, Cambridge, Massachusetts*

CITIES AND DEVELOPMENT
Series Editor:
Lloyd Rodwin, *Massachusetts Institute of Technology, Cambridge, Massachusetts*

OSHA and the Politics of Health Regulation

David P. McCaffrey

Graduate School of Public Affairs
State University of New York at Albany
Albany, New York

PLENUM PRESS • NEW YORK AND LONDON

Library of Congress Cataloging in Publication Data

McCaffrey, David P., 1950–
  OSHA and the politics of health regulation.

  (Environment, development, and public policy. Public policy and social services)
  Includes bibliographical references and index.
    1. Industrial hygiene—Government policy—United States. 2. United States. Oc-
  cupational Safety and Health Administration. I. Title. II. Title: O.S.H.A. and the
  politics of health regulation. III. Series.
  HD7654.M385 1982   353.0078′3   82-11201
  ISBN 0-306-41050-8

© 1982 Plenum Press, New York
A Division of Plenum Publishing Corporation
233 Spring Street, New York, N.Y. 10013

Printed in the United States of America

For Albert and Gertrude McCaffrey

Foreword

By way of introduction to this fascinating book, let me highlight two of its many contributions. First, it is a good example of something all too rare in sociology: testing competing general theories. Most of us either try to develop or refine theories about how the social world works, and cite convenient data as support, or we select and collect data that will fit some general theoretical position. In the first case, the data play a subordinate role—bits of evidence for our view of life. In the second, the theory plays a subordinate role—a way to make sense of the social behavior we have observed. McCaffrey's position subsumes these two. He has gathered data on an important social agency, but with an implicit problem in mind: which of the several theories about the social world he was exposed to in graduate school would do the best job of interpreting the data? Or, we might just as well turn it around. In a graduate department such as Sociology at the State University of New York at Stony Brook, there is a lively, never ending debate about the "truth" of competing perspectives on the political and social world. By selecting a data base and remaining alert to the kind of evidence each theory required, McCaffrey circumvented the usual "data for a theory" vs. "a theory for the data" dilemma that most of us live with.

McCaffrey went off to a staff position in the Bureau of Labor Statistics in Washington, D.C., which worked closely with the Occupational Safety and Health Administration (OSHA), to observe first-hand this controversial, burgeoning, headline-grabbing, and quite unprecedented government foray into the regulation of private enterprise. He gathered the kind of data most of us do not know exist—transcripts of obscure meetings with representatives of business and labor, notifications in the Federal Register, copies of the endless series of speeches by officials, "comments" of one agency upon the actions or memos of another, obscure mimeographed reports in great quantity. He then returned to graduate school and posed his central question: What can the first decade's experience of this government agency tell us about our theories of the social and political world? The major theoretical contenders that would seek to explain OSHA's confusing but unmistakable trend of development were conservative pluralism, radical pluralism, a capitalist state theory, and organizational imperatives.

They may sound unfamiliar to you, so let me put them in their more sensible colloquial form. Conservative pluralism says that we have a fairly open society and no group can be disadvantaged for too long. Sooner or later it will gain access to the courts, government agencies, or Congress and redress the inequities. Organized labor and liberals made a case for the safety and health of workers, and OSHA resulted. The play of various interest groups around OSHA—business and labor, primarily—will determine the outcomes. Over time inequities will be reduced (the current popularity of cost–benefit analysis fits with this view since it rationalizes the competition). Radical pluralism (or elite theory) says that workers and other underprivileged groups are bound to struggle against the dominant capitalists, and their struggles will result in some small victories such as OSHA, at least; but it is an uneven struggle and the resources of the capitalists are overwhelming.

A more extreme position on the radical spectrum is that of the "capitalist state." This view would say, in terms of the woman or man in the street, that elites have it all sewed up, and that even the small victories of the workers are nothing more than sops to keep them alive so they can continue to serve the capitalists. The capitalists can't have everybody dying from toxic chemicals, and the ruling class has to prevent the capitalists from gobbling one another up, so some mechanism is needed to preserve order for the sake of the survival of capitalism. The state is such a mechanism, and if something like OSHA comes along you can be sure it is there to serve the long-range interest of capitalists by preventing destructive competition among themselves and the disappearance of worker-consumers.

Finally, there is another widely held view, namely, that any behavior of a bureaucracy reflects the self-serving concerns of the bureaucrats involved. Bureaucrats don't want trouble, and they are not disposed to fight long battles with powerful business interests. They're not very efficient at organizing themselves, and even red tape that goes under such disguises as "extended policy analysis" is in their interest since it allows people to spend time on noncontroversial tasks. We dignify this description by labeling it "organizational imperatives." As McCaffrey makes clear, OSHA has had some successes, and if you are of the radical persuasion they must be considered stunning given the odds against the agency. But as McCaffrey also makes clear, OSHA has had many more failures. And if you are of the conservative pluralist persuasion, you can explain the failures to promulgate more stringent regulations in terms of cost–benefit analysis, or in terms of the extremity of the demands of labor activists within OSHA. McCaffrey patiently describes a number of significant areas that OSHA has been concerned with and gives us a detailed, blow-by-blow account of how some efforts succeeded while others appear to have failed. At each point he stops and asks, which of the theoretical perspectives would be supported by the behavior in question.

It is clear that neither OSHA nor the state in general manages to control many of the competitive excesses of capitalism in any rational way, and capitalists would prefer a much weaker or nonexistent OSHA. So the capitalist state theory receives little support (in the short run at least—note the developments reported in the last two chapters). Explicitly testing this theory has an important virtue, however; by posing an extreme case, McCaffrey is able to highlight the virtues and defects of the other theories much more effectively. Though he does not always distinguish between the conservative and radical branches of pluralism, except implicitly, the radical branch seems to come off best, but—and this is very important—only when it is moderated by the organizational imperative perspective. It is in this complex interweaving of theories that I find the greatest excitement and stimulation from this book. McCaffrey is about as undogmatic as a scholar can be, (until he comes to the current administration, where other issues concern him), and his open-mindedness allows him to play with the intermix of theories in a creative manner. None of them will ever be the same for me again now that I have read this work.

The other virtue of McCaffrey's book that I would like to emphasize is the approach to the topic of regulation. It has been a "hot" topic for some years now, after the great spurt of regulatory activity in the 1960s and early 1970s. We have many institutional histories of regulatory acts and agencies from political scientists, as well as numerous liberal and radical tracts concerning the need for or failure of regulation in myriad areas of life. And most important of all, since they occupy the high ground and receive the bulk of institutional support, we have the reactions of the economists, largely conservative, in the form of cost–benefit analysis, the "impossibility theorem" of Kenneth Arrow, and the mathematical symbols of the deductive logic analysts who would, as was said of Jeremy Bentham, plus or minus us to heaven or hell.

Not much sociological light has been spread in this area, and McCaffrey's book represents a considerable advance. It is not an institutional history, but uses institutional behavior to address some important and competing beliefs that we have about our world. It makes no simple-minded assumptions about "maximizing utilities," and substitutes political realities for cost–benefit analysis. It presents data that pose problems no cost–benefit analysis or formula could possibly cope with, at least as they are currently structured.

For example, it show how the requirement of cost–benefit analysis, so favored by the economists, made it easy for OSHA to weaken the proposed standards regarding cotton dust for the textile workers. OSHA explained that the costs of about 5,000 extra cases of byssinosis—a debilitating lung disease—were "less" than the costs claimed by the manufacturers of compliance with the proposed standards. The benefits of slightly cheaper textiles or slightly higher dividends "exceeded" the cost of lung disease for over 5,000 workers. Thus the requirement of cost–benefit analysis enabled OSHA to avoid an organizationally debilitating battle.

A more striking example of McCaffrey's too implicit raid upon the high ground occupied by the economists occurs in the remarkable Chapter 7. The sister agency and research arm of OSHA, NIOSH (National Institute for Occupational Safety and Health), inadvertently and rather unwisely disclosed that it had identified the names and addresses of at least 74,000 workers who had worked in plants handling carcinogens. About 123,000 other workers would be identified in future studies planned by NIOSH. Should it tell the 197,000 workers that they had been exposed to carcinogens? The answer would seem to be a clear "Yes." In fact to do so is a part of the official mandate of the organization. Once informed, the workers could know that they were at greater risk than the general public and monitor their health more closely, and perhaps cut down on smoking, have frequent examinations, and maybe even seek employment elsewhere if any jobs were available. (The chances of reducing the exposure limit were very slim.) Since OSHA (as revealed in another chapter) had bowed to industry pressure and refused to aggressively pursue the issue of putting warning labels on boxes and drums of toxic chemicals (one argument that industry used was that to mark a substance "Careful, carcinogenic" would scare the workers and possibly result in more accidents because of fright or low morale), many workers were unaware that the materials they were handling were carcinogens. It would be nice, someone suggested, to let them know.

The director of NIOSH, Dr. John Finklea, compiled a shopping list of truly extraordinary objections to any program to notify the 197,000 workers. The workers wouldn't get medical follow-ups because they would be afraid of losing their jobs with the company; there would not be enough health resources in their communities to treat them adequately; they "may become very, very disturbed;" others would "just seek to deny it" so "notification without an effective follow-up system might do more harm than good," and so on. The good doctor did not request funds to carry out a follow-up program, McCaffrey dryly notes, but instead labeled the problem a "major social issue," and major social issues are, as McCaffrey puts it, "not matters one works into this year's plans."

NIOSH admitted in an exhaustive report on the problem that "clearly, workers have the right to know" whether they had been exposed to hazardous substances; "however, this right is linked to a complex series of problems which must be faced and resolved if any worker notification program is to be successful." There were issues of cost–benefit analysis and trade-offs, of "inflationary impacts," and so on. Perhaps the most serious objection of all was that "a notification without counseling and adequate medical examination may prove socially disruptive and lead to an undermining of confidence in government and perhaps also in private industry and even labor unions." The policy paper took great pains to compile an exhaustive list of possible problems, but as McCaffrey notes, it never mentioned the *benefits* of notification.

McCaffrey quite sensibly analyzes this as a problem of organizational defense; for a variety of organizational reasons that he explores, this was a program that NIOSH and OSHA desperately wanted to avoid. But it is also instructive, and worthy of further reflection, that representatives of the steel workers' union pursued the matter in a low-keyed way, exhibiting a striking lack of vigor; liberal senators such as Schweicker and Javits let the matter drop after raising some mild objections; and that business interests had to do little more than lie low, hoping the other shoe would not drop.

This and other cases described by McCaffrey raise the possibility that yet another model might be usefully explored—the one that goes by the dreadful name "hegemony." This is a more sinister variant of the largely exhausted and discredited terms that sociologists have used for generations: "culture" and "belief systems." An analysis emphasizing hegemony would argue that elites have to work to preserve hegemony; premises are always in danger of being undermined or exposed, especially if the confidence in government and private industry and even labor unions might be undermined. There are some things about our social system that elites would prefer not to bring up as issues, and prefer not to confront, because they would destabilize ("prove socially disruptive" the good doctor put it) too much of the system. They might call the elites to account in ways they could not answer. Therefore, the unions, liberal senators, the press, and especially government agencies like OSHA must disregard those cost–benefit terms not admitted to the economic calculus. It is an example of the not-to-be-spoken premise that to be a powerful and productive and expanding nation (the "benefits" counted in the calculus), we must allow some people to be expendable, and above all not stir them into questioning the priorities of the system (since that would be counted as a "cost").

Thus this brief episode in the history of an agency entrusted with the health and safety of workers suggests a larger issue that needs exploring. We are led to it by this carefully reasoned and carefully researched study of the utility of the various social theories we live by.

Charles Perrow
Yale University

Preface

OSHA and the Politics of Health Regulation has two purposes. First, it describes the development of the Occupational Safety and Health Administration's (OSHA's) health regulations from 1971 to 1981. OSHA's best known image in this period was that of aggressive regulator; an organization which exaggerated the benefits of its decisions and was insensitive to their costs. The image justified the Reagan administration's extraordinary efforts to reduce occupational health regulation. The image is also—I think the evidence fairly shows—inaccurate. It is inaccurate because it neglects the network of political and legal constraints checking zealous regulation well before the excesses of the Reagan program.

Second, the book asks how OSHA's experience meshes with three perspectives on government policy. One view—which I will call the pluralist view—suggests that regulation reflects the balance of power among private interest groups. A second—the capitalist State perspective—suggests that regulation primarily modifies the competitive excesses of capitalism, but only enough to assure stable capital accumulation and the survival of the capitalist system. A third perspective—an organizational perspective—focuses on the ways that regulatory policies reflect the organizational properties of the agencies, rather than any sensitivities to interest-group pressures or to decisions' consequences for capitalism.

We project how OSHA would act if it functioned exactly as each perspective suggests, and then compare its behavior to the projections. The book does not "test" the perspectives—no single case could do so. However, I think that it raises some important questions about them.

Two individuals in particular extensively advised and supported this project. Charles Perrow urged me to link the history of OSHA with the broader issues of organizational and political theory, and to write

less like a bureaucrat. Lyle Schauer's knowledge of regulatory organization and governmental processes in general was invaluable; I suspect
that he would also disagree with some of my conclusions.

Mitchell Abolofia, Rose Laub Coser, Mark Granovetter, and Harry
Weiner helpfully commented on an early draft of the manuscript. Gary
Marx's later suggestions were very stimulating and made the final revi-
sion actually enjoyable. Jeanne Libby's suggestions made it readable.

The remaining weaknesses in the book certainly reflect those instances in which I did not take full advantage of the advice of all these
people.

I thank the publishers for permission to reprint certain materials
from the following works:

Accounting for Slower Economic Growth by Edward Denison
(Copyright © 1979 by the Brookings Institution, Washington, D.C.).

Crisis in the Workplace by Nicholas Ashford (Copyright © 1976 by
the MIT Press).

"Industry's Preemptive Strike Against Cancer" by William Reddig,
FORTUNE magazine, February 13, 1978 (Copyright © 1978 by Time,
Inc., all rights reserved).

*9th Annual McGraw-Hill Survey of Investment in Employee Safety and
Health* (Copyright © 1981 by McGraw-Hill Publications Company).

Occupational Safety and Health Reporter (Copyright © 1972 to 1980
by the Bureau of National Affairs, Inc., Washington, D.C.).

Red Tape: Its Origins, Uses, and Abuses by Herbert Kaufman
(Copyright © 1977 by the Brookings Institution, Washington, D.C.).

Stress and Contradiction in Modern Capitalism edited by Leon Lindberg, Claus Offe, and Robert Alford (Copyright © 1975 by D. C. Heath
and Company, Lexington Books, Lexington, Mass.).

"Substantive and Procedural Discretion in Administrative Resolution of Science Policy Questions: Regulating Carcinogens in EPA and
OSHA" by Thomas O. McGarity, *Georgetown Law Journal* (Copyright ©
1979).

The Triumph of Conservatism by Gabriel Kolko (Copyright © 1963 by
The Free Press, A Division of Macmillan Publishing Co., Inc.).

The Zero-Sum Society by Lester Thurow (Copyright © 1980 by Basic
Books, Inc., Publishers, New York).

David McCaffrey

Contents

Perspectives on Government Regulation

The Occupational Safety and Health Act of 1970 mandates that no worker should "suffer material impairment of health or functional capacity" from toxic chemicals in the workplace. In hearings on the Act, individuals from a variety of organizations testified that control of exposure to and monitoring of thousands of substances were necessary for workers' safety. In 1978, one study estimated that occupational exposure to toxic substances accounted for about twenty percent of all cancer cases (Bridbord, Decoufle, Fraumeni, Hoel, Hoover, Rall, Saffiotti, Schneiderman, and Upton, 1978). An industry-commissioned critique of that study by the University of Texas School of Public Health concluded that the estimate was roughly accurate (Stallones and Downs, undated). Yet, only twenty-one chemicals had been completely regulated by 1981. Unions, some academics, and public-interest groups argued persuasively that workers' health had been traded off for business's stability and convenience.

But businesses and a growing number of economists maintained, also persuasively, that OSHA's present regulations had substantially lowered industrial-productivity growth and therefore increased inflation. Edward Denison of the Brookings Institution and the U.S. Department of Commerce suggested that productivity in 1977 was .4 percent lower because of OSHA's regulations, although this estimate included the effects of *safety* as well as health regulations (Denison, 1979: 68; see also MacAvoy, 1979). Both advocates and foes of stringent chemical regulations agreed that OSHA's proposed health standards, if they ever went into effect, would be very costly.

The ten years of experience with regulations clarified the nature of the public health–economic tradeoffs that Congress only vaguely sensed in the late 1960's (Mendeloff, 1979: 20-1). This book discusses how the

1

tradeoffs were made, and what OSHA's experience suggests about the sources, effects, and direction of Federal regulation today.

1.1. VIEWS OF REGULATION

There are certain themes on how regulatory agencies, and perhaps government organizations in general, operate. One body of writings stresses that private-interest-group pressures determine government actions, and discusses how the State reflects the balance of power among interest groups. I will call this perspective *pluralism*. An alternative view suggests that the State is less a reflection of interest-group demands than an autonomous guarantor of a particular class of interests—the interests of capitalism. According to this view, the government often acts against the wishes of dominant private interest groups to assure capitalism's stability. This will be called the *"Capitalist State"* perspective. A third perspective, the *organizational* view, focuses on the organizational tendencies of the government's agencies. It suggests that these tendencies are not determined by private interest-group pressures or autonomous State support of capitalism. Rather, organizations' quests for autonomy, their ways of processing inputs, and the preferences of their leaders and staffs produce government behavior far different from that projected by the pluralist or capitalist State perspectives.

Each of these views organizes government actions around a central concept—interest-group pressure, State support of capitalism, or organizational tendencies, respectively. Analysts usually focus on one and treat the other two as complicating or limiting factors. Pluralists concede that the government acts somewhat independently of interest groups, but still emphasize private pressures when explaining specific government actions (Sakolsky, 1980: 4-5). Capitalist State theorists treat pressure groups and organizational factors as problems for the State, but they are its "problems" precisely because of its hypothesized core function of defending capitalism (Offe, 1975). Organizational theorists treat pressure groups and economic considerations as factors in decisions, but they discuss how organizations refract, ignore, misperceive, or otherwise process these inputs. They concentrate on the impact of organizational processes on government actions.

Yet, one perspective could conceivably make more sense out of what the government does than the others. Analysts compare the value of different perspectives by projecting the behavior of a government agency which acts exactly as a certain view suggests, and then identifying actual historical behavior which is consistent and inconsistent with the three perspectives. This is the method used by Nelson Polsby in comparing what he calls "pluralist" and "stratification" models of power (1963); by Graham Allison in comparing "rational actor," "organizational process," and "bureaucratic politics" models of State action (1971); and by J. Allen Whitt in discussing "pluralist," "elitist," and "class" models of power (1979). This book will assess which of the three perspectives outlined here is best supported by the Occupational Safety and Health Administration's (OSHA's) regulation of toxic substances. It will look for the central forces driving and constraining the agency, and infer what we can expect out of OSHA in the future.

1.1.1. Pluralism

1.1.1.1. "Active" Regulation: The "Interest Groups Run Amok" Theme

There is a new interest in interest groups. An increasingly developed view says that capitalism has serious problems of inflation, unemployment, and energy dependence largely because groups—right and left, community organizations and large corporations—have progressively demanded more from it, and been able to resist actions which are inimical to their interests. Diverse analysts agree on the nature of the condition but evaluate it differently. Some call for tighter restraints on demands in order to ease this "crisis of democracy" (Crozier, Huntington, and Watanuki, 1975). Others welcome "the fiscal crisis of the State" as a step toward socialist planning (O'Conner, 1973).

1.1.1.1a. The Growth of Pressures

The new "crisis" is only the latest stage in the historical expansion of pressures commencing with the labor movement. In the late nineteenth century, Social Darwinism counseled workers to strive individually for success, and to blame or look to no others if they failed. Economic inequality was said to reflect natural distributions of abilities and character—the survival of the fittest.

However, these exhortations could not prevent workers, gathered together in factories and confronted with objectionable conditions, from cooperating to fight common grievances. In 1897 American trade unions had 447,000 members; in 1904, the number had jumped to 2,072,700 (Bendix, 1956: 265). Unions gave businesses considerable trouble. After 1910 or so, a new managerial view arose to cope with the problem. Workers were advised that if they peacefully cooperated with management economic growth would gradually satisfy their material and status wants.

This promise was shaky (Bendix, 1956: Chapter 5); inequalities persisted, and the Great Depression threw millions back into miserable circumstances. The unemployed and industrial workers' movements turned militant once again. Militance forced concessions from business and government—the rights to organize unions and to strike were recognized and legally protected. This formalization of protest defused the labor movement's militance and diminished its impact but, as Frances Fox Piven and Richard Cloward argue, "the victory was worth winning." Real gains were made, and struggle for further gains was legitimized. The history of the civil rights movement and the welfare rights movement parallel that of the labor movement in their early militance and the subsequent formalization and legitimation of demands (Piven and Cloward, 1977).

In the last thirty years, partly as a result of the script written by these movements, special interest groups have multiplied. Lester Thurow writes:

> With the civil rights, poverty, black power, and womens' liberation movements, many of the groups that have in the past absorbed economic losses have become militant. They are no longer willing to accept losses without a political fight. The success of their militancy and civil disobedience sets an example that spreads to other groups representing the environment, neighborhoods, and regions (1980: 12-3).

The British economist Joseph Schumpeter forecast in 1942 that such groups would ravage capitalism. Further, "professional" social critics would aid and encourage them in this. Capitalism's support of education and rational organization produced, along with technically useful devices, a highly critical atmosphere. Intellectual critics had an easy target in capitalism's systemic limits—its inequality, for example—and an accessible forum in the expanding print media. What Schumpeter wrote of the labor movement applies to other movements as well—that while the labor movement was not the creation of intellectuals, "intellectuals invaded labor politics . . . they verbalized the movement, supplied theories and slogans for it—class war is an excellent example —made it conscious of itself and in doing so . . . radicalized it . . . (and) worked it up into something that differs substantially from what it would have been without them" (1942: 153-54). The critical atmosphere extended to legislatures, the judiciary, and government bureaucracies (1942: 156), (which the contemporary version of the argument calls "entrepreneurial Congressional staffs," "the imperial judiciary," and "wild to regulate bureaucrats".) Schumpeter concluded that

"The social atmosphere . . . explains why public policy grows more and more hostile to capitalist interests, eventually so much so as to refuse in principle to take account of the requirements of the capitalist engine and to become a serious impediment to its functioning" (1942: 154).

Schumpeter's ideas were extended specifically to the United States in the 1960s and early 1970s. Daniel Moynihan (1970) and John McCarthy and Mayer Zald (1973) outlined the growth of "professional social reform," arguing that the professional fostering of social criticism and change was a growing force with which conservative groups had to contend. Samuel Bowles and Herbert Gintis wrote in *Schooling In Capitalist America* that while higher education trained elites in "skills of domination," it also "gave birth to a powerful radical movement and critique of capitalist society" (1976: 12).

1.1.1.1b. Economic Strains

In the last two decades, interest groups demanded "social" regulation to reduce pollution, consumer and worker hazards, and discrimination; and benefit programs to reduce sickness, inequality, poor education, and other social problems. These demands got at least a sympathetic hearing in Congress and frequently resulted in new programs or agencies. Meanwhile, traditionally strong groups on the right, such as businesses and trade associations, have not diminished their political activity. Corporate opposition to economic deregulation of the transportation industries, the Chrysler loan guarantee, and demands for steel and auto import restrictions show how industry is just as willing to use the government as the Left is.

Interest-group demands for benefits, helpful agencies, and protection are expensive. The history of intergovernmental relations can be written as the progressive opening of the Federal treasury to state and locally-based groups (Wright, 1974). Also, benefit payments to individuals have increased twice as fast as the trend growth rate of the economy, and Federal loans and loan guarantees—not covered in the Federal budget—rose from $16.1 billion in fiscal year 1970 to $73.3 billion in fiscal year 1979 (Lubar, 1980: 82-83). In a report for the American Bar Association, Yale economist Paul Sommers estimated in 1978 that the annual costs of regulation were between $58 and $73 billion (Sommers, 1978).

Many analysts now argue that the capitalist system is in fact overloaded with demands. Because the supply of some goods, such as land, is limited, there are *inherent limits* on the amount of some wants that the system can satisfy. Also, demands for *conflicting* goods—cleaner factory

air and faster production of plastics—have multiplied. These circumstances "become an increasing brake on the expansion and extension of
economic welfare. Social scarcity tightens its grip. Economic liberalism
is in this sense a victim of its own propaganda; offered to all, it has
evoked demands and pressures that cannot be contained" (Hirsch, 1977:
11).

Western economies, such as those of the United States and Britain,
now face a zero-sum situation in which one group's gain is necessarily
another's loss. Economic growth once mitigated the strains of demands;
a surplus could be distributed without anyone directly losing income.
But now rapid economic growth produces double-digit inflation. There
are technically sound solutions to the inflation–unemployment tradeoff
and other problems. However, these policies would require that some
groups suffer substantial short-run losses (e.g., that Chrysler be allowed
to fail; that the United Auto Workers take a pay cut from $20 an hour;
that homes be torn down so that coal slurry pipelines can be built). But
"(j)ust as Democracy whips up expectations, it reduces the means available for fulfilling the expectations." Clamping down on British union
practices which are "inimical both to the standard of living and to the
stability of the social system" would be illegal (Brittan, 1978: 176). In the
United States, "solutions" run into laws intended to assure that individuals and group interests are not arbitrarily dismissed.

> All minority groups have gone through a learning process. They have dis-
> covered that it is relatively easy with our legal system and a little militancy
> to delay anything for a very long period of time. To be able to delay a
> program is often to be able to kill it. Legal and administrative costs rise, but
> the delays and uncertainties are even more important. When the costs of
> delays and uncertainties are added into the calculations, both government
> and private industry often find that it pays to cancel projects that would
> otherwise be profitable. Costs are simply higher than benefits (Thurow,
> 1980: 13).

Even if the solutions are legally cleared, they may be politically
disastrous for the offending officials and thus avoided (Bell, 1976: 239-
240). Congressional officials are reelected more for how much they
deliver to and protect their constituents than for how well Congress as
a whole handles economic problems. "Necessary" sectional losses are
thus prevented, and the economy deteriorates (Thurow, 1980: 212-213).

1.1.1.1c. OSHA as an "Active" Tool of Labor

A hypothetically strong Occupational Safety and Health Administration fits the "interest groups run amok" theme nicely. The physical
costs of production were previously dumped on employees as occupa-

tional disease. Unions and their supporters stopped tolerating this, requiring technical adjustments and retarding production. Yet higher productivity is needed to stabilize the economy and meet other demands. Thus, OSHA is an example of the relatively new strains plaguing capitalism.

Daniel Bell (1973), Francis Rourke (1976), Paul Weaver (1978), Paul Sabatier (1975), and Nichols and Zeckhauser (1977, 1978)—among others—say that agencies like OSHA are truly changing industry because of the influence of private groups. The agencies are goaded along by labor and liberal reform groups such as the "public interest" sector and activist Congressional staffs. Additionally, proregulation professionals within the agencies work closely with these groups. These analysts do evaluate environmental agencies somewhat differently among themselves. That is, Bell, Rourke, and Sabatier suggest that agencies protect interests that might otherwise be trampled for the sake of industrial production, while Weaver and Nichols and Zeckhauser argue that regulation is frequently an unnecessary weight on economic growth. All say that, for better or worse, regulators in the 1970's were significantly constraining production and OSHA, they argue, is a powerful agent of environmental interests.

1.1.1.2. "Passive" Regulation: The Intimidated Agency Theme

The "interest group crisis" argument clashes with what used to be a conventional view of regulation: that dominant conservative groups usually either capture or eviscerate regulatory agencies. Perhaps an only moderately strong "liberal" interest group or minority can delay and kill threatening policy *changes*. Perhaps they can also be given their own government agency. But, a fortiori, strong interest groups ought to be able to delay and kill changes which are threatening *to them*. In a zero-sum situation, a major social change will by definition threaten a dominant group. Strong interest groups may not prevent the establishment of an OSHA, a health-facilities planning board, or a Civil Rights Commission, all of which simply legitimate a weaker group's demands. But strong groups ought to be able to keep the new agencies from substantially changing hazardous technologies, the wasteful organization of health-care resources, or discriminatory practices. It is easier to prevent than to implement a change. Agencies eventually become passive and weak, and frustrate regulatory laws. Note that this view still functions within the pluralist model. It simply suggests that all interest groups are not powerful, particularly in implementing changes, and that some conservative groups influence government enough to usually benefit from its decisions. The balance of power tilts strongly in a conservative direction.

Louis Jaffe (1970) noted that the money, personnel, and political influence of regulatory agencies are limited in comparison to the industries they are supposed to regulate. A consistent adversarial posture quickly dissipates agency resources, making imbalanced compromises administratively rational.

Marver Bernstein wrote that "In its search for an equilibrium among interested parties, it is assumed that a commission will be guided by its legislative mandate." However, "Left largely to its own resources, which are apt to be weak relative to the strengths of organized parties, a commission will probably be guided by dominant interests in the regulated industry in the formation of the public interest. Thus, the public interest may become more private than public" (1955: 154).

James Landis's *Report on Regulatory Agencies to President-Elect* Kennedy in 1960 stated that "Irrespective of the absence of social contacts and the acceptance of undue hospitality, it is the daily machine gun-like impact on both agency and its staff of industry representation that makes for industry orientation on the part of many honest and capable agency members as well as agency staffers" (1960: 71).

Radical analysts of OSHA tend to view the agency as gutted and passive. Daniel Berman's book on "occupational health and safety struggles" argues that since the Occupational Safety and Health Act of 1970 was passed, corporations, insurance companies, and industry-backed safety associations—enlisting Congressional and Presidential support—have managed to dominate OSHA. Low budgets for enforcement, restrictions on enforcement, minimal fines, and decentralization of some enforcement functions to corporate-dominated State governments prevent OSHA from having any real impact on injuries (1978: 34-36).

Elliot Krause (1977: 317) writes that in OSHA "unions have a potential tool to work for change." However, "Interpretations of the new law by industry-favoring national administrations have led to federal government passivity which borders on sabotage of the intent of the law."

Again, both active and passive views of regulation work within a pluralist framework. They discuss the power of interest groups. They discuss circumstances that modify the exercise of power and influence, such as different levels of interest, awareness, and mobilization. They try to estimate the relative force exerted by different interest groups. Analysts differ on which way the historical preponderance of force goes.

There is no suggestion that the government inherently or structurally favors one set of interests over another.

This book will closely examine OSHA's behavior on the assumption that we ought to be able to judge whether OSHA fits the "new powerful tool of labor and environmental group" image or the traditional "intimidated passive shell" view. Or, is the condition of occupational health regulation much more than a reflection of interest group pressures? This brings us to the capitalist State perspective.

1.1.2. The Capitalist State Perspective

1.1.2.1. Bases of the Capitalist State

The capitalist State perspective views government organizations as part of a network of institutions, organizations, and social relationships. This network is called a structure (Wright, 1978: 210; Poulantzas, 1973: 115). The organizing principle of the structure of capitalist society is the maintenance and health of the capitalist economic system.

Government organizations are necessary because capitalist society generates irreconcilable class antagonisms. "The State arises when, where, and to the extent that the class antagonisms cannot be objectively reconciled. And, conversely, the existence of the State proves that the class antagonisms are irreconcilable" (Lenin, 1932: 8). Friedrich Engels wrote that the State functions as "a power apparently standing above society . . . whose purpose is to moderate the conflict and keep it within the bounds of 'order'." However, this does not mean that the State reconciles conflicting interests as a neutral arbiter. Interpreting Engels, Lenin says that the State "is an organ of class domination, an organ of oppression of one class by another; its aim is the creation of 'order' which legalises and perpetuates the oppression by moderating the collision between the classes" (1932: 8–9).

How does the State oppress the majority? The *parliament* or *Congress* mystifies and legitimates current political arrangements. They project an image of democracy, but in fact are "mere talking shops" concealing the fact that important government functions are actually controlled by the bureaucracy. Further, the majority of the population is barred from the political life of "representative" institutions because of a lack of time and resources, while the bourgeoisie have both (Lenin, 1932: 39-44).

The *bureaucracy* supports capitalism as well. It centralizes administration, perfecting the "instrument of domination" (Lenin, 1932: 29). Bureaucratic administration also excludes the majority of the population from participation in three ways. First, appointed officials are not subject to recall by voters. Second, officials are economically and socially distant from the majority because of their high salaries and privileges. Third, administration is conducted in a seclusion that cannot be broached by the oppressed (Lenin, 1932: 24-44).

Bureaucracy supports capitalism because bureaucracy is dependent on a stable capitalist economy. "Bureaucracy and the standing army constitute a 'parasite' on the body of bourgeois society—a parasite born of the internal antagonisms which tear that society asunder, but essentially a parasite, 'clogging every pore' of existence." Bureaucrats receive "a number of comparatively comfortable, quiet, and respectable berths raising their holders above the people" (Lenin, 1932: 26-27).

Others have noted the government's dependence on taxes. James O'Conner argued that the government is dependent on a healthy capitalism because "the source of its own power (is) the economy's surplus production capacity and the taxes drawn from this surplus (and other forms of capital)" (1973: 6). Clause Offe wrote that:

> In the absence of capitalist accumulation, everything, and especially the power of the State, tends to disintegrate. If we think of the budgetary obligation of the State in advanced capitalist societies, its extensive reliance on resources created in the accumulation process and derived through taxation through wages and profits, this becomes immediately clear. Thus, every interest the State (or the personnel of the State apparatus, its various branches and agencies) may have in their own stability and development can be pursued only if it is in accordance with the imperative of maintaining accumulation; this fundamental dependency upon accumulation functions as a selective principle upon state policies. The criterion of the stability of accumulation is thus incorporated in the pursuit of interests and policies that, considered by themselves, may have little to do with accumulation. Accumulation, in other words, acts as the most powerful constraint criterion, but not necessarily the determinant of content, of the policy making process (1975: 126).

This dependence is underscored by the extent to which the government tries to avoid "investment strikes" by business (Offe, 1976: 49; Habermas, 1975: 62). The point is a major and distinctive mark of the capitalist State view. It suggests that the government has an inherent and structural bias toward actions that will support the capitalist system. All of this suggests very tight ties between business and government organizations at the expense of the majority of people. But how does this view differ from the view that businesses enervate regulation?

1.1.2.2. Distinguishing the Capitalist State from "Passive" Regulation

Claus Offe says that such "elite" and "class" studies of government action "stick themselves to a pluralistic model of policy analysis." Such studies do consistently document that business preferences usually prevail in political disputes. However, they do not show that the State is *structurally* a capitalist State; that is, that under different pressures the State would not as readily perform anticapitalist actions (1974: 33). Nicos Poulantzas, a theorist associated with the capitalist State perspective, criticized radical pluralist analyses of State monopoly capitalism "on the grounds that they led to a vision of a State 'fused' with monopoly capital—a State with no autonomy that is purely at the service of the monopolies." These "instrumentalist" views reduce the State to a tool. Such a State could theoretically be used by the working class in a movement to socialism (1978: 129).

Not only could anticapitalist interest groups turn this pluralist State directly against capitalism, a pluralist State could also kill capitalism by overindulging business's special interests. "The concept of class interest as contrasted with the mere special interest of individual enterprises or capitalist groups clearly presupposes that the definition of interests possesses a degree of rationality cleansed of situational and particular coincidences and divergencies" (Offe, 1974: 33). However, because of the anarchy of competition, autonomous capitalist actions are not usually collectively rational. Oligopolies are set against small and medium-sized firms. The competitive pressures of the moment divert attention from any long-run, collective strategic orientation. Also, firms may not be interested in objectively important political matters. Poulantzas says that "everything happens as if the specific coordinates of the struggle of the dominant classes contribute to prevent their political organization" (1973: 284). In 1978, he noted the production of oil as an example of a critical function which can be distorted by firms scrambling after short-term profits; "the State—even Carter in the U.S.A.—was forced to take responsibility in the realm of energy. . . . It is thus a political necessity that the functions of general interest for the bourgeoisie as a whole should be discharged by the State" (1978: 181-182). The truly *capitalist* State must intervene in this confusion on behalf of private capital accumulation in four respects.

First, the capitalist State autonomously gives paramount importance to the profitability and stability of the capitalist system in policy controversies. If it is necessary to override business's special interests to assure capitalism's stability, the State will do so. For example, it will prevent legal or political agitation by workers by regulating working conditions enough to prevent major occupational disease epidemics, even over the complaints of businesses who find their short-run profits adversely affected. Of course, if there were no chance of worker agitation, the State would not regulate working conditions so long as the labor force remained sufficiently strong to continue production. The State, in short, regulates for *capitalism's* benefit, and any benefits to workers are incidental.

In contrast, a pluralist State goes along with the strongest pressures of the moment, even if they reflect anticapitalist sentiments. For example, if the consumer movement were a dominant force at a particular time, the pluralist State would avidly implement consumer protection measures *for the sake of consumer protection*, and not as a system-stabilizing tactic to be withdrawn as soon as pressures subsided (see the point on "defusing" pressures below). Also, a pluralist State would bend before business special-interest pressures destined to cause the capitalist system significant problems. For example, the pluralist State might grant to plants cost-saving emission control variances which would result in far more costly clean-up operations in later years.

Second, a capitalist State would *defuse* anticapitalist agitation if it did appear. By "defuse" it is meant that the State will grant concessions only when the system is threatened, and then only enough to cool out or coopt disaffected groups. Piven and Cloward's *Regulating the Poor*, which frequently takes a capitalist State position, maintains that the State granted welfare benefits only under the threat of violence, and then withdrew the benefits as soon as agitation had quieted and group leaders had been coopted. In contrast, a pluralist State would respond to a lower level of interest-group pressure because it has no inherent bias against anticapitalist interests. It would also not withdraw the benefits until a more powerful antiwelfare constituency materialized. In the capitalist State view the State, as an autonomous guardian of capitalism, *took the initiative* in reducing benefits (Piven and Cloward, 1971).

Third, the capitalist State, for the sake of private capital accumulation, tries to stifle potentially damaging controversies before they erupt into concrete conflicts. For example, the State would autonomously suppress information on past worker exposure to toxic chemicals, lest the information prompt law suits and agitation. In contrast, a pluralist State would make no effort to suppress the information on chemical exposures unless pressured to do so by business. If there is no pressure, the pluralist State will have no incentive to suppress the information because it nas no autonomous concern for business stability.

Fourth, the State makes no effort to discover and publicize objective latent interests that clash with private capital accumulation (Dahrendorf, 1959: 174-179; Lukes, 1974: 25). Of course, a pluralist State will not stir up interest agitation either, since its primary function is *responding* to active interest-group pressures. Thus, the pluralist and capitalist State perspectives must be compared using the first three types of behavior.

Generally, the capitalist State is not an arbiter and reflection of interest-group conflicts, as in the pluralist view. Rather, it is an autonomously active advocate of private capital accumulation at the expense of workers and individual businesses with only "special" interests.

1.1.2.3. Problems for the Capitalist State

Capitalist State theorists note that the State is a troubled guardian of the system. First, self-interested enterprises are not always willing to cooperate with the State. On the one hand, the State is supposed to override the interests of individual firms or capitalist sectors when these clash with the health of the system. On the other hand, the State authorities, who have little information or planning capacity, and insufficient coordination among themselves, are dependent on private firms for information and assistance. Further, the State cannot intervene significantly in the property structure without discouraging necessary private investment (Offe, 1976: 49). "Thus," writes Jurgen Habermas, "the State apparatus vacillates between expected intervention and forced renunciation of intervention, between becoming independent of its clients in a way that threatens the system and subordinating itself to their particular interests" (1973: 62-63).

Second, the growth of the public sector generates social phenomena and structural elements which are impediments, threats, and "ballast" to the creation of surplus value (Offe, 1976: 37). The public sector generates occupational spheres which are "oriented to use values." Public bureaucracies and educational, scientific, and research systems generate phenomena like "radical professionalism" which are "detached from privatistic career patterns and market mechanisms and can be oriented to concrete goals" (Habermas, 1973: 66). The regulatory processes of administrative power, which are foreign and yet to some extent necessary for the central, monopolistic sphere of the economy, can get out of control. These intrude on the capitalist system; according to Claus Offe, the "main problem" of late capitalist social systems is to not let the regulatory system go beyond simple maintenance of capitalism; "the more the capitalist economy is forced to utilize 'external regulatory services,' the more precarious its problem of prevailing against the dynamics of these 'extra-territorial' systems and of safeguarding itself against encroachments by them" (1976: 47, 51). In other words, there is the constant danger that government organizations will forget or disregard their ultimate dependence on capitalism and adopt anticapitalist goals or be effectively exploited by anticapitalist groups.

Third, the proportion of the population which "does not reproduce itself through the labor market"—such as students, schoolchildren, the unemployed, those living on annuities, welfare recipients, nonprofessionalized housewives, the sick, and criminals—grows with the State. These groups make demands which call for unproductive use of resources. This increases the chance of anticapitalist agitation and restricts the State's ability to act on behalf of private capital accumulation (Habermas, 1973: 66-67; Offe, 1976: 44-46; O'Conner, 1973).

These hypothesized problems of the capitalist State are clearly identical to those outlined in the pluralist view of interest groups straining the economic system. Capitalist State theorists agree that these circumstances impair the ability of the State to function as a capitalist State (Offe, 1975: 140). But the hypothesized reality of the capitalist State is 1. "the constant attempt to reconcile and make compatible" the protection of capitalism through certain regulatory and social programs—originally designed to stabilize the system—with the danger of their getting out of control and threatening the system; and 2. the attempt to override business's special interests while being vigorously resisted by business. Some argue that these attempts are doomed, that "The reality of the capitalist State can thus best be described as the reality (and dominance) of an unrealistic attempt" (Offe, 1975: 144). Müller and Neüsuss cite "the systematic (private) establishment of counter-apparatuses for evading and resisting (the State's) coercive power—businessmen's associations and lobbies, taxation 'advice' bureaus, etc." (1979: 37).

The critical difference between the capitalist State and the pluralist or organizational perspectives is the capitalist State's structural bias toward protecting the capitalist system. Poulantzas writes that "All measures taken by the capitalist State, even those imposed by the popular masses, are in the last analysis inserted in a procapitalist strategy or are compatible with expanded reproduction of capital." The State takes the resistances of dominated classes into consideration, but only makes concessions insofar as they aid in further private capital accumulation and the dominance of the bourgeoisie (Poulantzas, 1978: 185). In contrast, the pluralist State bends before the strongest pressures of the moment, even if these come from anticapitalist groups or from capitalists with only short-run and special interests. According to the organizational perspective described below, government organizations are primarily concerned with their own stability and autonomy, whether or not these conflict with the needs of the capitalist system.

1.1.2.4. Regulatory Behavior in a Capitalist State

What does the capitalist State perspective imply about occupational health and environmental regulation? First, it implies that regulatory agencies will seriously try to moderate the "anarchy of production" to keep the capitalist system from tearing itself apart. For example, weakly controlled handling of chemicals arguably damages the capitalist system. Clean-ups, compared to early chemical control, are very expensive (Green and Waitzman, 1979). Cancer and other diseases reduce profits as insurance premiums rise. They shorten workers' productive lives. They inflate prices in the medical-care system. The public support of disability adds enormously to government deficits and inflation. As businesses bear a share of compensation and damage costs, their profits—which could otherwise be used for capital expansion—are drained (Price, 1979; U.S. Department of Labor, Assistant Secretary for Policy, Evaluation, and Research, 1979; Leone, 1977). This is a situation in which a capitalist State would intervene to prevent diseases before they over-burden the system. Similarly, James O'Conner in 1973 argued that the capital-draining effects of environmental pollution foster strong pollution control regulations (1973: 175-177).

Second, in the capitalist State there ought to be some higher control—a monitor—to prevent regulators such as OSHA or the EPA from *over*-regulating. From this perspective, over-regulating means forcing businesses to control chemicals beyond the point that is necessary to maintain the productive and political stability of the workforce or to prevent expensive disease "epidemics." These monitors should also back or encourage regulations that *are* necessary to prevent expensive chemical difficulties and which have not been pushed by regulatory agencies. These monitors should not be tools which private corporations use to fight regulatory agencies because *necessary* regulations would then be prevented. Monitors which only reflected business pressure would characterize a *pluralist* and not a *capitalist* State.

The Council of Economic Advisors, the Council on Wage and Price Stability, the Office of Management and Budget, and other organizations encouraging "regulatory reform" after the mid-1970's are likely candidates for the role of monitor. They argued that regulatory agencies were paying too little systematic attention to economic cost-benefit calculations. They critiqued the economics of major regulations, and suggested that agencies be required to consider economic factors when initially designing regulations (Hopkins, 1976; DeMuth, 1980a). We will later examine the regulatory reform movement, and consider how it reflects Executive Office of the President concern for capitalism's health and stability (the capitalist State view), Presidential responsiveness to corporate pressures (the pluralist view), or interorganizational conflict and cooperation (the organizational perspective).

The suggestion that the State can override private special interests for the sake of private capital accumulation is distinctive. It is a clear alternative to the view of the State as an arbiter of private groups, the position shared by conservative, liberal, and radical pluralism. The capitalist State tries to be an integrating factor in the capitalist system, rather than a pluralistic reflection of disruptive private conflicts.

1.1.3. An Organizational Perspective on Regulation

There is no organizational perspective on regulation that is a self-consciously developed as the pluralist or capitalist State views. Rather, some common observations about regulation imply that organizational properties are important influences on how agencies operate. Analysts refer to the "single-mindedness" of agencies (American Bar Association, 1979: chapter 5), of how their leaders' or staff's backgrounds shape regulatory techniques (Kelman, 1980; S. Weaver, 1977), and how agencies resist change (Nichols and Zechhauser, 1977). If government organizations are singleminded, are tools of their personnel, and are inflexible, they will behave differently than they will if they are tools of interest groups or sensitive principally to economic considerations. An organizational perspective advises us that the State cannot be counted on to reflect the prevailing balance of power among interest groups or to pursue collective capitalist interests because of organizational tendencies. I will list six such tendencies.

First, organizations may resent attempts at coercion by other groups. Randall Collins notes that within an organization, "coercion leads to strong efforts to avoid being coerced." This applies to inter-organizational relations as well; he adds that "conflict against outsiders may be used to promote solidarity through participation in rituals that accompany stress" (1975: 298-299, 305). Hugh Heclo's study of decision-making by upper-level officials suggested that they are often more interested in preserving their autonomy and reputation than in the political implications of their actions (1977). John Quarles, former Deputy Administrator of the EPA, showed how an official can take different sides on issues—such as the probable job loss from a regulatory action—to deflect external pressures (1976: 67-73). Thus, interest group pressures may prompt resistence rather than acquiescence to demands. Organizations may also resist efforts to shift their programs to fit the needs of the economy. In fact, Claus Offe noted above that the tendency of organizations to get out of control is the "main problem" of capitalist social systems. The organizational perspective makes this concern for autonomy more than a problem for the system's driving force of capital accumulation; it is a driving force in its own right.

Second, organizations operate with limited rationality. When making decisions they disregard much of the available information and probable consequences. Organizations frequently ignore the claims of interest groups and also are not sensitive to the consequences of a decision for capitalism. This is the basis for the frequent claim that regulatory agencies make technologically impossible demands on business.

Third, and related to the idea of limited rationality, is the fact that decision making is not usually concerned with the optimal attainment of an organization's ends. Rather, an organization searches for satisfactory outcomes. March and Simon suggest that organizational persons do not search for the sharpest needle in a haystack, but rather one sharp enough to sew with (March and Simon, 1958). Cyert and March view the organization as a group of participants with varying demands, changing interests, and limited abilities to attend to all problems simultaneously. Bargaining among these participants produces a series of agreements that impose constraints on the organization. Organizational choice involves selection of the *first* alternative that people identify as satisfying these constraints, and not necessarily the *best* alternative (Cyert and March, 1963: see also Diver, 1980: 273-274). An organization might therefore settle for a state of affairs that does not accurately reflect the balance of interest-group pressures. Or the organization might settle for a state of affairs that fails to maximize capitalism's welfare; in fact, the organization may not even be concerned about it.

Fourth, organizations do not necessarily handle inconsistent constraints by trading them off rationally. Rather, organizations attend to the constraints sequentially. The choices may be quite inconsistent. An agency may first issue a regulation favoring capitalism at the expense of workers, and then turn around and issue one favoring workers at the expense of capitalism. Or a genuinely "protective" rule may be followed up with weak enforcement (Diver, 1980: 277-279). There is no real attempt to balance interests or to consistently pursue capitalism's welfare.

Fifth, organizations try to avoid uncertainty. They prefer standard procedures. When they have to change standard procedures, they prefer modifications that are only slight variations on the present. This is because people in organizations are very reluctant to take actions with uncertain results when options with more certain consequences are available (Cyert and March, 1963: 101-113; Allison, 1971: 91). Thus, an organization might favor a demand from a relatively weak interest group in conflict with a stronger one if the demand calls for an established organizational response. For example, a dependent and politically weak group of employees can call in the Occupational Safety and

Health Administration to inspect a workplace, and OSHA may aggressively do so over the objections and pressure of a large and influential employer. This is because OSHA is programmed to do inspections.

In the same vein, organizations may not attend to new problems which are important to interest groups or to capitalism if the problems require innovations. Thorstein Veblen made this point with his concept of "trained incapacity," according to which officials are so thoroughly trained in one set of responses that they cannot operate effectively in changed situations. For example, businesses and many economists today criticize OSHA for its insistent effort to control chemical exposure levels through machine design specifications. They charge that OSHA refuses to bend this traditional approach in favor of less expensive personal protective devices (masks, earmuffs, and the like) because of organizational rigidity, with businesses and presumably the economy suffering the consequences (Nichols and Zeckhauser, 1977).

Sixth, leaders may be able to shape the organization to fit their own ideology, even in opposition to powerful interest groups or the demands of the capitalist system. Chester Barnard said that the main function of leadership was to indoctrinate those at the lower levels with belief in the purpose of the organization (1938). Like Barnard, Philip Selznick emphasized the creation of socially integrating myths, that is, "efforts to state, in the language of uplift and idealism, what is distinctive about the aims and methods of the enterprise." Creative leadership "depends on having the will and insight to see the necessity of the myth, to discover a successful formulation, and above all to create the organizational conditions that will sustain the ideals expressed" (1969: 190).

Organizational analysts have suggested that a shift in leaders or staff backgrounds can significantly transform organizations. J. Kenneth Benson wrote that "The consciousness of organizational participants is partially autonomous from the contextual situations in which they exist . . . They are not in any simple sense captives of the roles, official purposes, or established procedures of the organization. The participants fill these forms with unique 'content.' Sometimes they do so in an automatic, unreflective way; in other periods they may become very purposeful in trying to reach beyond the limits of the present situation, to reconstruct the organization in accord with alternative conceptions of its purpose, structure, and technologies" (1977: 7). similarly, Charles Perrow suggested that appointments of individuals with different career lines or experiences can move an organization in new directions (1972: 154–155).

Many have commented that the appointment of "liberal" administrators has symbolic functions. It makes agency inaction—allegedly made inevitable by a conservative power structure—more tolerable (Edelman, 1977: 148–149). But can we consider the possibility that the person may get out of hand; that an administrator may turn on the most powerful groups or against what he or she regards as an opresive capitalist system? And might such conservative groups find it hard to get rid of such an administrator, once the person has the benefit of the job (making firing somewhat costly) and the support of the public-interest sector, labor, and the liberal media (making firing even more costly)? Or, from the other perspectives, does such a person modify his position to fit existing power distributions (Steinbruner, 1974: 124-139) or come to appreciate the necessity of "healthy economic growth" as a paramount goal?

These organizational factors may make the State a very imperfect reflection of interest-group pressures and may also make the State a highly untrustworthy guardian of capitalism. In fact, where organizational interests of ideologies clash with capitalism's long-run welfare, the latter may lose out.

1.2. OUTLINE OF THE BOOK

This chapter has reviewed three different hypothesized forces shaping regulatory behavior—interest-group pressure, concern for capitalism's stability and health, and organizational concerns for stability, autonomy, and preferences of leaders and staffs. Chapter 2 discusses central issues and uncertainties in chemical regulation. These issues involve tradeoffs among economic stability, income, and public health. Chapter 3 examines factors favoring and undercutting strong controls on chemicals. Chapter 4 describes the specific regulatory procedures of the Occupational Safety and Health Administration, and, given the power structure outlined in Chapter 3, estimates how OSHA might behave if it functioned exactly as each of the three perspectives suggest it function. With these "benchmarks" in mind, we will examine OSHA's history of chemical regulation in Chapters 5 and 6, and its handling of certain "service" issues in Chapter 7. These chapters will assess whether the pluralist, capitalist State, or organizational view best fits the development of occupational health regulation. Chapter 8 sums up the general conclusions about OSHA and relates these to other types of government intervention in the economy.

Occupational Disease: Magnitude and Issues of the Problem

Even when based on clear information, costly regulatory decisions will be controversial. When the decisions are costly and when the data on which they are based are uncertain—when the data do not come close to suggesting a technically "correct" path—the decisions are even more disputed. This uncertainty gives political and organizational factors considerable room in which to operate. This chapter discusses key issues and uncertainties in toxic-substance control prior to discussing political and organizational factors in Chapter 3.

2.1. SCOPE OF THE PROBLEM

In 1980, cancer was the second leading cause of death in the United States. The National Office of Vital Statistics reported that deaths from malignant neoplasms increased from 113.4 per 100,000 in 1930 to 133.2 in 1978 (see Table 2.A.). Earl Pollack and John Horm of the National Cancer Institute (NCI) released preliminary findings that the overall age-adjusted cancer incidence rate increased about 4 percent between 1947–48 and 1969–71 NCI surveys. They also suggested that, at least for white males, cancer incidence increased almost 10 percent between 1969 and 1976: "Age adjusted incidence rates for all sites combined increased from 346.6 per 100,000 in 1969 to 374.0 in 1976 among white males and from 271.5 to 301.2 among white females over the same time period. This represents an average annual increase of 1.3 and 2.0 percent, respectively" (Pollack and Horm, 1980).

NCI scientists, the President's Toxic Substances Strategy Committee, and others have argued that a substantial share of present cancer cases are due to increased exposure to toxic substances. The NCI's *Atlas*

Table 2.A.
Age-Adjusted Death Rates for Selected Causes of Death,
United States, 1900–1978 (per 100,000)

Year	Malignant neoplasms	Diseases of the heart	Influenza and pneumonia	Accidents	Homicides
1900	79.6	167.3	209.5	75.3	1.2
1910	97.0	201.7	163.0	88.4	4.5
1920	104.9	203.6	213.1	74.0	6.9
1930	113.4	252.7	108.2	84.6	9.2
1935	117.5	269.0	109.2	80.7	8.6
1940	120.3	292.7	70.2	73.1	6.3
1945	119.1	282.4	45.6	68.7	5.8
1950	125.4	307.6	26.2	57.5	5.4
1955	125.8	287.5	21.0	54.4	4.8
1960	125.8	286.2	28.0	49.9	5.2
1961	125.4	278.6	22.1	48.1	5.2
1962	125.6	282.7	23.7	49.7	5.4
1963	126.7	285.4	27.7	50.9	5.5
1964	126.7	276.9	22.8	52.1	5.7
1965	127.9	275.6	23.4	53.4	6.2
1966	128.4	275.8	23.8	55.6	6.7
1967	129.1	267.7	20.8	54.8	7.7
1968	130.2	270.0	26.8	51.1	8.2
1969	129.7	262.3	24.6	55.3	8.6
1970	129.9	253.6	22.1	53.7	9.1
1971	130.7	252.0	19.3	52.0	10.0
1972	130.7	249.3	20.8	52.0	10.3
1973	130.7	244.4	20.1	51.7	10.5
1974	131.8	232.7	16.9	46.0	10.8
1975	130.9	220.5	16.6	44.8	10.5
1976	132.3	216.7	17.4	43.2	9.5
1977	133.0	210.4	14.2	43.8	9.6
1978	133.2	207.3	15.4	45.3	9.9

SOURCE: President's Toxic Substances Strategy Committee, *Toxic Chemicals and Public Protection*, (Washington: U.S. Government Printing Office, 1980), p. 148.

of Cancer Mortality displayed a correlation between rates of cancer and industrial concentration (U.S. Department of HEW, National Cancer Institute, 1975). Another study by Hoover and Fraumeni found that "Geographic analysis of United States cancer mortality, 1950–69, revealed excess rates for bladder, lung, liver, and certain other cancers among males where the chemical industry is highly concentrated. The correlation could not be explained by confounding variables such as urbanization, socio-economic class, or employment in non-chemical industries" (Hoover and Fraumeni, 1975). An NCI study released in 1977 found that males experienced significantly higher rates of cancers of the lung, the nasal cavity and sinuses, and skin in counties with petroleum industries (Blot, Brinton, Fraumeni, and Stone, 1977). The President's Toxic Substances Strategy Committee said that only a minority of chemical carcinogens had been regulated by 1980 and that exposure to unregulated carcinogens would cause cancer incidence to continue to rise (1980: 118–122).

Reducing occupational exposure to harmful substances is one regulatory strategy. Chairman of the National Advisory Committee on Occupational Safety and Health Nicholas Ashford commented in 1976 that "In the four years during which I have been writing and speaking on these issues, I have witnessed study after study reveal more and more disease to be of occupational origin" (1976a: 12). The Department of Health, Education, and Welfare estimated that occupational exposure to toxic substances accounts for about 20 percent of all cancer cases (Bridbord, Decoufle, Fraumeni, Hoel, Hoover, Rall, Saffiotti, Schneiderman, and Upton, 1978). An industry-commissioned critique of that study by the University of Texas School of Public Health estimated the figure to be somewhere between 10 and 33 percent (Stallones and Downs, undated).

But other scientists deny that there is a chemically-induced cancer rate rise. John Higginson of the International Agency for Research on Cancer noted that

> . . . you cannot explain much of existing cancer patterns only in terms of simple general pollution by industrial chemicals in low doses. You can't explain why Geneva, a non-industrial city, has more cancer than Birmingham in the polluted central valleys in England. In the United States, reports are coming out that there are few differences in cancer patterns between the so-called dirty and clean cities. In fact, the only thing you may say is that air pollution may, and I emphasize MAY, increase lung cancer in cigarette smokers (Maugh, 1979: 1364); for a response, see the President's Toxic Substance Strategy Committe, 1980: 153–166).

Others criticized the 1980 NCI study by Earl Pollock and John Horm on the grounds that: 1) survey groups varied yearly because cities and regions joined or dropped out of the NCI survey program; 2) methods of cancer detection and reporting had improved and "inflated" the rate; and 3) the study underestimated the proportion of cancers due to smoking. Pollack and Horm responded that they made generous allowances for each of these factors before releasing the results.

The basic issue of whether or not cancer is increasing or decreasing will not be definitively resolved for years. It will also be difficult to draw conclusive connections between exposure to chemicals and the hypothesized increase. It *is* clear that a substantial group of scientists in policy-making positions have what they consider highly suggestive—if uncertain—data confirming that the rate of chemically-induced cancer is substantial and that occupational exposure is a promising policy target.

Regulatory agencies argue that they should be able to move against a toxic substance on the basis of such suggestive but inconclusive data. Toxicology, when dealing with low doses of chemicals, is a highly uncertain science. Conclusive studies require resources that are unavailable to agencies. For example, what kinds of evidence are necessary to firmly show that a chemical will not induce one or more cancer cases per million people?

> . . . to demonstrate with ninety-five percent confidence that the carcinogenic response rate is less than one in a million, an experimenter need only feed three million animals at the human exposure rate and compare the response with three million control animals that have been raised under identical conditions but with no exposure to the chemical. As a practical matter, however, scientists cannot conduct this "mega-mouse" experiment because it would require feeding and caring for six million rodents for eighteen to twenty-four months. Scientists therefore test significantly fewer animals at much higher dosage rates. Thus, the only data available to regulators are from experiments in which laboratory animals have been fed high doses of a chemical. The agency can never be certain whether a chemical that causes cancer at high doses will cause cancer at the lower doses to which humans are typically exposed (McGarity, 1979: 733-734).

Courts have in fact upheld regulations based on suggestive but uncertain information (McGarity, 1979: 730). Thus, studies such as those by the National Cancer Institute touch off regulatory pressures.

2.2. ISSUES IN OCCUPATIONAL DISEASE

The chemical–cancer link is not universally accepted. Even if it were, we would be left with the issue of what specific chemicals to regulate. Three issues repeatedly surface in regulatory debates over particular substances: (1) whether or not the substance causes cancer at *some* level of exposure; (2) whether there is a safe level of exposure to the substance; and (3) how exposure to the substance is to be controlled.

2.2.1. Does the Substance Cause Cancer?

Usually, epidemiological or animal data are used to test whether or not a substance is a carcinogen.

Epidemiological evidence, identifying excesses of disease among humans exposed to a substance compared to a statistically similar but nonexposed group, has triggered most of the controls on chemicals. Asbestos workers experienced much higher rates of cancer and other diseases. Coke oven workers were two and one-half times as likely to contract cancer of the kidney as other steelworkers. Workers exposed to vinyl chloride were found to contract an extremely rare form of liver cancer. Epidemiological evidence similarly justified government control of dibromochloropropane (DBCP) and acrylonitrile, although animal data were used as well.

Groups adversely affected by controls frequently criticize epidemiological data, charging that differences in illness experience stem not from the suspect chemical but from other agents. Manufacturers of Kepone, for example, once claimed that nervous tremors among workers resulted not from Kepone but from another, as yet unknown, substance. Similarly, industries frequently attribute high lung-cancer rates among certain workers to smoking habits (Shapley, 1977).

Those favoring regulations may in turn deny the contribution of other or "unknown" agents, or say that the specific occupational exposure was a strong factor in a multiphased, multicausal development of cancer. For example, exposure to asbestos coupled with cigarette smoking drastically increases the risk of lung cancer. According to Bridbord et al., ". . . if current theories of a multicausal process are correct, it seems likely that a large fraction of cancers which at first appear to be "attributable to' smoking should also be 'attributable to' asbestos, radiation, and/or other occupational factors" (Bridbord et al., 1978: 2–3). This issue surfaces in most regulatory proceedings.

Individual variability in response to a substance—related to genetic factors, diet, or metabolism—also clouds epidemiological evidence. Finally, the latency period, or the period of time between exposure to a substance and onset of cancer, ranges from five to forty years, further complicating interpretations. These uncertainties do not vitiate the use of epidemiological evidence. They do mean that the data used in an unpopular action are usually ambiguous and can be challenged indefinitely.

Animal data are also used to test a chemical's effects on humans. This assumes that a substance which causes cancer in animals causes cancer in humans. At least twenty-eight chemicals are known positively to cause human cancer; in most cases this conclusion came from epidemiological studies. With one or two exceptions all these substances also cause cancer in experimental animals. After hearings in 1978 on a proposed chemical control policy, OSHA noted that almost all witnesses in the cancer policy rulemaking hearing stated that animal data should be considered as suggestive for humans (U.S. Department of

Labor, OSHA, 1980: 5060-5067). OSHA did add, however, that the *potency* of an animal carcinogen could not be confidently extrapolated to humans; thus, weak animal carcinogens could be strong in humans, or strong animal carcinogens weak in humans (at the time, OSHA was justifying a rule lowering all carcinogen exposures to the lowest feasible levels).

In turn, industry representatives and other witnesses at OSHA's hearings, while granting that a relationship between animal carcinogens and human cancer exists, maintained that the relationship is extremely unclear. Therefore, they argued that expensive regulatory decisions should not be made "until conclusive positive human data are available" (U.S. Department of Labor, OSHA, 1980: 5061).

Thus, uses of epidemiological evidence and laboratory tests on animals involve certain uncertainties and assumptions. People with a stake in whether or not a chemical is treated as a serious threat can take one side or the other and usually appear reasonable, even if stubborn. (In some cases, such as that of vinyl chloride, the eventual evidence of human cancer was so strong that denying it would have been absurd.)

2.2.2. Is There a Safe Level of Exposure to the Substance?

A second critical issue is whether or not there is a safe level of exposure to the substance. Regulations usually set levels of exposure which must not be exceeded. The permissible exposure limit (PEL) will affect business's compliance costs and also the amount of disease that a harmful chemical will continue to cause.

People who are particularly sensitive to public-health considerations support the lowest technologically feasible PEL, even if this means high capital and operating expenditures for the controls. They maintain that there is no safe level of exposure to a carcinogen. Nicholas Ashford argued that cancer may be initiated by a single molecule of a carcinogen "hitting" a single susceptible cell, and that "Decisions about what standards to adopt for carcinogens have to be made with the recognition of the good possibility that a zero threshold (of harm) exists for these substances" (1976b: 119). OSHA's final carcinogen policy noted in 1980 that, because of individual variability in response to carcinogens, "even if thresholds for specific carcinogens could be demonstrated for certain individual humans, no reliable method is known today for establishing a threshold that could apply to an exposed group of workers." The agency argued that exposure should therefore be reduced to the lowest technologically feasible level (U.S. Department of Labor, OSHA, 1980: 5219-5220).

A contrary position says that thresholds should be presumed to exist until proven otherwise. Until evidence conclusively documents human cancer resulting from very low levels of exposure, standards should not require manufacturers to reduce exposure to chemicals—often at great cost—to the lowest feasible level. Monte Throdahl, Vice-President of the Environmental Policy Staff of Monsanto Chemical Company, said in a speech before the Manufacturing Chemists Association in 1977 that "Because of outside pressure, theories are being used to set policy: Theories that are unproven at this time, but are the bases of regulations . . . The one-molecule theory is a case in point: Thus far, the theory is being used by regulators as a basis for policy . . . even though no experimental proof of the theory has been set forth" (Throdahl, 1978: 294-296).

In 1978, industry groups contested in Federal court an OSHA standard for occupational exposure to benzene with a PEL of 1 part per million (ppm). They argued that there was no evidence that benzene induced cancer (leukemia) at any point below—or even near—the current standard of 10 ppm. In a decision later affirmed by a 5 to 4 vote of the Supreme Court, the Fifth Circuit Court in New Orleans agreed that OSHA had not shown that lowering exposure to benzene was "reasonably necessary or appropriate to provide safe and healthful employment." (The Supreme Court left open the question of how much evidence was needed to justify an exposure reduction.)

While one view argues that no exposure to a carcinogen should be presumed safe, the other maintains that low-level exposure should not be presumed to be dangerous. Generally, public interest groups and unions support the former position, and businesses and trade associations support the latter.

2.2.3. How Is Exposure to the Substance To Be Controlled?

A third important issue is how exposure to a substance is to be controlled. One major question is the relative mix of *engineering controls* and *personal protective devices*. Engineering controls include such methods as local exhaust ventilation, modification of processes to limit chemical release, or substitution of less hazardous substances. Personal protective devices include masks, respirators, or other devices to prevent a substance from contacting the body. (In the case of noise, another OSHA target, engineering controls would involve some muffling or alteration of equipment, and personal protective devices would include ear plugs or earmuffs.)

Regulatory agencies, unions, public interest groups, industrial hygienists, and some large companies like DuPont support engineering controls, largely because personal protective devices are flawed protections. Correct facial fit is crucial to the effectiveness of a respirator, but due to variations in facial dimensions, as well as facial hair, scars, or growths, it is difficult to maintain properly. Respirators tire workers because of increased breathing resistance, heat stress, and reduced vision. This means not only personal discomfort and fatigue, but also safety problems because of reduced vision and mobility. It is also very difficult to talk through a mask or a respirator (U.S. Department of Labor, OSHA, 1978b: 19617). Thus, these groups favor engineering controls to prevent initial chemical release. They say that respirators and the like should be used only if additional protection is needed after engineering controls have been adopted as fully as possible, and then only until the engineering controls can be improved.

Most businesses and many economists who are particularly concerned about the costs of standards dismiss these worries. Engineering controls are more expensive than personal protective devices, and they favor the latter. They claim that personal protective devices can be improved and that workers can be paid more to wear them (Levine, 1979; Morrall, 1979; Miller and Walton, 1980). (One problem with this position is that businesses object to chemical regulations partly because respirators and the like—to the extent they are required—would cut down productivity because of the discomfort and personal immobility of the workers wearing them; see the U.S. Department of Labor, OSHA, 1978b: 19611.)

The conflict comes down to whether workers, through discomfort and a less reliable method of protection, or businesses and the public, through higher capital-investment requirements and attendant higher prices, are to bear more of the costs of compliance with standards.

This chapter has focused on cancer and carcinogens. However, the general issues discussed here are also raised over substances that are not carcinogens but are highly toxic. For example, although some level of exposure to cotton dust—which causes a serious lung disease called byssinosis—was admittedly safe, groups fought over whether a 100, 200, 500, 750, or 1000 microgram per cubic meter of air PEL would be set. Also, there were serious disputes over the mix of engineering controls or personal protective devices to be used in controlling exposure to cotton dust.

2.3. SUMMARY

This chapter began by noting that when data do not unambigously suggest a technically "correct" path, political and organizational factors have considerable room in which to operate. Usually, we do not *know* that particular substances are carcinogenic or otherwise acutely harmful; whether some level of exposure to the substance is safe or what that level is; and whether or not engineering controls provide margins of protection and comfort over and beyond what personal protective devices provide which justify their higher cost. Therefore, while appearing reasonable, groups try to structure debates about regulations in ways favorable to them. This brings us to the forces favoring and opposing chemical control.

CHAPTER 3

Political and Economic Factors in Occupational Health Work

Chapter 2 described recurring issues in toxic-substance control. Groups have financial and health-related interests in how technically uncertain questions are decided. This chapter will describe the resources of groups with stakes in regulatory activity, including labor, public interest groups, business groups, and the government itself. What kind of political, technical, and legal influence do these groups have? What forces encourage and restrict chemical regulation?

Chapter 1 introduced three views of regulation—the pluralist, capitalist State, and organizational perspectives. The question of resources is central to each. The distribution of resources is a crucial variable in the pluralist perspective because that view focuses on the ability of different groups to get the State to act on behalf of their interests. It is also relevant to the capitalist State perspective. Assume that the State watches out for the interests of private capital accumulation. How much pressure does it receive from anticapitalist groups? How much pressure does it receive from capitalists with only special interests, and does the State have the ability to successfully oppose these for the system's good? Finally, a discussion of resources is relevant to the organizational perspective on State action. What resources does the State have to deflect external pressures? How powerful are these pressures, and what are the limits within which the State must function?

3.1. FACTORS ENCOURAGING TOXIC SUBSTANCE CONTROL

I will focus on five circumstances encouraging tight Federal regulation of chemical production. First, the United States has an influential social reform sector. Second, there is a significant link between this sector and activist congressional staffs, putting some Congressional force behind environmental considerations. Third, the General Accounting Office is an institutionalized Federal critic of lagging regulatory action. Fourth, agency bureaucrats do some autonomous regulating. Fifth, Federal courts give considerable weight to an agency's interpretation of its governing statute and to its judgements about facts. To be overturned, a decision must be more than "uncertain" or even "shaky"—it must be "arbitrary and capricious" or not supported by "substantial evidence."

3.1.1. There Is an Influential Social Reform Sector

Situations become social problems only when some group is able to express and publicize them and elicit some type of corrective response. In Chapter 1 we reviewed the growth of social reform in the twentieth century, specifically how it was stimulated by the scripts written by the organized labor and unemployed workers' movements, the expansion of education, and the accompanying proliferation of "social critics."

The new level of activity of public-interest research and law groups is a particularly important part of professional reform. Groups lobbying for liberal causes had been operating long before the term "public interest group" was coined. However, Jeffrey Berry found a spurt in their formation from 1968–72. He surveyed 83 public interest groups, and found that 47 percent of the groups originated after 1968, and that 63 percent originated after 1960. Eleven of the thirteen public interest groups working inthe consumer area, for example, appeared after 1968 (Berry, 1977: 34; see also Weisbrod, Handler, and Komesar, 1978).

According to Francis Rourke, groups such as Common Cause, the Natural Resources Defense Council, and the Nader-affiliated reform organizations have vocally criticized preferential treatment given to industry groups by regulatory agencies and "pressured them to expand their conception of their clientele to include the public at large and disadvantaged groups whose needs have previously not figured large in administrative decision-making . . . the reform spirit may be said to have become institutionalized. Under the watchful eye of these groups, the day-to-day decisions of regulatory agencies can be made to correspond more closely with the public interest" (1976: 57-59).

Also, several unions have established units to deal with occupation health issues, particularly since the OSH Act was passed (Bureau of National Affairs, January 16, 1975: 977-979). Lawsuits by the Oil, Chemical, and Atomic Workers' Union and the Public Citizen's Health Research Group prompted OSHA to invoke emergency controls on fourteen carcinogens in 1974. The Steelworkers, the Rubberworkers, the International Association of Machinists, and the Textile Workers were instrumental in the dispute over the now effective vinyl chloride standard. The Steelworkers fought for standards for coke oven emissions, chromium, lead, arsenic, and other substances. Unions have pushed for an OSHA noise standard of 85 rather than 90 decibels. The Textile Workers sued OSHA for a strong cotton dust standard. The Rubberworkers were active in disputes over the benzene standard (Health Research Group, 1976).

Labor–management contracts also reflect greater attention to occupational health issues. An agreement between the United Rubberworkers and management required certain companies to set aside a fraction of a cent per worker-hour to finance occupational health research at Harvard or the University of North Carolina. The university research found a new link between benzene and leukemia and was used as epidemiological evidence in the benzene proceedings. Also, there has been an increase in the number of union–management safety committees, although their substantive impact is unclear (Kochan, Dyer, and Lipsky, 1977).

3.1.2. The Link between the Professional Reform Sector and Activist Congressional Staffs

Michael Malbin argues that the electoral advantages of legislation which conspicuously demonstrates its sponsor's "great concern" has produced a "'legislative explosion:' If there is a problem then throw a law at it."The ever-increasing numbers of Congressional staff strive to sell competing causes to their Senator or Representative (1976; for figures on Congressional staff growth, see Fox and Hammond, 1977: 168-170).

Such entrepreneurial staffs pick up ideas elsewhere, usually from an interest group, and then sell them to a Congressman. These ideas frequently originate in public interest groups. Malbin says that "Much of the new power of public interest groups stems directly from the intermediary role played by entrepreneurial staffs. Young Democratic activists from the top Eastern law schools who work for a Congressional committee feel a basic kinship with their counterparts from the same schools who work for citizens' lobbying groups. Together they form a network every bit as intimate as the one tying business lobbyists to members of Congress on golf courses" (1976).

This coalition scrutinizes agencies very closely. Public interest groups and liberal Congressmen and their staffs help each other uncover possible regulatory failures which are picked up by the media as morally interesting. This forces publicity-conscious regulatory agencies to account for their behavior until some specific problem is solved or interest dies down (Rourke, 1976: 171-173); Berry, 1977: 243-250). For example, the Consumer Product Safety Commission was told by Robert Hehir, its director of biomedical science, on April 2, 1976, that an immediate ban on free asbestos in consumer products was necessary. It was only after a suit by the Natural Resources Defense Council, release of a discovered memo by Rep. Henry Waxman of California, and subsequent press coverage, that the agency publicly declared the condition hazardous, in April of 1977 (Curry, 1977a; 1977b). The tendency for agency action to follow law suits and Congressional inquiry has been noted for the Consumer Product Safety Commission generally (Curry, 1977c), the Occupational Safety and Health Administration (Ashford, 1976b: 477-479), and the Environmental Protection Agency (Quarles, 1976: Chapter 9; Smith, 1979).

3.1.3. The GAO as an Institutionalized Federal Critic of Lagging Regulatory Action

The General Accounting Office (GAO), an independent agency, was established by the Budget and Accounting Act of 1921. It assists the Congress in its legislative and oversight activities, audits the programs and financial operations of Federal departments and agencies, and suggests improvements in Federal financial management systems. Since the 1966 Federal attempts at Planning, Programming, and Budgeting, the GAO has done progressively more program evaluation work. This shift from an emphasis on financial accounting was accelerated by the Congressional Budget and Impoundment Act of 1974, which established an Office of Program Review and Evaluation in the GAO (Mosher, 1979: Chapters 6–7).

The GAO has given increasing attention to regulatory agencies. In fiscal year 1974 the GAO devoted eight professional staff years to a group of eight regulatory agencies (CAB, ICC, FMC, SEC, FCC, FTC, FPC, and NRC). This increased to twenty-one in fiscal year 1975 and to fifty in 1976. About 200 reports on all regulatory agencies were completed or undertaken between January 1, 1973 and April 30, 1976 (U.S. Senate Committee on Governmental Affairs, 1977: II-72-73). Between May 1, 1976 and January 31, 1977 the GAO completed 41 reports on regulatory agencies (U.S. General Accounting Office, 1977b: 69-85). About 12 reports were done on private-sector occupational health and safety regulation between 1973 and 1980.

The GAO has cooperative relations with the Congress, the press, and other media. The agency distributes its reports to the media quickly, and the reports often make news. These ties give much of its program evaluation work a critical tone. "The rise of two closely related phenomena in recent years—the accent on investigative journalism and the renewed interest in government accountability—has provided both the GAO and the media with a new set of common interests in their evolving relationship" (Mosher, 1979: 249). Congress has used the GAO as an investigative agent because its members, as indicated earlier, are interested in highlighting agencies' failures and thus making news. "Indeed," notes Mosher, "both Congress and the GAO have long realized that praiseworthy reports do not make 'news.' In addition to viewing the GAO in the capacity of an 'in-house Ralph Nader,' . . . Congress also tends to use the GAO audits to corroborate the charges made by public interest groups such as Nader's, or to investigate causes championed by the media. The use of Red Dye No. 2 in foods received immediate press attention because Congress claimed that (the GAO report on the subject) was the first independent examination of the issue, and because the GAO agreed with consumer advocates that the additive should be banned by the Food and Drug Administration" (Mosher, 1979: 249).

The GAO's reports on regulatory agencies tend to favor tight control of chemicals, often berating agencies for regulatory delays. Some titles are illustrative: "Slow Progress Likely in the Development of Standards for Toxic Substances and Harmful Physical Agents Found in Workplaces" (1973); "Federal Efforts to Protect the Public from Cancer-Causing Chemicals Are not Very Effective" (1976); "Better Data on Severity and Causes of Worker Safety and Health Problems Should Be Obtained from Workplaces" (1976); "Delays in Setting Workplace Standards for Cancer-Causing and Other Dangerous Substances" (1977); "Sporadic Workplace Inspections for Lethal and Other Serious Health Hazards" (1978); and "Workplace Inspection Program Weak in Detecting and Correcting Serious Hazards" (1978).

The reports are also influential, if only because they embarrass the investigated agency for a time. The Senate Committee on Governmental Affairs noted that "A backhand compliment was paid GAO by one Congressional staff member who said he would never request GAO to audit the agency he was responsible for overseeing. His feeling stemmed not from a dislike of GAO, but from the great impact a full GAO audit would have on the agency. This staff member was in agreement with the agency's policies, and he thought a GAO audit would turn up problems within the agency that would hurt his policy objectives" (1977: II-74). Thus, the GAO is an effective critic of lagging regulatory action.

3.1.4. Agency Bureaucrats Do Some Autonomous Regulating

The creation of an agency establishes a set of people in roles committed to regulation-oriented behavior. These bureaucrats, finding themselves on the side of business-controlling proposals by accident, fate, or design, will frequently defend the proposals for political, professional, or personal reasons (Heclo, 1977: 98-99; Heclo, 1974: 301-304; for similar comments on the Antitrust Division of the Justice Department, see Suzanne Weaver, 1977: 104-105). Also, "liberal" regulatory agencies will attract individuals with suspicions of and some antagonism toward business (Edelman, 1964: 52-53; Kramer, 1978a). Finally, while agencies are frequently pushed by the professional reform sector, they also *use* liberal groups as allies and countervailing pressures to offset business efforts (Smith, 1979) to prevent regulation.

3.1.5. Federal Courts Give Considerable Weight to an Agency's Interpretations and Judgments

In administrative law it is only required that "substantial evidence" support an agency's action or that the agency not be found to have acted in an "arbitrary or capricious" manner. The Supreme Court has said that "substantial evidence" means "such evidence as a reasonable man might accept as adequate to support a conclusion." (There are some differences between a "substantial evidence" standard of evidence and an "arbitrary and capricious" standard, but Professor Davis points out in his work on administrative law that "such refinements in the words have no effect upon what the courts do" (Davis, 1975: 62-63; Systemedics, 1977: B-10.)

The District of Columbia Court of Appeals said in 1974 that toxic-substance regulation involves questions "on the frontiers of scientific knowledge" and that decisions must "to a greater extent (depend) on policy judgements and less upon purely factual analysis." The Second Circuit Court for New York said in 1973 that when a regulation is challenged on scientific and technical grounds OSHA "has the burden of offering *some* reasoned explanation" (Systemedics, 1977: B-11-13). The OSH Act established worker "rights" to a safe and healthy workplace. When a policy decision is reached within the limits of the law and has a reasonable, even if shaky or incomplete, factual basis, a court will presumably not substitute its own judgement for that of the agency. In general, courts have upheld OSHA's and EPA's policy decisions

(McGarity, 1979: 730). (In 1979, Senator Dale Bumpers of Arkansas unsuccessfully tried to amend the Administrative Procedures Act. The amendment would have overruled the body of case law which established the presumption in favor of agencies' actions; see the Congressional Record, January 2, 1979, at S. 410.)

One important qualification of this point is that courts are politically diverse. For example, the Federal Third Circuit Court in Philadelphia tends to favor health and safety considerations, while the Fifth Circuit Court in New Orleans tends to favor economic considerations. Under the Administrative Procedures Act, groups can ask a Federal Court to review or overturn an agency decision. When different groups sue the agency in different courts, the court where the first suit was filed hears all of the suits. Thus, after an agency action is officially announced, adversaries literally "race to the courthouse" to establish a more sympathetic court as the court of jurisdiction. Even if a party does not oppose an action, it may want all suits consolidated in a particular court (Omang, 1980a). For example, organized labor did not oppose OSHA's standards for benzene and lead, but sued for review in the Third Circuit Court in Philadelphia to try to establish that court's jurisdiction in the case.

3.1.6. Evidence of Effects: The Costs of Health Regulation

The popularity among businessmen of polemics against "unproductive and excessive environmental regulation" is at least an indication that agencies like OSHA are not dominated by private industry. No one is quite sure how much it costs businesses to cope with OSHA's requirements; however, no one disputes that the amount is substantial.

Murray Weidenbaum and Robert DeFina suggested that complying with OSHA's safety and health regulations cost businesses about $3.2 billion in 1976 (Weidenbaum and DeFina, 1978: 4). The McGraw-Hill surveys of investment in employee health and safety from 1972 to 1980 estimated costs of roughly the same magnitude (see Table 3.A.). One problem with such estimates is that they include expenditures which businesses would have made whether or not OSHA existed. Most businesses have, at least in the last forty years or so, made some type of safety expenditures. Some firms have had quite extensive programs. Arthur Andersen and Company, in a study done for the Business Roundtable, estimated that the *incremental* costs (that is, over and above what businesses would have spent in any event) of complying with OSHA's health *and* safety standards in 1977 were $184 million for 48 companies. The study added that, if certain chemical standards were

Table 3.A.
Investment in Employee Safety and Health, In Billions of Current Dollars
and as Percent of Total Capital Spending (All Business)

Year	Amount	Percent of capital spending
1972	$3.3	2.7%
1973	3.6	2.6
1974	4.4	2.8
1975	3.8	2.4
1976	3.4	2.0
1977	4.3	2.2
1978	6.6	2.9
1979	4.3	1.6
1980	$4.1	1.4%

SOURCE: McGraw-Hill Economics Department, *9th Annual Survey of Investment in Employee Safety and Health* (New York, McGraw-Hill Publications Company, 1981).

implemented as planned, costs would increase substantially (Arthur Andersen and Company, 1979). Edward Denison of the U.S. Department of Commerce and the Brookings Institution estimated that the total incremental capital costs related to OSHA in 1975 were $522 million (1979: 73).

The costs of OSHA's standards fall heavily on certain industries. The wood, paper, metal, and automobile industries have particularly high costs (MacAvoy, 1979: 88), largely because these industries have many employees and, historically, numerous safety hazards (Table 3.B.). Similarly, the costs of health standards are particularly heavy in chemicals, petroleum products, and other industries with potential health hazards. Paul MacAvoy maintains that the high regulatory costs for these industries mean higher prices for their customers and lagging productivity as their investment is shifted to safety and health technology rather than the production of goods (1979: 88-93). *Total* GNP may remain temporarily stable because of the growth of industries producing safety and health equipment, but the overall rate of growth will slow. Edward Denison has estimated the cumulative effect of health and safety regulation on productivity:

> By 1975, the last year for which estimates were made, output per unit of input in the non-residential business sector of the economy was 1.8 percent smaller than it would have been if businesses had operated under 1968 conditions. Of this estimate, 1.0 percent is ascribable to pollution abatement and .4 percent each to employee safety and health programs and to the increase in employee dishonesty and crime (1979: 68).

Table 3.B.
Total Injury and Illness Rates, 1978 (per 100 workers)

TOTAL MANUFACTURING	13.2
Lumber and wood products	22.6
Paper and allied products	13.5
Chemical and allied products	7.8
Primary metal industries	17.0
Fabricated metal products	19.3
Transportation equipment	11.5

SOURCE: U.S. Department of Labor, Bureau of Labor Statistics, *Occupational Injuries and Illnesses in 1978: Summary*. Report 586, March 1980.

If this retardation of growth continues, MacAvoy notes, "the level of GNP could be as much as 5 percent lower by the mid 1980s" (1979: 140).

Reacting to such figures, a special *Business Week* section on government regulation claimed that "One of the most sweeping recent efforts to regulate industries for social ends came with the establishment of the Occupational Safety and Health Administration . . . businessmen point to the agency as the quintessential example of regulatory overkill" (April 4, 1977: 74). An Associate Editor of *Fortune* magazine, Paul Weaver, wrote in *The Public Interest* in 1978 that:

> The New Regulators (OSHA, EPA, and the Consumer Product Safety Commission) for the most part are mandated to pursue their goals more or less single-mindedly, with little or no concern for the cost and consequences of the pursuit. . . . By and large, the new regulatory agencies are true to the spirit of the laws, and, where they are not, suits by environmentalists, labor, or other such groups put them back on the straight and narrow. . . . If they are vulnerable to cooptation at all (and they are), it is to cooptation by safety and environment-oriented groups, not by business organizations (1978: 51-52).

Thus, the development of an influential "social reform" sector, the link between this sector and activist Congressional staffs, the General Accounting Office's independent criticism, autonomous regulation by agency officials, and liberal standards of evidence for justifying agency actions in court all encourage toxic-substance control. The costs of current safety and health regulations, and business complaints about OSHA, undercut any simple notion that the agency is dominated by those it regulates.

What, then, can we say for the conventional view of regulation— that regulatory agencies are usually captured or eviscerated by business-oriented groups? This brings us to the factors discouraging chemical control.

3.2. FACTORS DISCOURAGING CHEMICAL CONTROL

Businesses have historically tried to channel external pressures for regulation into relatively harmless directions. Gabriel Kolko's *The Triumph of Conservatism* noted that

> (Theodore) Roosevelt's view of the dangerous, potentially irresponsible character of the masses, and the need to channelize them along controllable lines was expressed by many others as well . . . Charles S. Mellon of the New Haven Railroad told the Hartford Board of Trade in 1904 (that) "A public must be led, but not driven, and I prefer to go with it and shape or modify, in a measure, its opinion, rather than be swept from my bearings with loss to my self and the interests in my charge" (1963: 162-163).

James Weinstein showed that businesses supported workers' compensation programs "to reduce the need for independent action by labor, as well as the appeal of unionism in large corporations." The programs also precluded increasingly successful suits for employer negligence which were given up by workers in exchange for assured—but meager—compensation for industrial injuries (Weinstein, 1968: Chapter 2; Posner, 1972).

Similarly, Alan Stone outlined how the food and drug industries tried to weaken food and drug advertising regulation by lobbying for legislation which would give the FTC, rather than the FDA, jurisdiction over the area. In fact, business efforts to weaken social and economic regulation are historically innumerable. I have already examined the pressures working in favor of the new wave of chemical regulation. What are the pressures business can bring to bear *against* it?

First, business controls employment. If workers believe that cleaning up workplace conditions will cost them their jobs, they will probably not support chemical control until their lives or abilities are clearly, imminently in danger. Second, business controls the bulk of scientific, technical, and legal resources in occupational health work. This means that businesses overwhelmingly influence what information is released to workers and the public and what issues are pushed hardest in regulatory proceedings. I will first discuss the control of employment, and then the dominance of resources.

3.2.1. Limited Union Commitment to Occupational Health

Unions *have* increased their occupational health-related activity since the OSH Act was passed, as shown in section 3.1.1. Nevertheless, resources committed to occupational health work by unions remain trivial. In 1976, the Health Research Group surveyed union efforts and concluded that "worker health is still not a top priority issue with many international unions. With wide variation from union to union, the impression is that occupational health is getting more attention today than it did years ago, but not enough. The clearest measure of activity is manpower and money spent on occupational health matters. In all areas, from doctors and hygienists to engineers and lawyers, the number of health experts working for unions is distressingly low" (1976: 15) (Table 3.C.).

Unions give economic issues much higher priority than health considerations. In 1975 A.F. Grospiron, the president of the relatively active Oil, Chemical, and Atomic Workers (OCAW) said that his union would not pursue new safety and health concessions because of "the priority given to economic considerations" and a desire to see what would happen to existing contract provisions. The Bureau of National Affairs commented that "It seems likely that other unions less active in the safety and health field will also ignore other issues to concentrate on economic matters" (January 16, 1975: 979). A report on copper smelting by INFORM, a nonprofit research organization, noted that while two-thirds of the copper smelters it studied had union–management safety committees, these "tend to concentrate on safety issues and pay little or no attention to occupational disease problems" (Bureau of National Affairs, April 12, 1979: 1649-1650).

3.2.2. Employee Reaction to Toxic Substances

Union bureaucracies' concern with economics mirrors employee concern on the shop floor.

The research on workers' adaptations to chemical problems has been of three types. First, there are valuable studies and review essays on the effects of the job on employee stress (House, 1974; Kasl, 1974; Katz and Kahn, 1978: Chapter 17). However, the descriptions in these studies of employees' reactions specifically to toxic chemicals are much sparser than the discussions of the pathological effects of job ambiguity, overload, monotony, and so forth. Such articles usually cite epidemiological data on particular hazards and surveys on employee perceptions of health and safety problems, but this information does not tell us very much or very exactly about how employees actually react to the problems.

The second major data source on this issue are the various surveys of workers' opinions. In these, thirty to thirty-eight percent of the employees in single places or buildings report "unpleasant physical conditions," or health and/or safety difficulties (Quinn and Staines, 1978: 99; Cambridge Reports, Inc., 1978: 38; Quinn and Staines report the former

Table 3.C.
Occupational Health Resources of Fifteen Major Labor Unions, 1976

Union	International health staff	Expenditures	*Ratio of staff/members	Other comments
Oil, Chemical, and Atomic Workers	1 industrial hygienist; 2 chemists; 3 union members.	over $100,000	1/30,000	district reps. trained in health and safety.
United Mine Workers	1 medical doctor; 4 public health workers; 1 lawyer	$170,000	1/30,000	
United Electrical, Radio, and Machine Workers	1 research director; 1 part-time hygienist; 1 part-time engineer; 2 part-time lawyers; 3 part-time union members	$15,000–$50,000	1/59,000	
Rubberworkers	2 industrial hygienists		1/85,000	extensive research contracts with Harvard and Univ. of North Carolina
Chemical Workers	1 part-time union member; 2 consulting medical doctors	less than $100,000	1/113,000	
United Steelworkers	1 epidemiologist; 1 industrial engineer; 8 union members	over $100,000	1/130,000	800 local health and and safety representatives
United Autoworkers	3 industrial engineers; 2 safety engineers; 1 lawyer; 1 part-time medical doctor; 1 part-time public health worker	over $100,000	1/147,000	300 health and safety reps. in plants; 20 international reps. with health and safety training
Painters	1 union member in economics	$15,000–$50,000	1/211,000	
Textile workers	1 part-time engineer; 2 part-time workers in economics	$15,000–$50,000	1/223,000	
American Fed. of Government Employees	1 full-time and 1 part-time union member	over $100,000	1/240,000	15 district reps. trained in health and safety
Electricians	3 part-time workers in law, publicity, and union work	$5,000–$15,000	1/397,000	
Paperworkers	1 part-time industrial engineer	$15,000–$50,000	1/1,204,000	
Machinists	1 full-time and 1 part-time union member; 1 consulting medical doctor	over $100,000	1/314,000	
Communications Workers	1 part-time economist	$15,000–$50,000	1/1,996,000	

*Part-time staff equals ¼ full-time staff.

SOURCE: Health Research Group, *Survey of Occupational Health Efforts of Fifteen Major Labor Unions* (1976).

figures and Cambridge the latter). These figures did not appreciably change between 1969 and 1977 (Quinn and Staines, 1978: 99). Chemical workers are particularly likely to be concerned: fifty-one percent report safety hazards and forty-eight percent report health hazards (Cambridge Reports, 1978: 92-94). The polls touch only lightly on the forms of employee and employer adjustment to hazards, and should be supplemented by case studies of plants.

Case studies of occupational disease epidemics by journalists, public interest groups, and Congressional committees are the third largest source of information. One could argue that such data are distorted because they reflect the investigators' personal crusades. They may, for example, exaggerate workers' grievances and managerial suppression of data.

Recognizing the critical intent of such journalists, groups, and investigators, and also that such data come from the unique population of "horror stories," it is nevertheless striking that a common core of employee and employer reactions appears at different times and places. The cases are also consistent with research on less charged situations, such as responses of patients to "regular" illnesses or normal organizational efforts to deal with competing problems.

3.2.2.1. Defining Symptoms: The Occupational Factor

Unpleasant, difficult, and irritating conditions are not necessarily defined as "problems," that is, as conditions that the individual feels ought to be corrected. Instead, they can be accepted as "normal" deviations from ideal states—as routine costs of living. Leonard Pearlin and Carmi Schooler of the National Institute of Mental Health gave three reasons for this (1978: 6). First, people often cannot identify a source of the suffering, and so they passively accept it. Second, even if they know a cause, they may not know what to do about it and so may resign themselves to the condition. Third, even if individuals can identify the cause, and know what would remedy the difficulty, the solution might have compensating disadvantages. Thus the situation would remain a "normal" cost of life. Pearlin and Schooler's survey of 2300 people in the Chicago area found that, compared to the stresses of marriage, parenting, and household economics, people are particularly likely to accept unpleasant occupational situations as normal or unalterable. They speculated that the respondents viewed their jobs as being "impersonally organized" and out of their control. Similarly, Ramsey and Joan Liem reviewed several studies showing that the overwhelming stresses of losing employment mean that job-disruptive actions are taken only for very compelling, clear, and immediate reasons (1978).

Cases of occupational disease outbreaks show that toxic substance symptoms may indeed be regarded as "normal" costs of employment. Employee and employer tolerance of the "wear and tear" of symptoms is reflected in the historical neglect of occupational disease by State workers' compensation systems. Arthur Larson has pointed out that the term "occupational disease," when used in the early years of the programs, was meant to exclude such cases from compensation. Diseases were not sudden and were in fact expected and accepted as part of the job; the hazards producing the diseases were considered uncontrollable (Larson, 1973: 257-276).

The capital and operating costs of chemical-control equipment are often very high. Consequently, high exposure levels are still frequently regarded as inevitable, and the physical effects remain part of the job. For example, the Director of Preventative Medical Services of the Virginia Department of Health, Dr. Robert Jackson, testified about the manufacturing of the nerve damaging and carcinogenic pesticide Kepone at a plant in Virginia:

> Everyone who came to work was informed that within a few weeks he would develop "The Kepone Shakes." Stories have been told of these men sitting around the table in the garage trying to drink coffee but unable to do so because of the shaking of their hands. It was clear that the men accepted this as part of their jobs. They did not at all, at least the earlier ones, the ones who were exposed relatively mildly, think of it as an illness so much as a phenomenon associated with Kepone (U.S. House Committee on Education and Labor, 1976: 10–11).

Until OSHA's enactment of a lead standard in 1979, lead workers were often given chelation drugs, which remove lead from the blood at the risk of mineral deficiency and intestinal damage. George Becker of the United Steelworkers said that:

> It was an accepted fact that everyone who worked in the lead smelter would eventually suffer some degree of lead poisoning. . . . The majority of the workers were required to take an oral chelating drug called versenate. A daily course of the drug usually consisted of six white pills—two pills with each meal. Many employees had taken versenate in this manner for years on end—it was an accepted way of life for the leadworkers. . . . (U.S. House Committee on Education and Labor, 1976: 435).

Red lumps on the faces, necks, and armpits of men who worked with 3,4,5-trichlorophenol at Hooker Chemical in New York were labeled "the Hooker bumps." One former worker commented that "This ain't no chocolate factory" (McNeil, 1979).

However, there is a threshold of functional impairments in oneself or in several coworkers beyond which the situation is no longer accepted as normal. Workers begin to discuss conditions among themselves, and possibly question the employer. Data from investigations cannot be used to predict the threshold. (It may be quite high, however. Quinn and Staines (1978: 117) indicate that 51.1 percent of workers "who had one or more hazards that they felt were 'sizeable' or 'great" did not report them to anyone.) Factors like income, ethnicity, costs sunk in the job, place in the organizational structure, and the curvilinear relation between anxiety and effective action complicate the link between growing anxiety and ensuing behavior (Rosenstock, 1975; Wright and Hamilton, 1978; Mechanic, 1979; Kasl and Cobb, 1966). But the information consistently indicates two very general types of adaptations once the situation becomes a "problem" for the workers: anxious discussion and resignation.

3.2.2.2. Anxious Discussion

Social support helps people overcome job stress. According to Daniel Katz and Robert Kahn, "the communication of positive affect— liking, trust, and respect—by significant others" such as peers and supervisors, "the affirmation of one's beliefs and perceptions, and certain kinds of direct assistance" help maintain employees "as functioning members of the organization" (1978: 602-604). Such social support— which may be valuable in company alcohol or drug treatment programs—could also encourage workers to accept chemical hazards. How so?

Remember that people generally avoid actions which could disrupt their jobs. Yet, the increasing visibility of symptoms suggests that either employees should press for production changes in the firm or quit. Awareness of the symptoms is, as psychologists say, "dissonant" —or incompatible—with continued job stability, and the theory of cognitive dissonance predicts a tendency for workers to redefine symptoms in ways which will not threaten their work (Aronson, 1978). The clustered illnesses might be interpreted as coincidences, or attributed to factors other than the working environment. If workers and management support each other in these cognitions, the situation may indeed become more acceptable (company medical personnel often reassure workers in this way; see Morton (1977) and Becker in the U.S. House Committee on Education and Labor [1976: 439-440]).

Even if workers do suspect an occupational hazard, the supportive group discussion may, through catharsis, reduce anxiety. In any event, the underlying source of the illnesses remains; the prolonged discussion delays the difficult choice between health and job stability. (In "regular" illnesses such inaction is a common reaction when the treatment for an illness is feared; see Rosenstock, 1975: 203.) For example, twenty-five employees exposed to bischloromethyl ether (BCME) in one building of a Rohm and Haas plant in Philadelphia died of lung cancer between 1960 and 1973. Family members had the following exchange with Senator Tunney of California in a 1975 inquiry:

> Senator Tunney: Ma'am, can I ask you: Did you or your husband, to your knowledge, have any understanding that he was working with a material that would produce cancer?
> Mrs. Aumen: No, he didn't . . . You think that when you see one man die, another man die, maybe he thought, because I know I thought about it, why are some men dying one right after the other? There has to be something, right? But where you work, men together on this one chemical, or all these chemicals, and they die one after the other . . . I don't think my husband would have (stayed) if he had known.
> Mrs. Karcher: I honestly don't think they wanted to believe it was due to chemicals. I know my husband tried to make excuses, saying a lot of men came from the coal mines . . . They kept making excuses and didn't have the knowledge that it was that serious (U.S. Senate Committee on Commerce, 1975: 62-63).

The questions and excuses raised at this plant indicate that there was a suspicion of a link between lung cancer and the chemicals used at work. But these and other statements at the hearing indicate that anxious discussion was a principal worker response to this danger over several years.

Similarly, the production of dibromochloropropane (DBCP) led to sterility among workers at a chemical plant in California. One worker said that "We've got young people here who don't have any family. We've got one 24-year-old kid who has already had a brain tumor. Another man bleeds from the nose . . . everyone was having trouble having kids. No one was using contraceptives, none of the wives were on the pill. The sad thing is that we didn't get to it earlier. We just talked about it a lot. I guess that we knew that we were sterile even before they took the tests. They just confirmed it" (Peterson and Shinoff, 1977). The same kind of reaction appears in other occupational illness epidemics.

3.2.2.3. Resignation to Recognized Hazards

Uncertainty about the symptoms encourages inaction. Nevertheless, workers have accepted clearly recognized hazards when they have minimal job mobility. For example, Deer Lodge County in Montana has an extremely high rate of lung cancer. This may be associated with a huge smelting operation in the county. A local union president told a reporter: "What bothers me is not what happens 20 years from now, but how I feed my kids tomorrow." Another union official said "Let's face it. Without the smelter this town couldn't support two cowboys and a saloon." The president added: "So the studies are right, what are my options? I'm 42 years, I've got six kids and a high school education. If the plants closes, what do I do?" (Richards, 1976).

In Minnesota, the local populations of Silver Bay and Babbit supported Reserve Mining's efforts to dump asbestos-rich taconite tailings nearby because the company had threatened loss of 3,200 jobs otherwise. Attorneys for the State and environmental groups called the threat a "'pernicious use of power that mocked Minnesota environmental laws" (Wehrwein, 1977).

3.2.3. Projecting Workers' Reactions

Two factors are central to these adaptations. One is the *level of information* about the suspected hazards of chemicals used on the job. In the anxious discussions mentioned above, workers did not have much of the available information on the hazard. Alternatively, if they know the specific risks, workers can link symptoms and possible causes. They can estimate the costs of the sitaution, and decide—within other constraints—whether or not to continue to accept them.

The second important variable is *the degree of the workers' job influence and mobility*. Both job influence and mobility shape the options that workers have when they suspect hazards. High job influence means that employees have a good deal of say about plant conditions. High job mobility means that they can easily change jobs. Workers with one or both can actually choose whether or not to accept further risks, or can at least press for fair compensation. Workers who have no such options are far more likely to resign themselves to toxic hazards.

Table 3.D. summarizes what I believe are likely adaptations to different combinations of these factors. The bischloromethyl ether (BCME) affair at Rohm and Haas in Philadelphia falls into Cell I (low information and low job influence and mobility). There was an accumulation of lung cancer cases in one building over several years, but employees had no information clearly linking BCME to human lung cancer. The plant was also not unionized; this limited employees' influence on the job. Thus, employees tolerated the situation for several years. In 1974—after undeniably strong evidence of BCME-induced lung cancer materialized—BCME was treated as an imminent health hazard.

The dibromochloropropane (DBCP) affair fits Cell II (low information but high job influence and mobility). Employees did not have the information that was available on the hazards of DBCP (Peterson and Shinoff, 1977; Shinoff, 1977), and some disabilities did result. But the

Table 3.D.
A Projection of Workers' Responses to Symptoms
Under Different Levels of Information and Job Influence–Mobility

HIGH JOB INFLUENCE AND MOBILITY

II	IV
Anxious discussion, but workers are likely to act before fatalities or numerous severe disabilities.	Workers are likely to force changes in hazardous processes, change jobs, or receive adequate compensation for extra risks taken.

LOW	HIGH
INFORMATION	INFORMATION

I	III
Prolonged anxious discussion. Severe disabilities and fatalities are likely to result before situation is rectified by workers or others.	Resignation to situation. Severe disabilities and fatalities are likely to result before situation is rectified by workers or others.

LOW JOB INFLUENCE AND MOBILITY

plant was unionized by the relatively health-conscious Oil, Chemical, and Atomic Workers Union. Through their union the employees eventually contacted the University of California for medical advice; they had a lower threshold of action than did the workers in the nonunionized Rohm and Haas plant.

Cell III combines high information and low job influence and mobility. Here the risks are acknowledged, but fatalistically accepted because there is no place to go or it is believed that nothing can be done. Such cases involve geographic areas with only one large employer.

Cell IV combines high information and high job influence and mobility. Here employees clearly recognize the risks and can either effectively press for production changes or compensation. I know of no such cases. This is partly because the public information on occupational disease incidents comes primarily from investigations, and such success stories are not investigated. Another explanation, also partial but probably true, is that employees rarely receive high levels of information about workplace hazards.

The potential impact of employee awareness deserves close attention from proponents of regulatory reform. OSHA's efforts could be efffectively supplemented—in some respects replaced—by employees taking an active part in risk assessment such as that played by workers in several European nations (Rubenstein, 1977; Geber, 1978). The agency could then focus on providing technical aid and intervening in irreconcilable labor–management conflicts. One reason that workers have not taken on such tasks is that they do not receive the relevant information in most firms. This brings us to the question of how managerial response to health hazards affects workers' responses.

3.2.4. Managerial Response to Suspected Health Problems

Richard Cyert and James March described organizations as coalitions of participants (1963: 29–32). The goals of an organization "are a series of aspiration-level constraints" argued for and imposed on the organization by members of the coalition. "Local rationalities" of the participants shape their aspirations and arguments. The sales, production, and pricing departments, for example, have different and frequently competing aspirations (1963: 115-116).

Occupational health has no comparable advocate in most organizations. I have maintained that, at present, workers in general do not actively press for occupational health concessions from employers. In return, their jobs are more stable. Thus, the routine monitoring of occupational health conditions is defaulted to employers.

But managers have little incentive to argue that effective chemical control ought to be an important organizational constraint. Steinbruner (1974: Chapter 3), Lindblom (1959), Cyert and March (1963: 118-119), and others have shown that organizational decisions usually turn on short-term feedback from certain critical variables. The needs of production, pricing, and sales are likely to be compelling constraints because their performances are quickly reflected in the firm's income. In contrast, occupational health is not a critical variable because there are only small probabilities that the firm will suffer from neglecting it. Possible OSHA intrusion is not an overwhelming problem. OSHA has completed regulations for only twenty-one substances, and inspections are relatively infrequent and penalties low (U.S. General Accounting Office, 1978a; 1978c).

Nor are employee claims, filed under State workers' compensation systems, effective incentives for substance controls. While these systems now nominally cover all occupational diseases, in practice statutory barriers severely limit such coverage. Two are especially notable. First, the time limits for filing claims are often less than the long latency periods of diseases such as cancer. Second, there are statutory presumptions against compensating many diseases. About thirty States exclude "ordinary diseases of life," and twenty-one States restrict coverage to diseases which are "peculiar to" or "characteristic of" a workers' occupation. Yet, "ordinary diseases of life," which are not traditionally or statutorily linked with certain jobs, may well be induced or promoted by occupational exposures. What also depresses compensation claims is the fact that workers do not have the information on exposures necessary to build a claim (Mancuso, 1979).

The Office of the Assistant Secretary for Policy, Evaluation, and Research in the U.S. Department of Labor notes that because of these factors "large segments of the population suffering from work-related diseases are unaware of the attendant occupational origin, while still other potential applicants are discouraged from filing claims because of the difficulties inherent in establishing the employment relation" (1979: Chap. II-14). About three percent of workers' compensation claims are for occupational diseases, and the overwhelming proportion of these involve obvious skin disorders (U.S. Department of Labor, Bureau of Labor Statistics, 1979). The 1972 Social Security Administration Survey of the Disabled, and Discher, Kleinman, and Foster indicate that workers' compensation claims are filed for only about three percent of the work-related diseases in the United States (U.S. Department of Labor, ASPER, 1979: Chapter II; Discher, Kleinman, and Foster, 1975).

The chances that the firm will suffer from employee pressure, an OSHA health inspection, or a wave of workers' compensation disease claims are relatively small. Should an occupational health issue surface in the firm, it will not effectively compete with the demands of production, pricing, and other key functions. At best, we can expect exposure reductions to a point just below where the chemical is known to cause toxic effects. Also, managers may restrict knowledge of the issue to prevent "overreactions" of workers.

Note that these expectations do not presume "bad faith" or immorality on the part of managers. They follow from managers' authority in the firm, their control of information, and their concern with pressing financial constraints on the company. Remember also that even highly suggestive data on health hazards are rarely conclusive. When businesses have a large stake in a suspect substance, a small degree of uncertainty will—to them—often justify withholding the information until it can be exhaustively checked, or until alternative substances can be developed. The incentives facing the firm, coupled with any uncertainty in the data, bias managers toward errors of underprotection (indeed, just as regulatory agencies tend to be biased toward errors of overprotection).

There are cases where firms came upon data that incriminated production staples. What technological changes were made? How was the information managed?

3.2.4.1. Technological Changes

Firms respond to data suggesting health hazards by autonomously reducing exposure to the hazard. However, they often reduce exposure considerably less than eventually recommended by public health agencies.

When the manufacturers of vinyl chloride found that several of their workers died of a rare form of liver cancer, many voluntarily reduced exposure to 50 ppm; others followed when OSHA issued an emergency standard of 50 ppm. After six months of hearings on vinyl chloride, OSHA issued a permanent standard of 1 ppm. The manufacturers sued on the grounds that the standard was infeasible and would entail massive job cuts. They lost, and then developed the technology to meet the 1 ppm limit without substantial job loss (B.F. Goodrich, 1977; Perry, 1980).

Similarly, firms which discovered problems with dibromochloropropane and the pesticide Leptophos did autonomously reduce employee exposure to the substances. However, when public health agencies and outside researchers discovered and investigated the hazards, the firms shut down the operations entirely and introduced substitute processes or products (U.S. Senate Committee on the Judiciary, 1976: 38-39; Bureau of National Affairs, 1977: 710). Morton Corn, the former Assistant Secretary of Labor for Occupational Safety and Health, noted that firms and trade associations routinely contest toxic substance standards in court because they find the costs of litigation to be lower in the short run than the costs of complying with the standards (1977: 26). Thus, autonomous technological changes by firms often do not adequately protect workers.

3.2.4.2. Management of Information

Employers have often not really told workers thoroughly about hazardous chemicals, reasoning that current exposure levels were not dangerous. "Alarmed" employees agitate for what firms regard as excessive or unsupported technical changes and compensation. A trade association representative at the meeting of the National Advisory Committee on Occupational Safety and Health on February 17, 1977, expressed these concerns well. Protesting a requirement that a sign explicitly stating "CANCER SUSPECT AGENT" be posted where regulated carcinogens were used, he said that:

> . . . if you put this word "cancer" on the sign, that cancer is the most
> fear-provoking word in the English language, and this has been established

in academic studies and in tests that have been surveyed among people—
that you create anxiety and stress among the employees. The end result is
that you have greater accidents, you have greater absenteeism, and it reduces the employee's morale and is deleterious to the employee's health.

He testified that at one plant the union supervisor threatened to
pull his people off of work, saying that "I'm not going to have my people
working where they are exposed to cancer." "One of our plants," the
representative testified, "had to put this sign up, and the businesses
next to him—the employees in that business were threatening to quit
because they had this cancer substance next door . . . Now, the use of
the word 'cancer,' as I say, is not necessary for safety, but the havoc that
played in the workplace, and specifically where you have small businesses involved, is fantastic."

Such business objections are common. In 1978, OSHA issued a final
standard for inorganic arsenic, a known carcinogen. Part of the standard
required that a sign saying "CANCER HAZARD" be posted where
arsenic was used. A number of businesses objected that "Such signs
would cause unnecessary alarm" (U.S. Department of Labor, OSHA,
1978b: 19622). Similarly, the standard for benzene required that cancer
warnings be placed on containers holding benzene. A large corporation
protested the requirement on "the basis of its potential adverse market
impact" (Bureau of National Affairs, June 19, 1978: 100). Even if information on carcinogens in the workplace is published, however, few
workers follow the appropriate scientific journals.

Thus, information somehow "fell through the cracks" in the vinyl
chloride case (Edsall, 1975: 690), in the DBCP case (Shinoff, 1977; Peterson and Shinoff, 1977), and in the Kepone case (U.S. House Committee
on Education and Labor, 1976: 269-270). Dow Chemical chose not to tell
its workers of an internal study suggesting chromosomal damage
among workers exposed to benzene. The company disagreed with the
findings and did not want to "err by finding a false positive, placing an
undefined albatross on the back of the worker. This is very unfair to the
employee" (Scott, 1978; more will be said on this particular case in
Section 3.2.5.1. below). Senator Harrison Williams of New Jersey wrote
to Senator Richard Schweiker of Pennsylvania regarding the BCME case
at Rohm and Haas:

> . . . the evidence does indicate that Rohm and Haas indeed may not have
> adequately informed their workers of a very serious health hazard. Like
> many other industry employers, Rohm and Haas refused to accept the data
> on animal carcinogenicity of bischloromethyl ether as sufficient proof of
> human carcinogenicity. The company was unwilling to tell their workers of
> the relationship of bischloromethyl ether to human lung cancer until epide-
> miological studies of human lung cancer experience had been completed in

May of 1974. . . . Hence, while some workers were told of the animal studies and possible unspecified health hazards in the environment, Rohm and Haas showed great reluctance to inform workers of the specific hazard presented by their exposure to BCME (Bureau of National Affairs, August 7, 1975: 320).

Other judgements are harsher. A former supervisory engineer for a large chemical company said that it was company policy "not to tell workers the dangers of the chemicals they worked with" (McNeil, 1979). Also, billions of dollars of suits have been filed against the asbestos industry for its failure to warn employees about the hazards of asbestos (Richards, 1978).

Every single investigation of an occupational disease epidemic demonstrates that, for one reason or another, workers did not have much of the available information on suspect substances. This prolonged the employee uncertainty which, in combination with economic concerns, encouraged anxious inaction.

One would expect the people potentially harmed by hazardous substances to be a powerful force in favor of controlling them. However, the circumstances outlined above—low information, low job influence, and low mobility—stifle this potential political force, and the default strengthens those opposing controls. Can we expect public interest groups, union health organizations—such as they are—and liberal legislators and bureaucrats to fill this gap in political support for chemical regulation? I have already discussed the contributions of these groups, and they are significant. But how do the resources of industry compare?

3.2.5. Control of Resources

Businesses dominate, but do not monopolize, three key resources: scientific and technical resources, lobbying resources, and legal resources.

3.2.5.1. Scientific and Technical Resources

Research on environmental and workplace hazards, once a neglected area, is thriving. In particular, large firms have stepped up their toxicology programs. "Getting the jump on regulators," William Reddig of *Fortune* points out, businesses are spending much more on toxic-substance research. "What they are worried about, of course, is that their best-selling products may be condemned as cancer causers, and so they are turning to the toxicologists for help . . . Budgets in this area, once just a corner of corporate safety work, are rising by 30 percent or

more a year, especially at the chemical and consumer product companies that feel most exposed to public censure and private lawsuits"
(1978).

In fact, most industrial hygienists (specialists in the effects on
health of workplace substances) and doctors in occupational medicine
are employees of private industry; many others, linked to universities,
are consultants to industry (Health Research Group, 1976; Edsall, 1975;
Schnaiberg, 1977). The concentration of these resources in industry
means that manufacturers are usually relied on to test their own products for safety.

Under the 1976 Toxic Substances Control Act, the director of the
EPA has the *option* to require testing prior to mass production, but
testing by the manufacturer. Proponents of stronger legislation advocated that all mass-produced chemicals be tested, but similarly left the
testing function with the manufacturer. The Act requires that manufacturers submit any information that they have that suggests that a chemical might be dangerous, whether or not the EPA asks for it. Steven
Jellinik, the Assistant Director of the EPA for toxic substances, told the
National Advisory Committee on Occupational Safety and Health in
February, 1978 that EPA had received only 80–90 such notices, that most
of these were inconsequential (such as a published study), and that the
EPA hoped that guidelines it was developing would increase business
response. An OSHA official told the Committee on May 11, 1979 that the
provision was "of little use in the early detection of substances that have
insidious chronic disease risks." Although people routinely suggest
that testing be done by outside parties, the concentration of research in
industry and the number of substances to be tested mean that a non-
partisan testing organization would literally "choke" on the project (see
Washington Post editorial, January 10, 1977).

Despite the increased technical activity of proregulation groups,
compared to industry they remain very weak. John Quarles, former
deputy administrator of the EPA, stated that "Industry usually has
ready access to information and can hire the best experts in the country.
Environmentalists generally must rely on limited or volunteer help and
have little ability to even question the data submitted by industry"
(1976: 170). The limited union capabilities in the health field were already discussed. Morton Corn, former Assistant Secretary of Labor for
Occupational Safety and Health, said in January, 1977 that "organized
labor has assumed a watch-dog role for the agency. Unfortunately, only
a very few of the unions have a level of expertise necessary to the
watch-dog role they desire" (1977: 16). John Sheehan of the relatively
active Steelworkers union admitted that "None of us were real experts

on safety and health. Now we have an industrial hygienist on our staff, but we still don't have the capabilities to have much input into a new (chemical) standard. That's why we want a heavy government presence in this area" (Mendeloff, 1979: 16).

However, Assistant Secretary Corn also noted OSHA's own "technical incompetence" in the occupational health area:

> With the resources currently planned for the Health Standards Directorate of OSHA, I estimate that a productivity rate of 15 to 20 health standards promulgated per year is a noble ambition in 1977 or 1978. Obviously, there are thousands of chemicals in the work environment and this rate of productivity will not adequately address the problem. However, this rate of productivity will, I believe, saturate the ability of the compliance staff to follow up with inspections related to the standards which have been promulgated. Nonetheless, the public will undoubtedly judge the Agency on the basis of standards promulgated rather than on adequate enforcement until such time as the sophistication of the public permits it to call attention to the mismatch between compliance activities and standards promulgation (1977: 24-25).

OSHA is now training industrial hygienists internally for both standards development and compliance work. Businesses can be expected to raid the agency for these people just as they have raided other agencies for lawyers with regulatory experience. An official in a related organization said that:

> It'll take them two years to train industrial hygienists and as soon as they're trained why should they stay around? Business needs them. An industrial hygienist can make a lot more in private industry than in government, and he's got OSHA experience as an extra selling point (Personal conversation, 1978).

OSHA has had some such troubles. In 1977 six OSHA hygienists tried to sound out their marketability by informing businesses about a "new service about to be offered by a staff headed by ex-OSHA compliance officers with masters degrees in occupational health." OSHA, punitively, transferred the six after learning of the clumsy market survey. The case illustrates the pull of the market on OSHA's health personnel (Bureau of National Affairs, November 10, 1977: 821).

OSHA has been able to retain, at least for a time, its industrial health trainees. The number of OSHA's health inspectors increased from 248 in 1976 to about 600 in 1980, and the number of health inspections from 9,217 in 1976 to 11,160 in 1979. But OSHA had been falling so far short of adequately monitoring health hazards that even large increases in compliance activity may not adequately address the problem. From 1973 to 1976, OSHA performed inspections for inorganic lead covering 1.1 percent of the workers handling lead; benzene inspections for .1 percent of the employees handling benzene; and vinyl chloride inspections for 1.2 percent of the workers handling vinyl chloride (U.S. General Accounting Office, 1978a: 11). OSHA recommended in 1979 that South Carolina increase its industrial hygienist staff from 8 to 61; North Carolina, 8 to 118; Wisconsin, 7 to 74; and Wyoming, 3 to 10. The States called the suggestions economically and politically ridiculous (Bureau of National Affairs, October 18, 1979: 469).

Thus, industry controls most of the industrial health research in the United States. This creates a bias against the discovery of occupational health problems. Firms—which are understandably interested in stable production—may not release suggestive data until most of the uncertainty about a suspected problem is removed. "Removing uncertainty" usually requires strong epidemiological data; that is, a noticing of several fatalities or serious disabilities. Subsequently, industry heavily influences the level of attention others give to studies of a particular substance.

Allied Chemical performed studies in 1961 suggesting the hazardousness of Kepone and filed them with the government in a routine application for pesticide registration (U.S. House Committee on Education and Labor, 1976: 92; for a criticism of the U.S. pesticide registration program, see the U.S. Senate Committee on the Judiciary, 1976). When several disabilities from Kepone surfaced, almost accidentally, Allied Chemical actively advertised studies presumably showing the safety of a chemically comparable substance. The company contacted industrial hygienists from the National Institute for Occupational Safety and Health in August of 1975 about a meeting where these latter studies would be discussed. Congressman Daniels asked one hygienist, Dr. William Lloyd, "why Allied, which had made definitive studies on Kepone, had not called this meeting to discuss its own studies of Kepone conducted in the early sixties?"

> Dr. Lloyd: I don't think I can speculate on that sir. I must say that at the time I received this call I was not too familiar with Kepone and the problems associated with it. The news was just developing. I think I had seen the 1960 and 1962 reports a few days before and only looked at them very briefly.
> Mr. Daniels: did you think it important at any time that Allied was manufacturing this product Kepone, especially after what had occurred at Hopewell, Virginia, at the plant of Life Science, that it did not call a conference on its own report?
> Dr. Lloyd: I think that would have been appropriate, to review all the evidence, to consider what might be causing this disease experience . . . the 1960 and 1962 reports were not discussed at the meeting, but, if they were, they may have been mentioned briefly. The whole point of the discussion there was to present to the people gathered there what was then known about the experiences of workers at Life Science (U.S. House Committee on Education and Labor, 1976: 269-270).

According to Lloyd's notes on the meeting, the discussants brought together by Allied Chemical suggested that the German studies showing Kepone's safety were valid. They said that the samples used in the damaging studies of the early 1960's were possibly contaminated, and that Life Science's workers may have been exposed to other, as yet unknown, toxic agents. Lloyd noted that no toxic agents other than Kepone had been found in the workers' blood, and so it "would not seem reasonable to conclude that other agents were involved" (U.S. House Committee on Education and Labor, 1976: 269).

Some industrial scientists do underline the implications of their research to management, although they stop short of covertly releasing the data. A medical consultant warned Velsicol of a series of possible Leptophos-related diseases on June 9 and June 20, 1975. The consultant recommended that a "discrete investigation be made of all the employees who have been in contact with Leptophos," and that the company monitor exposure to the substance. Meanwhile, based on evidence gathered overseas, the EPA proposed to revoke Leptophos's registration as a "safe" pesticide. Velsicol did not include its consultant's reports in its June 24, 1975 protest of the EPA's action (U.S. Senate Committee on the Judiciary, 1976: 37-38).

In June, 1977, Dr. Dante Picciano of Dow Chemical told the company that a study he had completed showed that benzene concentrations of less than 10 ppm induced chromosone damage in workers. One Dow consultant called the research a "really important study . . . by a first rate investigator." Three consultants agreed with the thrust of Picciano's conclusions. Dr. D.J. Killian, Picciano's supervisor at Dow Chemical, told the company's Director of Medical Services in July, 1977 that "the results are not what we expected, but (the study) identifies an unsuspected occupational health hazard and, therefore, appropriate steps must be taken to disseminate the information through EPA, NIOSH (the National Institute for Occupational Safety and Health), or the medical literature." At the time, OSHA was actively considering an exposure limit for benzene.

At hearings on the proposed standard, Dow officials did not mention Picciano's findings. Instead, they submitted three other corporate studies showing "no significant abnormalities . . . that would relate to benzene exposure" (Scott, 1978). OSHA learned of the Picciano study when Picciano quit Dow and joined OSHA's Office of Health Standards. Reacting to press reports of the incident, a Dow spokesman said that the company had not submitted the study to the Summer 1977 OSHA benzene hearings because it considered the study "incomplete." However, in May, 1978—almost one year after Picciano told Dow of the findings—it submitted the study to the EPA. "Even though the study was not complete, we thought it would make a contribution," said its spokesman (Bureau of National Affairs, June 22, 1978: 59). Dow later argued that Picciano's study was methodologically deficient. The Manufacturing Chemists Association asked James Jandel, a hematologist at Harvard Medical School, to evaluate the data. Jandel asked a cytogeneticist, Peter Tishler, to comment also. Both criticized the study, Tishler saying that "The sloppy way in which this was handled is offensive to me." Another of Picciano's chromosomal studies—this one on the residents of Love Canal—was both scored and accepted by outside reviewers (Kolata, 1980; Omang, 1980b).

One could argue that the corporate treatment of uncertainty biases the system to errors of underprotection. It is not that corporations withhold conclusive data on the hazards of a chemical. Rather, they are selective about the uncertain data they release, distributing the corporate studies showing the safety of chemicals and "discretely checking" incriminating studies. Here Dow was apparently very reluctant to give an "incomplete" study indicting benzene to OSHA when the agency was about to issue a standard for benzene, in spite of the recommendation of Picciano and his supervisor at Dow.

Thus, ultimately management does decide the disposition of research, and there is no evidence that internal scientists are rebelling in significant numbers. According to Dr. Samuel Epstein, one trade association member commented in an OSHA advisory committee meeting that "these are just scientists. They have no authority to pass judgements on regulatory matters. This is the responsibility of top corporate management and lawyers" (U.S. House Committee on Education and Labor, 1974: 197).

There are certainly many examples of corporate cooperation with outside researchers or agencies. These arrangements, however, are often slow in developing. Firms subsequently publicize them as evidence of their responsibility in quickly handling chemical problems.

One such case was the handling of the BCME (bischloromethyl ether cancer "epidemic" by Rohm and Haas. The president of Rohm and Haas told the Subcommittee on the Environment of the U.S. Senate Committee on Commerce in 1975 that ". . . when we had the meeting with (a New York University research team), they indicated they were going to undertake an epidemiological study of the entire industry and we, of course, said 'You have our complete cooperation on this'. . ." (U.S. Senate Committee on Commerce, 1975: 75).

Senator Tunney later asked the NYU researchers—who since 1966 had been studying BCME—"Could either one of you comment generally on the extent to which Rohm and Haas or any other company cooperated with you in making data available on BCME during the time you did your studies?"

> Dr. Albert: I think it is fair to say that companies put in this position are extremely defensive and they feel extremely threatened, which they are, and it really required overwhelming evidence, experimental evidence, as well as common knowledge about suspicion of increased numbers of lung cancer cases to bring them around, but the meeting that was held was a room full of angry men. When finally the die was cast and the study went as the epidemiologic study, there was good cooperation. We had reason to think that all the available data was given to us . . . They were not very happy, naturally, about the whole business. This is really a very traumatic affair.
> . . . Part of the unhappiness was being forced into the position of having to go ahead with a study of this sort.
> Dr. Wagoner: Well, I think there was great consternation among the members of the industry at the meeting. Actual disbelief by some and denial of the validity of the NYU studies on the part of others. I think it was in that setting that we went away from the meeting convinced that there had to be immediate resolution of the problem both in terms of its scientific merit and in terms of its public health impact (U.S. Senate Committee on Commerce, 1975: 110-111).

It is not that Rohm and Haas did not cooperate in the investigation. The point is that the later company interpretation overstated the ease with which Rohm and Haas cooperated. We are asked to believe that firms are falling over themselves to quickly redress chemical problems.

A second case of "cooperation" with outside researchers was the handling of the vinyl chloride affair by the plastics industry. In late 1972, Dr. Cesare Maltoni of Italy found cancerous tumors in rodents exposed to vinyl chloride concentrations as low as 50 ppm. At the time, the U.S. exposure limit was 500 ppm. In October, 1972, the Manufacturing Chemists Association had agreed with a consortium of European chemical companies to share information, but not to disclose it without prior consent. In January, 1973, the Manufacturing Chemists Association (MCA) and the associate director of the carcinogenesis program of the National Cancer Institute learned of the Maltoni study. The NCI scientist later told a Senate committee that he felt the work should be included in a report to the World Health Organization's Agency for Research on Cancer.

Some members of the Manufacturing Chemists Association responded to the news of the Maltoni study by reducing exposure to vinyl chloride and studying the mortality of plastics workers. The MCA also recommended to NIOSH a precautionary label for vinyl chloride that did not mention its toxic effects on animals or people (Epstein, 1978: 103).

In January, 1974, one study by MCA member B.F. Goodrich indicated that three employees had died in the past two years from a rare form of liver cancer. Goodrich told OSHA, which issued an emergency standard of 50 ppm. When OSHA issued a permanent standard six months later of 1 ppm, the Society of Plastics Industry sued, threatening massive job losses. The Society lost, and industry had little difficulty complying with the standard.

Four things are clear. First, the Manufacturing Chemists Association members knew of the Maltoni data and regarded them as ominous enough to reduce exposure to vinyl chloride. Second, the MCA did not immediately tell workers of the possible cancer danger.

Third, government scientists did not follow up on the leads by immediately asking for tighter regulation of vinyl chloride. The NCI scientist suggested that Maltoni's work be presented to the World Health Organization. NIOSH, which—according to B.F. Goodrich—had been told of the Italian studies by the MCA, did not actively pursue the lead.

Fourth, the MCA—in not telling workers of the suspicion of vinyl chloride's danger based on animal data—had behaved in the fashion that had earned Rohm and Haas the wrath of Senator Harrison Williams in the BCME affair (pp. 52-3 above). In both cases, animal data raised suspicions, but workers were not immediately informed.

In February, 1977, MCA member B.F. Goodrich interpreted this history in an article titled "Vinyl Chloride—A Study in Prevention." The article was published in *Job Safety and Health*, the magazine of the Occupational Safety and Health Administration. Goodrich made three pertinent observations.

First, it said that the epidemiological evidence released in January, 1974, was the first proof of human carcinogenicity. Even if this were true, the fact remains that the MCA members did not tell workers of their suspicions of human carcinogenicity based on the animal data.

Second, Goodrich emphasized at several points that it had contacted government scientists and gotten no substantial response. This repeated defensive claim contrasted sharply with the image of aggressive industry–government cooperation that the article was trying to project. It read like a signal that governmental inactivity made the MCA's own failure to notify workers, for which it had been criticized, more tolerable (Edsall, 1975).

Third, the article explained the suit over the permanent standard of 1 ppm as a belief, in good faith, on the part of the plastics industry that the standard could not be met. Even granting this, the suit underlines the fact that industries autonomously lower exposure to toxic substances only insofar as it is technically convenient. OSHA's health standards are challenged in court precisely because they force exposure controls that industry would not otherwise install. Thus, the fact that the MCA members reduced exposure to vinyl chloride somewhat does not mean that the workers were removed from danger. (It is also ironic that two years after Senator Williams—a coauthor of the OSH Act—criticized Rohm and Haas for not fully informing workers about the human implications of the animal data on BCME, the OSH Administration magazine published an article by B.F. Goodrich praising a similar situation as a "study in prevention".)

Workers may obtain full information on suspected hazards only after strong evidence removes uncertainty about the substance or there is external pressure on the firm. Until such evidence or pressure materializes, and when firms have a substantial investment at stake and the controls would be costly, management has strong incentives to not fully inform workers about hazards. That industry dominates research resources in this area is a powerful force operating against toxic-substance control.

3.2.5.2. Access to Lobbying Resources

Like information, lobbying resources are imbalanced in favor of business. John Quarles, the former Deputy Administrator of the EPA, points out that industry is represented in Washington by a "vast aggregation" of trade associations, lobbyists, and other agents whose salaries are deductible as business expenses. Environmental groups, on the other hand, are financially able to maintain only a small number of full-time active lobbyists in the city. Their lobbying efforts are curtailed by tax laws which preclude lobbying by organizations receiving tax deductible, charitable gifts (Quarles, 1976: 169-170). I have already discussed the limited resources given occupational health matters by labor unions (Section 3.2.1.).

Agencies sense this imbalance. In 1977, public interest groups accused the EPA of loosening registration requirements for categories of pesticides. Edwin L. Johnson, head of the EPA pesticide registration program, responded that "If we don't register (these pesticides, the businesses) run to their congressman and he comes to use. We end up spending all of our resources on the Hill arguing this and there's nothing left over to do the job" (Richards, 1977).

The director of Policy Planning for the Federal Trade Commission, Robert Reich, pointed out that "it is estimated that corporations and trade associations account for eighty-five to ninety percent of about $1 billion a year spent on grass roots efforts" (1979: 3). Douglas Costle, the administrator of the EPA during the Carter administration, spoke of the EPA's struggles with "the rape, pillage, and burn crowd," which includes "members of a number of industries with very special agendas —the auto industry, coal, and steel. Some of them exercise more prudent judgement than others." Although noting that the nation's air and water were cleaner in 1980 than in 1976, and that it was now "possible to burn coal in this country" within EPA standards, he said that "My successor has my total sympathy and empathy—You win very few victories. It's just varying degrees of defeat" (Omang, 1980c).

Common Cause surveyed thirty-nine regulatory commissioners in 1976, asking them to record their contacts with outside groups. Forty-three percent of the 2,786 recorded contacts were with industry representatives. Four percent were with representatives of public interest groups, consumer organizations, or concerned individuals. Also, seventeen of the thirty-nine commissioners who made their records public recorded no contact with public interest groups or consumer groups during 1976 (Kramer, 1977).

3.2.5.3. Access to Legal Resources

Court orders frequently determine national policy. Industry can always use litigation to stall action if it thinks a suit will be helpful, and it has available "the best and most expensive" lawyers to argue its case (Quarles, 1976: 171). Dr. Morton Corn's report on OSHA in Janaury 1977 stated that:

> . . . the uncertainties (in occupational health) which we attempt to treat in our standards documents are fertile grounds for legal challenges by those who are not committed to abiding by the standard in question. It is clear that delay of implementation of a standard saves a great deal of money for those impacted by a standard. Indeed, rough estimates by OSHA indicate that the legal costs of ensuring delay through the courts represent a small fraction of the costs of compliance, costs which would have been expended during the period that the challenge holds the standard in abeyance (1977: 26).

Environmental organizations, on the other hand, are generally strapped for funds. "They have won a large number of striking court victories," says the EPA's Quarles, "but have overcome tremendous odds in doing so" (1976: 171). Jeffrey Berry's study of public interest organizations noted that, while litigation by such groups has increased in recent years, litigation is still very limited, tends to be very expensive, and is used only as a last resort (Berry, 1977: 225–230). What increases there have been in public interest litigation must also be kept in perspective by remembering the continuing flow of top lawyers to regulated corporations. Sixty-nine percent of the 1977 graduating class of Harvard Law School went into corporate law, while only one percent joined public interest groups (Auerbach, 1977). It is not surprising, then, that the U.S. Senate Committee on Governmental Affairs *Study on Federal Regulation* found that, compared to public interest groups, industries committed as much as 50 to 100 times the resources for outside counsel to represent them in regulatory proceedings (U.S. Senate Committee on Governmental Affairs, 1977: III).

3.2.6. Pressure for Cost-Benefit Analysis of Regulations

The previous factors working against chemical control principally involved the private sector—the economic vulnerability of workers, their inability to obtain all available information on hazards, and industry's domination of scientific, technical, lobbying, and legal resources. However, just as certain government organizations tend to support strong chemical controls, other public organizations tend to oppose them. The most effective public criticisms come from the Executive Office of the President—specifically, from the Council on Wage and Price Stability (CWPS) and, to a lesser extent, from the Council of Economic Advisors (CEA) and the Office of Management and Budget (OMB).

The regulatory laws of the late 1960's and early 1970's gave little explicit weight to the economic costs of controls. The Occupational Safety and Health Act of 1970 mandated that, "to the extent feasible," OSHA should assure that no worker suffer disabling injury or illness. The agency has, at least publicly, maintained that "feasibility" is more a technological than an economic issue. That is, it can order firms to install expensive controls even if many firms cannot afford them on the grounds that a firm that must expose workers to serious hazards to survive should not be operating. Further, OSHA can order an industry to install expensive controls to prevent even indeterminate numbers of illnesses. According to this view, the OSH Act weighted the decision-making process heavily in favor of protecting workers; the balancing of health and safety benefits with economic costs has little role to play in the Act's enforcement.

Since 1974, however, economists in the Executive Office of the President—particularly in the Council on Wage and Price Stability and the Council of Economic Advisors—have tried to inject explicit cost-benefit calculations into agency decisions.

In 1974, inflation was a raging economic problem. The Consumer Price Index increased 12.2 percent in 1974, 1.3 percent during August alone. The Council on Wage and Price Stability was established in August to monitor private-sector actions that might increase the rate of inflation. Also, CWPS was directed to review Federal activities and programs to determine whether or not they were inflationary. The Council interpreted this as requiring cost-benefit analysis of important Federal regulations (Miller and Yandle, 1979: 5).

On November 27, 1974, President Ford issued Executive Order 11821, telling executive agencies to certify "that inflationary impact . . . (has) been carefully considered" when they issued major legislative proposals, rules, or regulations. The Office of Management and budget (OMB) was told to guide agencies' impact statement programs. OMB Circular A-107 (January 2, 1975) provided the guidelines. OMB's criteria for a "major" action included the action's 1) cost to consumers, businesses, markets, or government; and 2) its effects on competition, important materials or services, employment, productivity, or energy supply and demand. An agency was to review how a proposal might affect each of these, and also consider the costs and benefits both of the action and reasonable alternative actions. CWPS came to serve as the principal monitor of the inflation impact statements.

CWPS did not want "inflationary impact" to mean only the effect on the Consumer Price Index. Individually, even major regulations do not directly affect the CPI substantially. Rather, an inflationary proposal was considered one in which the costs exceeded the benefits, and an antiinflationary proposal one in which the benefits exceeded the costs. According to a 1976 CWPS report:

> This approach recognizes that the primary determinants of the rate of inflation are monetary and fiscal policy. However, holding these constant, any regulatory or legislative action which misallocates resources is, in and of itself, inflationary. This can be seen by observing that, if resources are misallocated, the real supply of goods and services which the economy can produce is reduced. Thus, for any given level of nominal output, the price of final goods is increased (Hopkins, 1976: 5).

One of the CWPS analyses—a critique of OSHA's cotton-dust standard—noted that "To the extent that the costs of the proposed regulation exceed the benefits, resources would be withdrawn from other markets where their use is valued more highly . . . We note also that the 'cost of a regulation may be the foregone opportunity of adopting a better one. Therefore, to the extent that the goals of a proposed regulation could be achieved in a less costly manner than the regulation contemplates, that regulation is inefficient. The costs which are associated with such a proposed regulation ultimately are translated into higher prices. Thus, such costs may become reflected in and add to the overall price indices (such as the consumer price index) more than is necessary to accomplish the same regulatory goals" (U.S. Council on Wage and Price Stability, 1977: 4). An "economically efficient" regulation was usually one that permitted firms to make workers wear personal protective devices to control chemical exposure, rather than one which required engineering controls. Also, "economically efficient" regulations did not reduce chemical exposure limits far below the threshold of known toxic effects; CWPS was far less likely than OSHA, for example, to conclude that "there is no safe level of exposure to a carcinogen."

The inflation impact statement program was extended by President Ford in 1977 with Executive Order 11949; this simply changed the term "inflation impact" to "economic impact." President Carter ordered a similar program with Executive Order 12044 on March 23, 1978. This program required economic analyses of regulations having an annual impact of at least $100 million on the economy or requiring a major price or cost increase for an industry, region of the country, or level of government. The "Improving Government Regulations Program" also established a Regulatory Analysis Review Group (RARG) to independently review ten to twenty major regulations each year. While nominally an interagency organization including regulatory agencies, RARG was in practice a joint venture of CWPS, CEA, and the OMB (DeMuth, 1980a: 16).

After critiquing an agency's economic impact statement, or after reviewing the proposed regulation itself, the Council on Wage and Price Stability wrote comments for either the public docket on the regulation or for internal regulatory agency use. CWPS also testified at hearings on proposals.

From 1974 to 1980, CWPS's comments usually severely criticized OSHA's proposals. The conflicts of the agencies reflected different orientations toward health and safety regulation. OSHA's primary purpose was to regulate health and safety problems. If there was a danger of erring, OSHA maintained that it preferred to err in favor of workers' protection. It often proposed reducing toxic exposures to levels providing maximum feasible protection, and it favored engineering changes over personal protective devices as controls (see Chapter 2).

The agency also resisted using cost-benefit calculations in its decisions. Arguing that the OSH Act instructed the agency to maximally protect workers, OSHA asserted that cost-benefit ratios had little part to play in regulatory decision making. Even if cost-benefit analysis had a role, OSHA maintained that calculating benefits is a highly uncertain and arbitrary exercise, and that policies should not be guided by such a flimsy tool.

The Council on Wage and Price Stability's primary mission was to control inflation. CWPS was thus sensitive to how much regulation would cost businesses or consumers, and inveighed against any expenditures without measurable benefits. What OSHA called a "protective margin of error," CWPS called an "economic misallocation." The President's economic advisors argued that businesses, which face a complex web of monetary incentives and economic interactions, are more likely to comply with "economically efficient" regulations. Also, assuming compliance, "then it is a recognized scientific principle that more employees can be protected by a standard based on cost-effectiveness principles than one not based on cost-effectiveness grounds" (U.S. Council on Wage and Price Stability, 1977: 8). Indeed, regulation channeled resources away from investments in new plants and equipment, diminishing productivity and thus the resources needed to attain other regulatory goals; "economically efficient" regulations minimized the unproductive use of resources and retarding of growth. The Chairman of the Council of Economic Advisers under President Carter, Charles Schultze, noted that such conflicts between regulatory agencies and CWPS and the CEA only indicated a balanced and healthy debate (U.S. Senate Committee on Environment and Public Works, 1979: 335).

Still, many regulatory officials, public interest groups, and labor treated CWPS and CEA interventions into regulation as something other than efforts to optimally meet health and safety goals. They charged that, if regulatory agencies often seemed obsessed with health and safety, CWPS and CEA were obsessed with businesses' preferences for stability. One EPA official noted that the economic advisors relied overwhelmingly on industry information, thus "giving industry one more shot at weakening the regulations after the record is closed" (Shabecoff, 1979). Wanting to see whom the CEA spoke to when analyzing Interior Department regulations on strip mining, the Natural Resources Defense Council checked the list of its contacts. "Virtually all were initiated by CEA staff members. Of the more than seventy such contacts disclosed, two were with environmental organizations. The vast majority were with industry, officials from states that had opposed the Surface Mining Act, or consultants hired by the Department of Energy to demonstrate that the regulations would adversely affect coal production. Aside from two calls to environmental organizations, none of the contacts showed any concern with the potential benefits of the regulations or the objectives of the Surface Mining Act" (U.S. Senate Committee on Environment and Public Works, 1979: 107).

It is clear that the CWPS and the CEA attempted to prevent very tight regulatory controls, whether one regards their involvement as a healthy different point of view or as a conduit for industry pressure. We will later evaluate which image best fits CWPS and CEA intervention into health regulation.

3.3. SUMMARY

This chapter has outlined the forces encouraging and discouraging strict controls of toxic substances. Public interest groups, union health organizations, activist Congressional staffs, the General Accounting Office, the proregulation tendencies of agency officials, and standards of evidence in judicial review of agency actions generally encourage controls. However, industry, which tries to minimize the disruptions caused by chemical-industry controversies and regulation, considerably offsets those factors. Businesses control employment and access to information about hazards, thereby minimizing pressure or protest by affected workers. Businesses also dominate scientific, lobbying, and legal resources in occupational health work and regulatory proceedings. Finally, the Council on Wage and Price Stability and the Council of Economic Advisors in the Executive Office of the President, in trying to retard price increases, tend to support regulations with relatively high exposure limits ("high" meaning limits not much below the point where toxic effects are known to occur) and regulations which rely on personal protective devices as controls. CWPS and CEA support these industry positions far more often than they support regulations with low exposure limits ("low" meaning limits which allow a large protective margin of error) and which rely on engineering changes as controls.

What implications does this "force field" have for the pluralist, capitalist State, and organizational perspectives on regulation outlined in Chapter 1?

According to the pluralist perspective, which treats the State as a reflection of private interest-group pressures, the resource imbalance against chemical control leads us to expect that OSHA will tend to compromise in favor of business. If it does, and how it goes about trading off the goals of the OSH Act for business's convenience, will be discussed in Chapters 5–7. Remember, to test this view we have to see if the government is a reflection of interest-group pressures.

At first glance, the capitalist State perspective does not explain a weak OSHA. If OSHA is overwhelmed by stronger industry groups, how can we say that it patches up the particularly oppressive aspects of capitalism? There are at least two responses. First, one could say that businesses' control of jobs and information has effectively prevented any mass agitation about unhealthy working conditions; therefore, capitalism does not have much of a structural weakness for OSHA to repair, and so OSHA can be passive. However, if this were the case, why would we have an OSHA in the first place? This capitalist State response does not convincingly explain a weak OSHA. There is a second possible capitalist State response; that is, the capitalistic nature of the State would be demonstrated in the activities of other State organizations vis-a-vis OSHA. Organizations of the State reflect society-wide class conflict. A weak OSHA represents workers' interests in the State apparatus; it is a concession to labor and anticapitalist groups. When OSHA generates too much pressure on business, stronger procapitalist State organizations will step in to safeguard the interests of private capital accumulation, overriding workers' interests (Poulantzas, 1978: 137, 142-143).

For example, let us say that OSHA, opposing powerful businesses, attempts to implement a particular expensive chemical standard which is of little value to collective capital accumulation but may prevent diseases, the costs of which are internalized by workers. Presumably, CWPS and CEA—concerned about capitalism's welfare—will step in and successfully pressure OSHA to drastically revise the standard. Therefore, one could say that the State *apparatus* is truly a conscious, active guardian of capitalism. We will see if there are such cases as we review OSHA's standards activity.

Of course, the second capitalist State interpretation assumes that OSHA *does* represent workers' interests. Does OSHA in fact actively try to protect workers' from dangerous chemicals? Or is it primarily interested in surviving as an organization, any benefits to workers being secondary effects? This brings us to the organizational perspective.

The organizational perspective would see a weak OSHA not as an arbiter of competing interests; not as an agency trying to repair the structural weaknesses of capitalism; and not as an active guardian of workers' interests overwhelmed by procapitalist State organizations. Rather, OSHA's creation would be a societal recognition of an occupational disease problem, a product of intergroup bargaining. Once set up, however, the agency is above all an organization and as such is interested in autonomy and procedural stability. Perhaps it is also susceptible to radical (and destabilizing) redirection by activist leaders. Also, it does not act in a comprehensively rational way; it may behave inconsistently.

An organizational perspective leads one to the following questions about a weak OSHA. How does OSHA adjust its procedures in response to pressures, recognizing that these adjustments will not simply reflect the balance of power among interest groups? How does it present these adjustments to the outside world; what are the changing definitions of goals, successes, and failures? How does OSHA respond to new, potentially straining situations—such as very promising public-health leads —which clash with stable operations? Can activist leaders turn a weak agency effectively against powerful businesses or the allegedly dominant value of private capital accumulation and survive?

This chapter has scanned what appears to be the power structure in occupational health work, and outlined questions the different perspectives raise about the power distribution. Chapter 4 reviews OSHA's standards-setting procedures, and then projects how OSHA would behave, *given the circumstances outlined in this chapter*, if it functioned exactly as the pluralist, capitalist State, or organizational views imply.

Procedures of and Predictions about OSHA

4.1. REGULATORY PROCEDURES: THE ADMINISTRATIVE PROCEDURES ACT AND THE VALUE OF RATIONAL PARTICIPATION

The Administrative Procedures Act of 1946 is a codification of procedural fairness requirements governing all Federal administrative agencies. It applies to proceedings which produce rules, orders, and licenses. Its purpose is to give people affected by decisions an opportunity to make their views known so that their interests will not be overlooked or arbitrarily dismissed.

Agencies must inform people about the responsibility for rules, orders, and licenses. The authority behind an agency's decisions, the exact wording, and where and how to protest decisions must be published in the Federal Register. The agency must publish a description of its organization, authority structure, rules and methods, and reasons for its decisions. Agencies must make available for inspection by those persons "properly and directly concerned" all final opinions or orders in the adjudication of cases. Notices of proposed rule making must be published, and the agency must give "interested persons an opportunity to participate in rule making" through written comments. All comments must be considered by the agency. An interested person is given the "right to petition for the issuance, amendment, or repeal of a rule." The Act specifies how proceedings are to be conducted. Final decisions must include "findings and conclusions, as well as the reasons or basis therefor, upon all the material issues of fact, law, or discretion presented on the record." The Act adds that "any person suffering legal wrong because of any agency action, or adversely affected or aggrieved by such action . . . shall be entitled to judicial review thereof" (Kaufman, 1977: 43-46).

How do OSHA's standards activities live up to the requirements of public participation set by the Administrative Procedures Act? How is a standard implemented?

4.1.1. The National Institute for Occupational Safety and Health

The OSH Act of 1970 created the National Institute for Occupational Safety and Health (NIOSH) in the Department of Health, Education, and Welfare (Now the Department of Health and Human Services) to do research on hazards and related work, such as evaluation of suspected workplace dangers when requested by specific employers or employees. On the basis of its research, the Institute recommends occupational safety and health standards to OSHA. NIOSH forwards these recommended standards and related information to OSHA in packages called "criteria documents." These describe the effects of specific toxic substances and suggest protections. Officially, NIOSH hopes that this will stimulate voluntary action by employers and give employees a basis for petitioning the Labor Department to issue compulsory standards.

NIOSH obtains its information by reviewing research literature as well as through its own or contracted laboratory and field research. NIOSH is headed by a director and is part of the Center for Disease Control in the U.S. Public Health Service in Health and Human Services.

4.1.2. OSHA's Health Standards

The OSH Act of 1970 also authorizes the Secretary of Labor, through OSHA, to establish national occupational health and safety standards, to promote information and education programs, and to enforce standards through workplace inspections and impose penalties for violations.

OSHA issues three types of standards—Interim, Emergency Temporary, and Permanent.

4.1.2.1. Interim Standards

Interim standards are the national consensus standards which existed at the time the OSH Act was passed. In 1968, the American Conference of Governmental Industrial Hygienists (ACGIH), a private standards-setting organization, had established recommended exposure limits for about 400 substances. Under the Walsh–Healy Act, the Labor Department in 1969 made the limits compulsory for firms doing government-supported work.

These standards are only threshold limit values (TLVs). They do not require work-practice measures, compulsory air monitoring, medical examinations, retention of medical and exposure records, and other requirements characterizing more stringent standards proposals since 1971.

Also, the limits are high. According to Nicholas Ashford, the TLVs "merely define the limits beyond which exposure is known to be hazardous. Because TLVs are often based on poor data and are not designed to protect all those exposed, they afford minimal protection for workers. Only about 400 TLVs were included in the initial standards package, even though it has been estimated that literally thousands of agents and substances found in the workplace pose health hazards" (1976b: 296). The TLVs are particularly high for carcinogens. In fact, the American Conference of Governmental Industrial Hygienists had issued an appendix calling for zero exposure levels for carcinogens itemized in the main TLV list. However, OSHA did not include this appendix in the 1971 regulation adopting the TLV list. The regulation extended the Walsh–Healy requirements to all regulated industries, and OSHA argued that this appendix had not been included in the Walsh–Healy Act (Ashford, 1976b: 154).

In 1974, recognizing the deficiencies of the TLV list, OSHA and NIOSH announced the Standards Completion Project, which was supposed to supplement the Threshold Limit Values by adding requirements for medical surveillance, exposure monitoring, and other preventative measures. The Project is not intended to change the TLVs themselves. The exposure limits are retained unless NIOSH develops a criteria document for a completely new standard. At the end of 1981, NIOSH had completed and sent to OSHA supplementary requirements for over 250 substances. OSHA had *proposed* such requirements as standards for seventeen of the substances. None of the proposals had actually been implemented.

4.1.2.2. Emergency Temporary Standards (ETSs)

Section 6(c) of the OSH Act says that when the Secretary of Labor determines that "(A) employees are exposed to grave danger from exposure to substances or agents determined to be physically harmful or from new hazards, and (B) that such emergency standard is necessary to protect employees from such danger," the Secretary "shall" issue an emergency temporary standard (ETS). The ETS is effective immediately upon publication in the Federal Register. A permanent standard must follow within six months.

4.1.2.3. Permanent Standards

Section 6(b) describes how a permanent standard should be set. After determining that a standard is needed, the Secretary may request the recommendation of an advisory committee. The advisory committee must give the Secretary its recommendations within 90 days or some other period established by the Secretary, in no case to be longer than 270 days.

OSHA must then publish the proposed standard in the Federal Register, give interested parties time to comment, and, if requested, hold hearings. The comment periods are thirty days long. Within sixty days after the comment period or sixty days after the hearings OSHA must issue the final standard or determine that the standard should not be issued.

Grover Wrenn, then the chief of the Division of Health Standards within OSHA, described how OSHA actually implemented 6(b) in a court affadavit filed with the U.S. District Court in the District of Columbia in 1975. He listed nineteen steps in setting a standard (The affadavit is summarized as an Appendix.) The affadavit outline a rambling series of reviews and requests for "public inputs" which could be extended indefinitely. For example, after step 12,

> . . . here, as at all other stages requiring direct approval by the Assistant Secretary (for OSH) . . . or staff, new developments or the full expert inter-disciplinary scrutiny of top-level panel examinations may, and frequently do, reveal significant deficiencies or require altered regulatory choices necessitating further drafts before a proposal is approved for publication. Several of the above steps may accordingly be repeated several times before the next milestone is needed.

With its multiple layers of review and likely repetition of steps the standards process is, in practice, amorphous. Clearly, the degree of review is not a legislative requirement. The process Wrenn described extends standards development far beyond what one would expect on reading 6(b) of the OSH Act. This part of the process does provide extensive public input. Because toxic-substance control is fraught with uncertainties, and because the standards involve large sums of money, "input" and debate could conceivably be extended indefinitely. Literal enforcement of the OSH Act would cut off this debate, committing OSHA to act on "substantial" even if shaky or incomplete evidence to protect workers.

However, there is a clear conflict between literal enforcement of the Act and the values of participation and "full rational deliberations." Participation, notes Herbert Kaufman, increases the rationality of decision making.

> Lack of comprehensiveness in weighing alternatives can result in a course of
> action inferior to available alternatives. It may eventuate in decisions that
> powerful public agencies and political leaders, excluded from the process of
> deciding, cannot support. It may produce policies offensive to a segment of
> the community capable of offering strong resistance and even of overturning
> them (1977: 46-47).

If businesses—which generally want to avoid tight regulation of
their processes—dominate technical, political, and legal resources, and
if OSHA and proregulation groups are comparatively weak, the value of
participation by interested groups might override the value of moving
quickly on public-health problems. For example, recall the statement by
former OSH Assistant Secretary Morton Corn that the costs of insuring
delays of standards through the administrative and legal process are a
small fraction of the costs of compliance with the standards themselves
(1977: 26). We will see if this occurred as we examine OSHA's history in
Chapters 5, 6 and 7.

4.2. WHAT DO THE PERSPECTIVES ON REGULATION IMPLY?

Three views of regulatory agencies were described earlier. The
pluralist view suggests that regulatory agency behavior reflects the balance of power among private interest groups. The capitalist State perspective suggests that the State overrides anticapitalist groups, and
businesses with only special interests, for the sake of the capitalist
system. The organizational perspective suggests that the agencies desire
autonomy and stability, and therefore deflect interest-group pressures
and care little about the welfare or profitability of businesses. Given the
circumstances outlined in Chapter 3, what could be expected of OSHA
if it was best explained by 1) interest-group pressure, 2) concerns for
capitalism, or 3) organizational desires for stability and autonomy, or its
leaders' personal agendas?

4.2.1. Pluralism

The pluralist perspective, emphasizing interest-group influence,
suggests that businesses will dominate regulatory activity. OSHA will
not regulate many chemicals because of industry pressure.

But, periodically, comparatively weak interest groups will prod the
government to strictly control toxic substances. This is because historical conditions sometimes favor regulation. For example, businesses
may not be mobilized on some issue, and groups favoring regulation
would be the main pressures for the moment. Or proregulation groups
might be irritated, challenged, and mobilized by some government

action favoring business. Their organization, effectiveness, and influence would temporarily increase. Or a particular substance or condition may be so lethal, or substitutes so readily available, that firms would not vigorously oppose a regulation.

What would not be consistent with the pluralist perspective? *Long* periods of aggressive, effective chemical regulation would run against the balance of interest-group pressure because dominant business pressures oppose effective regulation, and such "overregulation" should mobilize their adverse response. By long I mean one or two years. If an agency tries aggressively to control toxic substances for longer than two years at a time, the pluralist view is seriously incomplete.

Also, the complete failure of regulatory activity would be inconsistent with the pluralist perspective. Interest-group pressures fluctuate, and once in a while they ought to favor regulation. Businesses will not always be mobilized. Public interest groups, unions, etc., will occasionally take advantage of that. If there is no effective regulation of toxic substances, then interest-group pressures are probably not the main force driving the regulatory system.

Finally, given the political economy of toxic-substance control, if OSHA even-handedly balances the interests of public health and stable production, the pluralist view is flawed. If interest-group pressures drive the system, in the majority of cases business should win.

Thus, the pluralist perspective suggests that we will see a history of probusiness delays and compromise, but one punctuated by "liberal" regulatory initiatives which quickly spend themselves or stimulate counteracting corporate influence.

4.2.2. The Capitalist State View

What does the capitalist State perspective predict about OSHA's activity? Assume, first, that OSHA itself is primarily interested in protecting the health of the capitalist system. OSHA ought to make a reasonably strong effort to control chemicals, since its role is to moderate the effects of excessive competition—specifically, costly occupational illness epidemics and chemical clean-ups.

What evidence would support the view that OSHA is a token guardian of workers' interests and as such is dominated by procapitalist State organizations such as, hypothetically, the Executive Office of the President? Beyond assuming that OSHA does try to effectively regulate chemicals, this view presumes three things about "monitoring" procapitalist organizations. first, they would have to consciously oversee OSHA. Second, they would have to have review procedures which distinguish those regulations which unnecessarily hurt short-run profit (and therefore are to be suppressed) from those that, while costly, are needed to preserve the system. These reviews should consider both the economic and political effects of regulations. Third, and this is important for the pluralist-capitalist State comparison, the State should have *autonomously* established these review procedures. They should not have been established and run in response to business pressures. The Council on Wage and Price Stability would be an *autonomous* guardian of the capitalist system. Alternatively, if CWPS or the CEA are conduits for interest-group pressures, we have a pluralist and not a capitalist State.

What would be inconsistent with the capitalist State perspective? To the extent that the State's actions are dictated by the demands of interest groups, or its own organizations' tendencies, the view is flawed. But doesn't this just restate the perspectives' differences? No, and for the following reason. The pluralist and organizational views of regulation explain government action in terms of processes. In one it is interest-group influence, and in the other it is organizational self-defense and assertion. The distinctive characteristic of the capitalist State is its support of a particular goal—encouraging private capital accumulation. The government attempts to achieve this goal precisely by protecting capitalism from the processes that run the governments outlined by the pluralist and organizational views. The State has to ward off the influence of interest groups with anticapitalist or with other "special" interests, and also the influence of its own self-interested or "antibusiness" organizations. To the extent that these factors do shape State actions we cannot say that the government functions to support private capital accumulation.

4.2.3. The Organizational Perspective

What does the organizational perspective suggest about OSHA's probable behavior? Organizations try to preserve their autonomy, and they will resist coercion. Once a decision is made, OSHA will resist altering it in response to interest-group pressures or political–economic conditions. In fact, pressure might intensify the agency's defense of the decision. However, the defense could be costly because the agency might be sued, lobbied, publicly castigated, etc. OSHA would learn from this, and it would consider these consequences when framing future decisions and policies, not because it is interested in arbitrating disputes among interest groups or protecting capitalism, but because

OSHA wants to avoid coercive pressures, and will shape procedures accordingly so as to minimize pressure and conflict.

Organizations also try to avoid uncertainty and to pursue policies and actions that maintain stability. The top personnel of the agency are usually in close agreement on, or at least can tolerate, any resource shifts due to some change. Changes are thus manageable within present resource and political limits (Lindblom, 1959). This means that, contrary to the image of an entrepreneurial bureaucracy, OSHA will not work up damands for its services. It will not make a concerted effort to force chemical controversies into the public spotlight. OSHA and related agencies will avoid stimulating or reacting to large changes or crises, even if the work overload could eventually lead to major resource increases (Bardach, 1977: 159). The organizational perspective suggests that, even if a significant public-health lead materializes unexpectedly, OSHA and related agencies will not pursue it if to do so would clash with stable procedures and plans.

The view of this tendency to suppress demands on the agency is a key difference between the organizational and pluralist perspectives. The pluralist view takes interest-group demand as a given; the State responds to it. The organizational perspective suggests that the State organizations will try to *shape* demand because shaping demand is an organizational tactic and a way to avoid stressful situations. (A capitalist State will also try to shape demand if the uncontrolled demands would call for action inimical to capitalism. In such a case we have to judge whether organizational considerations or concerns for capitalism's welfare were the central factors in the government's behavior.)

Of course, the possibility that leaders can redirect and shake up the organization complicates the image of a stable, uncertainty-avoiding OSHA. A new top administrator could commit OSHA to vigorously attacking chemical problems regardless of the strain and uncertain conflict it would bring to the agency.

What kinds of historical patterns, then, support the organizational perspective? Initially, OSHA should be willing to regulate chemicals because this is what the OSH Act, its first guide to procedures, sets it up to do. OSHA should do so autonomously, and not in response to interest-group pressures. When early conflicts develop, autonomy-valuing OSHA should first resist changing its decisions, but then gradually bend its procedures to favor the dominant pressure sources. But isn't this pluralism? Partially, yes. It *is* a recognition that an organization interested in autonomy, certainty, and minimizing conflict will take its political and economic environment into account. Note, however, that the focus is on how the organization is defending itself, and not on how it is arbitrating disputes. The defense image has implications; for example, it suggests that the organization will suppress interest-group demand where possible rather than just react to it.

The organizational perspective suggests that new, liberal, vigorous leadership will revitalize regulation. In 1977, such an aggressive Assistant Secretary for OSHA, Eula Bingham, was appointed. She could have conceivably turned the agency against dominant pressure groups or any general governmental concern for maintaining capitalism at all costs. Thus, after 1977 there could have been accelerated regulatory activity because of Bingham.

Table 4.A.
Expectations and Tests of The Perspectives

	Main force behind state inspection	Expectations of the perspective	Patterns inconsistent with the perspective
PLURALISM	Interest groups	Business dominates regulation, but there is some intermittent regulation. State is a reflection of the balance of interest group pressures.	Generally effective regulation. No effective regulation. Eula Bingham turns OSHA into an aggressive agency for an extended period.
CAPITALIST	State concern for private capital accumulation	OSHA itself should try to regulate to check capitalism's excesses. There is much agency–industry conflict with State usually winning. Or procapitalist State organizations autonomously review and support or destroy regulations based on their utility for system. State wards off anticapitalist or "special" interest groups.	State actions are driven by interest-group pressures, organizational quests for stability and autonomy, or leaders' personal agendas.
ORGANIZA-TIONAL	Organizational autonomy and stability, and leaders' agendas.	In the short run OSHA defends its own decisions in the face of pressure. OSHA has an early period of regulation, then evolves procedures to minimize destabilizing pressure and conflict. However, Eula Bingham may turn OSHA around, after 1976, to effective regulation. OSHA manipulates interest-group demand to its own advantage. OSHA avoids destabilizing, even if potentially profitable, programs.	OSHA willingly backs down on its decisions. Historically aggressive regulation which destabilizes the agency. OSHA and related agencies willingly take on new and challenging programs without the intervention of a new, dynamic leader.

What patterns are not consistent with the organizational view? If OSHA makes decisions and then quickly retracts them under interest-group pressure, it is not insisting on organizational autonomy. This behavior would tend to undercut the usefulness of the organizational perspective.

A history of aggressive regulation would weaken the organizational perspective because aggressive regulation will stimulate many destabilizing conflicts and pressures for a weak OSHA. According to the organizational view OSHA will try to avoid these conflicts and adjust its aspirations accordingly. If OSHA does not cool off its regulatory aspirations, concern for stability may not be that important in explaining a regulatory agency's behavior.

Radical changes in programs to meet new opportunities would not fit the perspective. For example, suppose that OSHA finds itself with information that is an important public-health lead but which does not fit in with its current capabilities or procedures. It should bypass the lead out of concern for stability. If OSHA does not, the organizational perspective is weakened.

There is an exception to the above points. New, dynamic leaders may suspend organizations' tendencies toward stability, at least for a time. Should such a leader come to an agency, we may see a period of destabilizing regulation and innovation. Radical policy change under new leadership is consistent with the organizational perspective.

Table 4.A. summarizes the key expectations and tests of the perspectives. Chapters 5–7 describe OSHA's occupational health activities. Chapter 8 will take a final look at the factors that seem to best explain this history, and then estimate the promise or limits of health and safety regulation.

OSHA'S Chemical Regulations, 1970–1976

5.1. OSHA'S ACTIVITY

5.1.1. Asbestos

The adverse effects of asbestos were well documented long before the Occupational Safety and Health Act. By 1918, U.S. and Canadian insurance companies had stopped selling life insurance policies to asbestos workers. In the early 1920's, a new disease involving progressive scarring of the lungs leading to respiratory disability and heart failure was noted, and it was called asbestosis. By the 1930's, there were suspicions that asbestos was a carcinogen; this was confirmed by British and American studies in the 1950's and 1960's.

By 1969, Dr. Irving Selikoff and others had produced data conclusively showing that asbestos workers had developed cancer by working in areas with concentrations of asbestos fibers below the twelve fiber per cubic centimeter of air standard then recommended by the American Conference of Governmental Industrial Hygienists (ACGIH). In 1970 the ACGIH revised the recommendation down to five fibers.

In 1971, the Occupational Safety and Health Administration adopted the twelve-fiber limit as one of the 400 Threshold Limit Values (TLVs). On August 3, 1971, Dr. Selikoff urged OSHA to revise the standard, noting his research that showed that exposure to two or three fibers per cubic centimeter greatly increased the risk of asbestosis and cancer (Brodeur, 1974: 43-44). In November, 1971, the AFL–CIO asked that OSHA adopt an emergency standard of two fibers. In December, OSHA issued an emergency temporary standard (ETS) limiting exposure to five fibers, the same level then recommended by the private ACGIH.

After March, 1972 hearings, OSHA issued a permanent standard in June. The standard continued the five-fiber limit for four years, to be revised down to two fibers after that time. Selikoff criticized the standard, and the AFL–CIO sued OSHA over it. The suit said that the OSH Act assured workers of a healthy workplace, and it charged that the asbestos standard was diluted for the convenience of business. In 1974, the D.C. Circuit Court said that OSHA had the right to take compliance costs into account in setting standards.

OSHA was sympathetic to business complaints about the compliance difficulties of an immediate two-fiber standard, difficulties outlined by a widely criticized economic feasibility study by the consulting firm of Arthur D. Little, Inc. (Brodeur, 1974: 157-217). Thus, the standard had the four year phase-in period. However, a final standard— even if in diluted form—was issued fairly quickly after Selikoff, unions, and public interest groups petitioned OSHA. OSHA moved quickly. This should be contrasted with later standards which were stymied—in many cases indefinitely—because of corporate opposition.

The two-fiber limit was originally developed in 1969 by the British Occupational Hygiene Society for the limited purpose of minimizing asbestosis, and not cancer, which could conceivably be induced by lower levels of exposure. Studies since 1969 indicated that the two-fiber limit permits a significant incidence of even asbestosis (Bureau of National Affairs, April 17, 1980: 1067). In 1980, OSHA was considering lowering the exposure limit to .5 fibers per cubic centimeter of air. At the end of 1980 the revised standard had not yet been implemented.

5.1.2. Certain Carcinogens

On May 22, 1972, OSHA asked the National Institute for Occupational Safety and Health (NIOSH) to obtain information on nine chemicals that were suspected carcinogens. In a Federal Register notice on July 6, 1972, NIOSH reported fifteen substances as chemical carcinogens, including the nine on OSHA's list, and requested that the public provide any available information on the substances. In December, the Health Research Group and the Oil, Chemical, and Atomic Workers' Union (OCAW) petitioned OSHA to establish emergency temporary standards for ten of the carcinogens. In February, 1973, OSHA asked for comments on the petition and received written comments from about fifty manufacturers, trade associations, unions, and other parties. On May 3, 1973, OSHA issued an ETS for fourteen of the fifteen carcinogens on NIOSH's early list.

OSHA appointed a standards advisory committee, which met from June until August, 1973, to recommend a permanent standard. The committee's suggestions were published in the Federal Register on September 7, 1973.

After hearings on the substances, OSHA told the General Accounting Office that "Public hearings have failed to produce clinically significant evidence that a latent carcinogenic danger does not exist for each substance covered by the emergency temporary standards." OSHA concluded that there were insufficient medical, technical, and economic data to justify the risk of continued exposure to the substances. Note that this policy was "protective." OSHA did not try to accumulate an overwhelming file of evidence that the substances were carcinogenic to humans. Rather, OSHA said that there was substantial evidence that the chemicals were hazardous and that opponents of the regulation would have to prove that continued exposure would not be harmful. OSHA put the burden of proof on the businesses that were manufacturing or using the carcinogens.

OSHA stated that the standard would affect limited numbers of employees and establishments:

> Only seven of the carcinogens are currently produced in commercial quantities and the remainder are presently used only for research or appear as contaminants in other chemicals. Most of these latter seven were commercially produced at one time, but have fallen into non-use since they have been proven to be human carcinogens. . . . Approximately 250 firms with about 1,200 employees are known to be affected by the proposed regulations. It is estimated that the number of firms is closer to 1,700 and the number of employees is closer to 12,000, with over 80 percent of those working with 4,4'-methylene-bis (2-chloroaniline, or MOCA) (U.S. General Accounting Office, 1975a: 4-5).

Business nevertheless objected to the proposals. At a meeting of the U.S. Chamber of Commerce in Washington on January 8, 1974, Assistant Secretary of Labor for Occupational Safety and Health John Stender said that OSHA hoped for a "new openness of communication with the business community." Anthony Obadal, a Washington attorney, told the Chamber that the proposed permanent regulations were much more significant than industry originally realized. He claimed that parts of the proposal would lead to a "lack of due process" although "I don't think that the Labor Department intended this." He suggested that the "Labor Department should contemplate carefully this process, and should favor open standards arrived at through open procedures." Leo Teplow of Organization Resources Counselors, Inc., claimed that "those with responsibility for the proposal had little understanding of the utilization, the number of people affected, and the real hazards involved, and did not expect the severe reaction and disruption that the standards caused."

Both objections were actually groundless. Publicly open and announced meetings of the carcinogen advisory committee had considered these issues at length; business simply disagreed with the committee's conclusions. Teplow argued that highly technical people representing employers on scientific advisory committees should be replaced by people with "a broad management view" who "could negotiate." He urged business to monitor public meetings "very carefully and submit carefully prepared statements." Thus, the imminence of the carcinogen standards stimulated and broadened industry's interest in OSHA's health standards activity (Bureau of National Affairs, January 10, 1974: 1008-1009).

The *final* carcinogen regulations, issued on January 29, 1974, were weaker than the *proposed* regulations based on the advisory committee's recommendations. They deleted several requirements recommended by the committee. The final standards did not contain "use-permit provisions." Under such a system, firms would be required to apply for permission to use a substance after documenting that they could effectively control it and that the substance had no substitute or that its use could not be avoided. OSHA stated that this would give it the power to close down a facility, and argued that only the courts could do that. Also, OSHA claimed that developing and enforcing the system would be too time consuming and costly. The carcinogen advisory committee, the Health Research Group, and the Oil, Chemical, and Atomic Workers' Union had actively supported the system. Businesses had opposed it.

The final standards did not cover mixtures containing less than 1 percent by weight or volume of eight of the carcinogens and .1 percent for the remaining six. The eight had been shown to be carcinogenic in animals, the six in animals and humans. OSHA said that, while it agreed with the position that "a safe level of human exposure to any of the 14 carcinogens cannot be established by application of present knowledge," it was "not prepared to draw from this state of knowledge the conclusion that such levels do not exist." OSHA clearly came down on the side of business in handling this uncertainty (Ashford, 1976b: 157-158).

Although OSHA's advisory committee recommended required monitoring of the chemicals "by the most sensitive, feasible methods available," the final standards did not require monitoring; again, this was an easing of the standards' requirements.

The Health Research Group and OCAW charged that the final standards "were written to ease industry's compliance with them rather than to protect the workers' lives and health" (Bureau of National Affairs, January 31, 1974: 1100). The public interest group and the union asked a court to review the standards. Two industry groups—the Synthetic Organic Chemical Manufacturers and the Polyurethane Manufacturers Association—did also on the grounds that the standards were too restrictive. The Third Circuit Court of Appeals in Philadelphia upheld the standards for the most part. However, it vacated the standard for MOCA (4,4′-Methylene(bis)-2-chloroaniline). The court did not question MOCA's carcinogenicity, but said that the standard had been illegally published because a special advisory committee had not reported on the substance in a timely fashion. The court also vacated the standards for laboratory use of the chemicals, again on procedural grounds. The public had not been given adequate time to comment on the MOCA report, or adequate notice of the laboratory standards (U.S. General Accounting Office, 1977a: 34).

As in the asbestos case, the standards were issued fairly quickly. OSHA responded to the petition from the Health Research Group and the Oil, Chemical, and Atomic Workers in issuing the emergency standards. OSHA then bent before industry's objections and was willing to dilute the final permanent standards compared to the earlier *proposed* standards.

5.1.3. Pesticides

In February, 1972, President Nixon's environmental message said that agricultural worker protection was essential to a sound pesticide policy. The President told the Labor Department to develop a pesticide standard. Standards advisory committees were appointed at the Council on Environmental Quality (CEQ) and at the Labor Department. In December, both committees told OSHA that an emergency temporary standard for pesticides was unjustified. Nevertheless, the Labor Department told its committee to develop a standard. The committee did so with the understanding that it would not be issued as an emergency temporary standard.

In March, 1973, farmworker representatives sued OSHA for failing to issue an ETS on pesticides. A counselor for the White House suggested that OSHA issue a "one time" emergency standard—that could lapse after six months—as a defense against the farmworker suit. The counselor also suggested that in the future the EPA be primarily responsible for protecting workers from pesticides.

In April, OSHA sent a proposed emergency standard to NIOSH for comment. NIOSH responded by saying that workers greatly needed protection from certain pesticides and that the standard was as valid as possible in view of the available scientific data. Assistant Secretary for OSH John Stender issued the ETS on June 18, 1973. The farmworker representatives dropped their lawsuit.

Within three weeks the Florida Peach Growers Association and other grower associations petitioned ten circuits of the U.S. Court of Appeals to vacate the standard. The petitions were later consolidated into one suit before the Fifth Circuit in New Orleans.

After the business lawsuits were filed, the Labor Department suspended its initial standard and said that it would be revised. OSHA issued a revised standard on July 13, 1973, deleting nine of the original twenty-one pesticides covered and loosening controls on the others. Not satisfied, the grower associations asked the court to delay the effective date of the revised standard. The court did so.

The farmworker representatives then asked the U.S. Court of Appeals for the District of Columbia to reinstate OSHA's first standard. The court did not do so.

Early in 1974, as requested by the peach growers, the Fifth Circuit permanently suspended the pesticide standard. The farmworkers again asked the Court of Appeals in D.C. to order the Labor Department to issue a permanent standard for the original twenty-one pesticides. They also asked that the EPA not be allowed exclusive authority to regulate worker exposure to pesticides, apparently figuring that—in the long run—farmworkers would obtain better protection from the Labor Department. In May, 1974, EPA published a permanent standard for twelve pesticides. In June, OSHA asked the D.C. court to dismiss the farmworkers' suit because the EPA had the authority to regulate pesticides and had done so. In October, 1974 the court agreed, and the OSHA pesticide standards were eliminated (U.S. General Accounting Office, 1975b).

5.1.4. Vinyl Chloride

Nicholas Ashford has noted that:

> . . . the legal and political problems encountered by OSHA in attempting to issue permanent carcinogen standards and then, later, pesticide standards led OSHA in subsequent standards activity—and especially in the case of vinyl chloride—to proceed with considerable care in collecting adequate technical data to support the standard's requirements and in setting forth the basis for the standard. . .

After three workers died from vinyl chloride-induced liver cancer at a Goodrich plant, "OSHA did not move quickly in either adopting a temporary emergency or a permanent standard" (Ashford, 1976b: 159, 252). (This was written in 1975; OSHA subsequently became even more cautious.) Marcus Key, the director of NIOSH, said that no safe level of vinyl chloride could be established, and recommended that exposure be reduced to below measurable limits. In March, 1974, OSHA issued a temporary emergency standard of 50 parts per million.

"The vinyl chloride standard," OSHA said later, "provides a striking example of the effort which has been required for standard promulgation under optimum circumstances" under a chemical-by-chemical approach (U.S. Department of Labor, OSHA, 1980: 5013). The vinyl chloride standard was developed on a top-priority basis with resources borrowed from other projects. Dr. Irving Selikoff told a House subcommittee on Labor that ". . .when the Division of Clinical Field Studies, which does the fieldwork for NIOSH, was alerted on January 23 to the vinyl chloride problem and they assigned their few people to it, they have dropped every other piece of research that they are doing" (U.S. House Committee on Education and Labor, 1974: 142).

Vinyl chloride was indisputably a human carcinogen. Nevertheless, there were disputes over the permissible level of exposure, over whether or not there was a safe level of exposure, over whether animal data could be extrapolated to humans, and over the standard's requirements. These debates led to 600 written comments, 200 written and oral hearing submissions, and a 4000 page record. OSHA concluded that, although the record did not definitely answer any of these questions, a protective permanent standard of 1 ppm was necessary. OSHA issued the standard in September, 1974.

The Society of the Plastics Industry claimed that the standard would shut down the industry and, in a case heard by the Second Circuit Court in New York, unsuccessfully sued OSHA over the standard's feasibility. The firms manufacturing or using vinyl chloride subsequently had little difficulty complying with the standard (Perry, 1980).

5.1.5. Coke Oven Emissions

Coke is a residue from the destructive distillation or carbonization of coal. It is used as a fuel and reducing agent in blast furnaces and foundries. The production of coke generates gases and particles—"coke oven emissions"—which are carcinogenic (U.S. Department of Labor, OSHA, 1976: 46744-46748).

NIOSH issued a criteria document on occupational exposure to coke oven emissions in February, 1973. The Occupational Safety and Health Administration established an advisory committee in August, 1974, to study coke oven emissions and to design a standard to control them; the committee suggested the standard on May 24, 1975. OSHA— under acting heads Deputy Assistant Secretaries Marshall Miller and Bert Conklin—proposed a standard in July, 1975, which differed from the advisory committee recommendations in several respects.

The advisory committee recommended specific engineering controls to moderate coke oven emissions. OSHA's proposed standard only required employers to develop their own program based on any engineering controls they chose, gave no date by which the engineering changes were to be in place, and permitted firms to control exposures by making workers wear personal protective devices until the engineering changes were implemented. The proposal stated that:

> As part of its recommended standard, the Advisory Committee included detailed requirements mandating specific engineering and work practice controls. OSHA prefers, however, not to include detailed specifications on possible methods of compliance in the standard in order not to limit the development of new technology or necessitate frequent revisions of the standard (cited in Bureau of National Affairs, August 7, 1975: 335).

The advisory committee also recommended that medical exams be made available to employees; that workers showing symptoms of disease related to or aggravated by coke oven emissions be removed from the coke oven area; and that they be given other work without loss of pay or seniority ("rate retention"). The committee reasoned that coke oven workers ought to be regularly examined and that they ought to be transferred if they were developing symptoms, but that workers would not allow themselves to be examined if they ran the risk of losing income from a transfer. The "rate retention" clause guaranteed that workers would not lose income from a medically related transfer.

OSHA's proposed standard, on the other hand, included the medical exam provision but dropped the job transfer and rate retention clauses. The proposal "question(ed) the extent of the employer's responsibility to guarantee the present income of an employee where, for medical reasons which may or may not be related to an occupational exposure, a physician recommends that action should be taken to avoid either a health hazard or aggravation of an existing condition." OSHA added that, with rate retention, employers might be unwilling to remove workers from the ovens "because of the impact on the wage and salary systems currently in existence," and that OSHA may not have the legal authority to order such income maintenance (Bureau of National Affairs, August 7, 1975: 338).

Organized labor scorned the proposed standard. Stephen Wodka of the Oil, Chemical, and Atomic Workers Union (OCAW) called it "the worst standard ever proposed by OSHA." Wodka noted that nothing in the proposal would force coke battery operators to install engineering controls within a given period of time, and that to comply with the standard all they had to do was "file a vague plan with OSHA" and then equip their workers with respirators while the plan was casually implemented. "When you are dealing with a known carcinogenic substance such as coke oven emissions, there must be a sense of urgency to the abatement procedures related to it."

The OCAW representative also criticized OSHA's failure to guarantee workers transferred from coke ovens for medical reasons their regular pay rate. "OSHA is fooling itself if it thinks that workers will submit to medical exams when the results might cost them their job, their seniority, or present pay rate. Many of them have some form of (medical) abnormality." "In the past," Wodka concluded, "OSHA has gone halfway to satisfy worker demands in issuing standards. This proposal doesn't even throw them a bone. . . . If this is a sample of (acting OSHA heads Marshall Miller's and Bert Conklin's) work, workers in this country are in trouble." The Steelworkers union echoed Wodka's objections to the proposed standard (Bureau of National Affairs, August 7, 1975: 316–318).

At hearings on the proposed standard, the steel industry—while not claiming that the standard threatened the existence of coke oven operations—questioned whether it was justified "given the magnitude of the hazard and the cost of complying with the standard." For example, the American Iron and Steel Institute (AISI) said that the standard would cost $1.28 billion annually (U.S. Department of Labor, OSHA, 1976: 46748–46749). (Inland Steel, which was financially strong and in fact would "tend to gain a competitive edge from the regulation" came in with a low estimate of $160 million in annual costs; see U.S. CWPS, 1976: 3–4.) The American Iron and Steel Institute also charged that the exposure limits on coke oven emissions could not possibly be regularly met, that several requirements of the standard were unnecessary, and that the proposal was technically deficient (Bureau of National Affairs, July 22, 1976: 244–245).

The Council on Wage and Price Stability also intervened in the coke oven proceeding, primarily to criticize OSHA's inflation impact statement. The Council charged that while OSHA had adequately considered the costs of the proposal, which CWPS—as a best estimate—put at $200 million annually, OSHA's analysis of benefits (lives saved and illnesses prevented) was flawed and discussion of alternatives to the proposal missing. CWPS dismissed as based on unreasonable assumptions OSHA's estimate that 240 workers died per year from coke oven emissions exposure, and claimed that the actual figure was between 8 and 35 workers per year. The Council argued that the standard would thus cost between $4.5 and $158 million per life saved. It then cited studies using "willingness to pay" methodology—which estimates the extra income people accept as compensation for some higher probability of death as a way of deriving the monetary value people give to life— placing the value of life at $200,000 (Thaler and Rosen, 1973) and $1.5 million (Smith, R. S., 1976). "Again," CWPS noted, "the numbers are important only because they strongly suggest that there may be less costly ways of reducing the risk of death or that for a given expenditure more lives could be saved;" it suggested that money might be better spent on cancer research. Finally, the Council argued that OSHA ought to have considered relying on respirators rather than on engineering controls to control exposure to coke oven emissions, as industry had suggested (U.S. CWPS, 1976).

The proposed coke oven standard was issued in July, 1975. In December, 1975, Morton Corn was named Assistant Secretary of Labor for Occupational Safety and Health, taking the agency-director job from Marshall Miller and Bert Conklin. On October 22, 1976, OSHA issued the final coke oven emissions standard.

The differences between the proposed and final standards tightened the rule. Unions had complained that the proposal required no specific engineering controls, but the final standard mandated detailed engineering changes on old coke oven batteries, although not on new batteries so as not to "freeze" technology. Also, the final standard ordered that the changes be made by January, 1980, while the proposal had no time limit on installation of changes. Jack Sheehan, legislative director of the United Steelworkers, said that the union felt "very good" about the standard. The union was "disappointed" that the rate retention clause was not included, but would not sue the Labor Department over the issue (Bureau of National Affairs, October 28, 1976: 620).

The preamble to the final standard also extensively criticized the CWPS suggestions that OSHA do a cost-benefit analysis of the standard, and particularly rejected any attempt to calculate the value of life. The agency noted that the Council had criticized the assumptions from which OSHA had calculated that 240 lives would be saved per year by the standard, and that CWPS instead estimated that 8 to 35 lives per year would be saved. In turn, OSHA criticized the Council's assumptions, and concluded that "As can readily be seen, estimates of the mortality benefits of the reduced exposure will vary significantly depending upon the assumptions utilized." Thus,

> OSHA finds that compliance with the standard (even if the higher cost estimate were used) is well within the financial capability of the coking industry. Moreover, although we cannot rationally quantify in dollars the benefits of the standard careful consideration has been given to the question of whether these substantial costs are justified in light of the hazards. OSHA concludes that these costs are necessary in order to adequately protect employees from the hazards associated with coke oven emissions" (U.S. Department of Labor, OSHA, 1976: 46750-46751).

The American Iron and Steel Institute and six steel companies later asked the U.S. Third Circuit Court of Appeals in Philadelphia to suspend the standard. Industry's principal objections were that the exposure limit could not be attained, that the standard forced industry to develop impractical technology, and that the standard was generally not feasible; the American Iron and Steel Institute argued that it was "technologically and economically infeasible for an already economically crippled industry." OSHA responded that there was "overwhelming epidemiological evidence" that coke oven emissions were carcinogenic and that most of the technology for attaining the exposure limit was already available—industry simply did not want to be forced to invest in it. The United Steelworkers also argued on behalf of the standard. Their lawyer noted that industry had not adopted all of the controls currently available and that the union was "cautiously optimistic" that the standard would not cost any jobs (Bureau of National Affairs, January 12, 1978: 1237-1238).

On March 28, 1978, the Third Circuit Court unanimously upheld the exposure limit and other key provisions of the standard. The Court declared that OSHA had a sufficiently reasoned case showing that the limit could be met and that the industry would not be imperiled. The Court also said that it "attached significance to the United Steelworkers' support of the standard" (Bureau of National Affairs, April 6, 1978: 1659). The industry appealed the case to the Supreme Court but, in August, 1980, admitted that the required controls were already in place in most plants and dropped the suit.

5.1.6. OSHA's Early Treatment of the Economic Impact of Standards

The coke oven emissions case was the first major clash over a health standard between the Occupational Safety and Health Administration and the Council on Wage and Price Stability.

OSHA did not resist analyzing the inflationary impact or technological feasibility of its standards, although organized labor protested and unsuccessfully sued the government over the Executive Order 11821. According to former Health Standards official Grover Wrenn in 1977,

> Since OSHA has existed, it has from time to time engaged in economic analysis and cost studies associated with its developing regulations long before there was an executive order or requirement to do so. But there was little made about that because OSHA had complete management freedom and flexibility to decide when and how to do such studies, when they were needed and when they weren't and when to introduce them into the record and so forth, or whether to do them before a proposal was issued or in the aftermath of a proposal after information began to become available, and certainly there was no prescribed analytical matrix that had to be complied with in doing such studies (Wrenn, 1977: 79).

The Executive Order required more systematic treatment of the costs and benefits of regulations. Before the Office of Management and Budget issued guidelines on the Order, OSHA "had substantially completed the staff work and policy decisions on about a dozen major regulatory proposals. . . . We didn't have the kind of detailed inflation impact statements to accompany the proposals that the (Executive Order) at that time required." OSHA contracted out the required studies until it developed its own economic staff and had, by 1976, completed inflation impact statements for the coke oven, arsenic, and lead standards (Wrenn, 1977: 79–82).

In 1976, the Council on Wage and Price Stability surveyed agencies on how they were handling the Inflation Impact Statement (IIS) program. Regarding OSHA, CWPS spoke to three agencies—the Assistant Secretary for Policy, Evaluation, and Research in the Labor Department (ASPER), which internally reviewed OSHA's impact statements; the Solicitor of Labor, which defended OSHA's standards in court; and OSHA itself.

Economists in ASPER told the Council that "very little economic analysis of high quality was done by OSHA before the IIS program; what was done was on the technical feasibility of proposed standards, with some attention paid to cost considerations. . . . Hardly any attention was paid to quantifying the benefits of regulatory proposals." (Several individuals charged that ASPER's dissatisfaction with OSHA's economic work delayed the impact statements and, thus, the health standards. However, ASPER's influence depended on the Executive Order and the involvement of the Council on Wage and Price Stability; see Hopkins, 1976: 69.) The Solicitor's Office said that the IIS program improved the information on the costs of standards. However, like OSHA, the Solicitor's Office maintained that analyzing the benefits of standards was difficult, if not impossible, and "not relevant to OSHA's mission" because of the weight given workers' safety by the OSH Act.

Summarizing the review of OSHA's program, the Council on Wage and Price Stability said that OSHA's cost and feasibility analyses were adequate, but that the treatments of benefits and alternatives were extremely weak. CWPS felt that the quality of the analyses seemed to be improving because "OSHA does appear to be quite conscious of its image and its critics and thus the public hearing format has been instrumental in improving the quality of the proposed regulations. CWPS participation in four public hearings over the past year and a half has apparently had a major impact on the quality of these analyses. Both ASPER and OSHA representatives mentioned OSHA's sensitivity to CWPS public criticisms."

While the analyses may have improved, the IIS apparently did not affect the one standard completed between 1975 and 1977—the coke oven emissions rule. OSHA did not modify the standards as CWPS suggested, and in fact dwelled on the flaws of cost-benefit analysis in occupational health regulation. The Council suggested that OSHA looked on the IIS as a "hurdle to overcome in promulgating regulations" rather than as a "management tool for improved regulatory decision-making" (Hopkins, 1976: 68-69).

OSHA's commitment to the Executive Order actually fell between ethusiastically embracing cost-benefit analysis and treating the IIS as a mere "hurdle." OSHA did resist, at this time, calculating the benefits of regulations. As the coke oven case demonstrated, calculating the number of lives saved by a standard was a controversial exercise; changes in assumptions could reduce a figure of 240 lives saved per year to 8. A flat statement that the OSH Act committed the agency to protect workers' health even at very high cost per life saved was easier to defend than any cost-benefit ratios that OSHA could produce to justify standards. (However, as we will see later, OSHA gradually backed off from the "protection at high price" stance and began justifying regulations in cost-benefit terms.)

OSHA did not want to estimate regulatory benefits. But the agency's transition paper to President-elect Carter said that the careful consideration of costs and alternative technologies helped ward off "criticisms of arbitrary actions in the standards development process, particularly from industry groups." Further, the fact that an Executive Order mandated the more extensive economic analysis—rather than an autonomous decision by OSHA—took some of the political heat on the subject off the agency; "Should Executive Order 11821 expire, OSHA may find itself under considerable pressure not to perform the very sort of economic analysis that is becoming increasingly important in the rulemaking, regulating, and judicial processes" (Bureau of National Affairs, December 16, 1976: 884). Thus, the Council on Wage and Price Stability's review of the IIS program stated that "Both OSHA and ASPER representatives expressed a desire to have the IIS program continue as it is without modification. However, the Solicitor's Office spokesman recommended that EO 11821 not be renewed since he feels that it could be used to reduce OSHA's discretionary control over the standard-setting process. He doesn't feel that this has happened yet" (Hopkins, 1976: 69). OSHA's transition paper to President-elect Carter said that "OSHA has taken actions to internalize the requirements of the order by establishing agency procedures to make it an integral part of standards development, without delaying the rulemaking process.

It is important to continue this sort of analysis whether the Executive Order expires or is extended" (Bureau of National Affairs, December 16, 1976: 884).

Grover Wrenn reported four months later—after the change of administrations—that the transition document was no longer "the official policy of the Labor Department and OSHA" (Wrenn, 1977: 92). However, a key force pushing OSHA to analyze the technological feasibility and cost of standards—"criticisms of arbitrary actions in the standards development process, particularly from industry groups" (see preceding paragraph)—did not leave with the Ford administration. This continuing force made the transition document to President-elect Carter the working, if not the "official," policy of OSHA.

5.1.7. A Regulatory Slowdown

In 1974, OSHA and NIOSH announced the Standards Completion Project, Remember (Section 4.1.2.1.) that this was to supplement the exposure limits of the Threshold Limit Value list adopted in 1971 with rules for chemical monitoring, medical examinations, etc. At the end of 1980, OSHA had proposed supplementary requirements for seventeen substances. None of the proposals has been implemented.

In 1975, in addition to the coke oven emissions standard, OSHA proposed standards for controlling MOCA, beryllium, lead, toluene, trichloroethylene, arsenic, ammonia, and asbestos as a carcinogen. Of these, beside the coke oven standard which was finalized in 1976, final standards have been issued only for lead and arsenic (1978).

In 1976, OSHA proposed a standard for cotton dust after the Textile Workers' Union sued. OSHA did not issue the final standard until June, 1978, after another textile workers' suit and a judge's pressure. I will discuss the lead, arsenic, and cotton dust proceedings in Chapter 6 because most of this activity occurred after Eula Bingham was appointed Assistant Secretary for Occupational Safety and Health.

Post-1974 proposals specified the details of monitoring and medical examinations, and the types of controls required, in more detail than earlier standards. Unions and public interest groups had criticized the looseness of earlier standards. Also, tightening the standards was not in itself controversial. The requirements never went into effect without long—and, in most cases, continuing—delays. OSHA, after implementing fifteen permanent health standards by 1974, had issued only one additional final standard (coke oven emissions) by the end of 1976. Unions, public interest groups, the liberal media, some Congressional committees, and the U.S. General Accounting Office criticized this pace.

On May 10, 1977, the General Accounting Office (GAO) charged that OSHA issued health standards too slowly:

> The Occupational Safety and Health Administration's application of two provisions in the 1970 Act has not been responsive to the need to protect workers from dangerous substances as soon as possible. These provisions relate to (1) the issuance of temporary emergency standards to protect employees from grave dangers and (2) issuing standards, as soon as possible, on the basis of the best scientific data available (U.S. GAO, 1977a: 26; unless otherwise noted, parenthesized numbers below refer to pages of this GAO report).

I will outline both of the GAO's charges.

5.1.7.1. Failures to Use Emergency Temporary Standards

Up to the time of the draft report (March, 1977), OSHA had issued emergency temporary standards (ETSs) for asbestos, fourteen carcinogens, pesticides, and vinyl chloride (the emergency temporary standards for pesticides and one of the carcinogens—MOCA—were vacated by court decisions). The GAO noted that OSHA had issued the ETSs because the chemicals were carcinogenic or very toxic.

However, the National Institute for Occupational Safety and Health (NIOSH) criteria documents covered at least nine additional carcinogens by November, 1976, and OSHA had issued emergency standards for none of these. In 1976, the director of NIOSH sent OSHA a memorandum saying that "We strongly recommend that OSHA establish emergency temporary standards for benzene, hexavalent chromium, and MOCA." (NIOSH did not recommend emergency temporary standards for the other substances because either 1) the recommended exposure levels were not much different from the limits which had been adopted as interim standards in 1971; or 2) OSHA had proposed permanent standards or was close to doing so for a substance; or 3) NIOSH did not think that OSHA would take on the added workload (26-27).)

An OSHA official remarked that the agency had not issued ETSs for benzene or chloroform because evidence of their carcinogenicity was not strong enough. However, NIOSH maintained that the evidence was as strong as, or stronger than, the evidence which OSHA had used to justify the earlier ETSs for carcinogens.

On December 27, 1976, OSHA wrote to NIOSH that it would use the permanent standards process rather than the quicker emergency temporary standards process to control benzene, hexavalent chromium, and MOCA. The acting director of OSHA's standards development staff declared that the "grave danger" in the ETS clause might be interpreted as meaning a threat of death, and so OSHA would have trouble upholding an emergency temporary standard without clear evidence of fatalities from the three substances (27-28).

This interpretation of "grave danger" was much more conservative than the position OSHA took in earlier ETSs on carcinogens. For example, a 1974 Fifth Circuit Court of Appeals decision had vacated the ETS for pesticides, but nevertheless upheld the more protective interpretation:

> We reject any suggestion that deaths must occur before health and safety standards may be adopted. Nevertheless, the danger of incurable, permanent, or fatal consequences to workers, as opposed to easily curable and fleeting effects on their health, becomes important in consideration of the necessity for emergency measures to meet a grave danger (28).

Because cancer is irreversible, and benzene, hexavalent chromium, and MOCA were carcinogens, they were more than "easily curable and fleeting" dangers to health. Thus, OSHA had become much more conservative in interpreting the meaning of "grave danger" to employees.

In January, 1977, Assistant Secretary for OSH Morton Corn said that OSHA had not yet issued the ETSs—and had no plans to do so— because of OSHA's "lack of success in defending emergency temporary standards in court." *It was not true that OSHA had been unsuccessful in defending ETSs in court*. The asbestos emergency standard was not challenged. The ETS for vinyl chloride was not challenged, and OSHA had successfully opposed industry over the permanent vinyl chloride standard. OSHA's difficulties with the permanent carcinogen standards were over procedural matters and not on the technical merits of the standards. The one judicial setback on the substance of a health standard to that point involved the pesticides standards. Thus, it does not appear that Corn's judgement reflected OSHA's objective history of legal successes or failures. Rather, the high political and resource costs of court battles—successful or unsuccessful—made OSHA reluctant to issue the ETSs. Industry did not have to win in court to inhibit regulatory actions; making actions very expensive was sufficient.

OSHA gave other reasons for not issuing the ETSs, all of which the GAO dismissed as being very flimsy. Corn said that OSHA would not issue emergency standards for any of the approximately 400 substances included in the *Threshold Limit Value* (TLV) list (see Section 4.1.2.1). As pointed out earlier, these limits were not set with the carcinogenic potential of the chemicals in mind. In fact, OSHA never adopted the American Conference of Governmental Industrial Hygienists appendix modifying the carcinogen limits. Congress had expressly given OSHA the freedom to modify the limits when appropriate.

OSHA also told the GAO that it would not issue ETSs unless it was sure that employers could comply within six months. This was not a consideration in earlier ETS actions. Again, OSHA had become more sensitive to imposing costs on business. There was no legal basis for this inhibition. The OSH Act specifies that the only criteria for issuing an ETS are that 1) employees are exposed to grave danger; and 2) that the standard is needed to protect them. OSHA could be flexible in fining employers for violations if the employer seemed to be making a good faith effort to comply, but the GAO argued that the emergency temporary standards—according to the Act—should have been issued (31-32).

Thus, according to the GAO, OSHA had failed to use emergency temporary standards often enough to protect workers. Additionally, the General Accounting Office criticized OSHA's failure to issue permanent standards based on the best available—as opposed to the best possible—evidence.

5.1.7.2. Failure to Issue Permanent Standards on the Basis of the Best Available Evidence

OSHA's standards prescribe exposure limits and other protective measures. NIOSH and OSHA felt that data on many substances did not support certain requirements. In such cases the Institute recommended standards that *would* be supported by available data. However, instead of issuing standards based on the best available evidence, OSHA wanted to wait until more and better data were developed. "In our opinion," the GAO said, "OSHA's approach is not responsive to the Act's intent that standards be promptly issued based on the best available data and improved later as more and better data become available . . . it is clear that Congress did not intend that any standard represent for all times the means by which to provide safe or healthful employment; the Congress recognized the need for standards to be constantly improved and replaced as new knowledge and techniques are developed" (32-33). The General Accounting Office cited five examples of delay by OSHA—for MOCA and laboratory use of certain carcinogens, benzene, inorganic arsenic, chloroform, and cotton dust.

5.1.7.2a. MOCA and Laboratory Activities Involving Thirteen Other Carcinogens

In 1973 OSHA had proposed emergency temporary standards for fourteen carcinogens, including special provisions for laboratory use of the chemicals. The D.C. Court of Appeals vacated the standard for MOCA and the laboratory provisions for all the substances. It did not question MOCA's danger or the lab provisions' usefulness. Rather, it suspended the standard and lab provisions because adequate time had not been allowed for pubic comment on both. OSHA could have immediately republished the standards, given the public adequate time to comment, conducted hearings if necessary, and issued the standards it was willing to issue in 1973.

In 1976, OSHA had still not done this. In April, the GAO asked why. In July, 1976, OSHA wrote the Office a letter replying that 1) the standards were delayed because they were given lower priority than other projects; 2) the delay on MOCA was related to OSHA's effort to establish an exposure limit for MOCA (exposure limits were not included for any of the other thirteen carcinogen standards included in the 1974 package); 3) OSHA would move as quickly as possible to publish a proposed amendment to the thirteen carcinogen standards to cover their laboratory use; and that 4) a revised draft of the MOCA standard was being prepared and would be published pending completion of an inflation impact statement which was due in four months.

Following up on that OSHA letter, the General Accounting Office noted that:

> As of November 1, 1976, the acting director of OSHA's standards staff told us that OSHA 1) did not have a basis for setting an exposure limit for MOCA; 2) had not taken action to include laboratory activities in the standards for the other thirteen chemicals; and 3) had not made significant efforts regarding these matters because the staff was working on other standards (35).

At the end of 1981, OSHA still had not issued final standards for MOCA or the laboratory use of the other chemicals.

5.1.7.2b. Benzene

In July, 1974, NIOSH sent OSHA a criteria document calling for a reduction in the exposure limit for benzene. Although conclusive evidence was not in hand, it said that there was a strong possibility that benzene caused leukemia because bone marrow and blood changes had been observed in humans and animals exposed to benzene. The Institute also recommended medical monitoring of employees, education on benzene hazards, warning signs, engineering controls, and work procedures to minimize contact with benzene.

After receiving the criteria document, OSHA asked NIOSH to clarify whether or not benzene caused leukemia. The Institute responded that bone marrow and blood changes would precede leukemia and that the standard was designed to prevent such changes.

OSHA still did not issue the standard. Instead, OSHA argued that

NIOSH had neither given adequate evidence supporting the recommended exposure level nor indicated whether the standard should include gasoline service stations because of the high levels of benzene in unleaded gasoline. OSHA and NIOSH proceeded to collect more data. In August, 1976, NIOSH recommended a reduction in benzene exposure from 10 ppm to 1 ppm because of new evidence that benzene caused leukemia and damaged blood-forming organs. OSHA still did not issue either an ETS or a proposed standard until the draft GAO report was released in March, 1977, and after the change in administrations. I will discuss the benzene proceedings in Chapter 6.

5.1.7.2c. Inorganic Arsenic

The exposure limits adopted by OSHA in 1971 permitted exposure to arsenic of .5 milligrams per cubic meter of air as an eight-hour time-weighted average. These interim standards, as noted earlier, included no other protections.

In January, 1974, NIOSH sent OSHA a criteria document that recommended exposure to arsenic be limited to .05 milligram. Strong but not unequivocal evidence showed that arsenic was a factor in lung cancer. The criteria document also recommended medical surveillance, warning labels, and other controls. In November, based on new evidence that arsenic caused cancer, NIOSH revised the suggested limit down to .002 milligram.

OSHA proposed a standard in January, 1975, with an exposure limit of .004 milligram. It held hearings in April. The wood-preservative industry claimed that the evidence did not apply to its operations because it used a different arsenic compound from the one used in the researched industries. NIOSH argued that there was no evidence that the wood-preservative industry's arsenic compound was not carcinogenic. The General Accounting Office commented that:

> As of October, 1976, OSHA had not finalized the arsenic standard and was still considering whether the standard should include the arsenic compound used in the wood preservative industry. We believe that the applicability of the proposed standard to the wood industry does not justify delaying protection of employees in other industries where arsenic has been shown to cause cancer. Further, the possibility that the wood industry's compound causes cancer would, in our opinion, justify a standard to require, at a minimum, medical surveillance of exposed workers and monitoring of exposure levels in that industry (41).

OSHA did not issue a final arsenic standard until May of 1978. I will discuss this standard in Chapter 6.

5.1.7.2d. Chloroform

The limit on chloroform adopted by OSHA in 1971 permitted exposure up to 50 ppm and included no other protections. In September, 1974, NIOSH recommended a new limit of 10 ppm and additional protections. NIOSH said that it based the new exposure limit on the finding that chloroform caused liver and kidney damage, although the cancer danger was uncertain. In June, 1976, based on new evidence, NIOSH told the Occupational Safety and Health Administration that chloroform did cause kidney and liver cancer, and it lowered the recommended exposure limit to 2 ppm.

At the end of 1980, OSHA had not proposed a revised chloroform standard, arguing that NIOSH had not adequately shown that chloroform caused cancer. NIOSH disagreed. It is noteworthy that in 1978 the Environmental Protection Agency (EPA) moved to require filters on city water systems partly on the grounds of removing chloroform, which it considered carcinogenic (Epstein, 1978: 370).

5.1.7.2e. Cotton Dust

Cotton dust causes a serious, sometimes irreversible lung disease called byssinosis. The exposure limit adopted in 1971 permitted exposure up to 1 milligram per cubic meter of air, and included no other protections.

In September, 1974, a NIOSH criteria document recommended additional work practice controls. In December, 1974, NIOSH recommended a lower exposure of .2 milligram of cotton dust per cubic meter of air along with further protections.

Until November, 1976, OSHA maintained that the criteria document was inadequate because it covered only part of the textile industry. NIOSH responded that the research covered most of the industry and that employees in those segments should be protected. OSHA did make a study of the cotton industry from November, 1974, through January, 1976. In December, 1976, after the textile workers' union sued the Labor Department, OSHA proposed a cotton dust standard lowering the exposure limit to the same levels suggested by NIOSH two years earlier. In June, 1978, almost four years after NIOSH suggested a new standard, one and one-half years after the standard was proposed, one year after the GAO report, and after two lawsuits by the textile workers' union, OSHA issued the final cotton dust standard. This proceeding will be discussed in Chapter 6.

5.2. A BRIEF EVALUATION OF OSHA'S EARLY ACTIVITY

OSHA's early behavior fits neither the "servant of industry" nor "youthful zealot" regulatory images. Petitions from organized labor and the Health Research Group prompted the asbestos and carcinogen standards. The emergency asbestos standard was issued one month after the AFL–CIO request. The permanent asbestos standard was issued six months after the emergency standard. The emergency standards for carcinogens were issued five months after Labor's petition, and the permanent standards eight months after the ETSs. Although perhaps as a defensive maneuver, OSHA responded to a farmworkers' lawsuit by issuing emergency standards for pesticides within three months. From the perspective of 1981, these were remarkably quick actions.

However, the early standards stimulated business's attention to OSHA. At the Chamber of Commerce meeting in Washington in January, 1974, for example, speakers discussed how business had not made OSHA "aware" of the "disruption" such standards caused, and how industry could avoid this in the future by carefully monitoring the agency's activities. The permanent asbestos and carcinogens regulations were modified to ease firms' compliance. After issuing the pesticide emergency standards, OSHA spent more time fighting the farmworkers than the growers' associations, and tried to jettison all responsibility for controlling pesticides (something OSHA would later reclaim under Eula Bingham).

Therefore, one could not say that OSHA was born "dominated" because it quickly conceded too much to organized labor and public interest groups. But certainly the quick regulation of asbestos and the carcinogens cannot be attributed to the zeal of a young agency because the standards were loosened too quickly.

Rather, after the Occupational Safety and Health Act was passed OSHA simply acted in a reasonably responsive manner toward its legislative mandate. When petitioned to issue a health standard, the agency did so much as the OSH Act prescribed. But business's reaction to this early regulatory activity firmly demonstrated that occupational health regulation would be politically and economically costly, even though OSHA quite successfully defended the technical grounds for standards in court. Thus, after 1974, OSHA would not regulate a toxic substance unless it had overwhelmingly documented the chemical's harmful qualities and thoroughly justified the economic and technological feasibility of the controls. This is indicated by the progressive lengthening of the preambles justifying and explaining the standards. The preamble to the standards for the fourteen carcinogens took four pages of the Federal

Register (January 29, 1974); vinyl chloride, six pages (October 4, 1974); and coke oven emissions, forty-one pages (October 22, 1976). These documentations would not prevent court challenges, but they would make the challenges more manageable.

The tradeoff for such caution was that few chemicals were regulated. The GAO claimed that OSHA's caution had evolved into timidity and administratively comfortable delay. The GAO also claimed that OSHA was not issuing emergency temporary standards when needed, was not issuing permanent standards based on the best available evidence, and was therefore undercutting the OSH Act.

How does this early activity fit the pluralist, capitalist State, and organizational perspectives?

5.2.1. Pluralism

Pluralism fares reasonably well. Much of what OSHA did in these early years were reactions to interest-group pressures. Labor's and public interest groups' pressures produced early chemical regulations. The Oil, Chemical, and Atomic Workers' and the Steelworkers' unions also closely monitored the coke oven standard, and their objections apparently weighed heavily in the tightening of the final standard compared to the earlier proposal. Labor participated in the vinyl chloride proceeding, although clear epidemiological data on worker deaths triggered the regulation. The *loosening* of the early standards (asbestos, carcinogens) followed business's objections.

However, industry, had little impact on the vinyl chloride and coke oven regulations (Grover Wrenn later said that if companies knew that OSHA would maintain a particularly strong vinyl chloride standard— as OSHA did not with previous standards—"they would have descended on (Assistant Secretary for OSH) John Stender) with such pressure that he would have backed off from the 1-ppm standard" [Mendeloff, 1979: 55]). Industry unsuccessfully sued OSHA over both.

But constant litigation over the economic and technological feasibility of regulations had an effect. OSHA exhaustively analyzed and documented these regulations to cope with lawsuits, as its transition document to President-elect Carter indicated (Bureau of National Affairs, December 16, 1976: 884). Grover Wrenn added that the "dialogue on the public policy issue . . . the economic issue . . . has been raised to a higher level of discussion, emotion, more time and energy directed them in recent proceedings than in earlier ones, and I suppose that was inevitable with or without an executive order. . . ." (Wrenn, 1977: 83-84).

5.2.2. The Organizational Perspective

The fact that OSHA issued early standards quickly could indicate that it was following its first procedural guide—the OSH Act—closely. However, the suggested drive for organizational autonomy does not appear. OSHA did not defend its early standards in the face of opposition, but weakened them. Another hypothesized force driving organizations is a desire for stability. As outlined in 5.2.1., OSHA *did* tailor its procedures to minimize the difficulties and costs of litigation.

That development was an organizational effect of interest-group pressures, suggesting a combination of the pluralist and organizational views. It suggests that interest groups set constraints for a regulatory agency. They do this by direct pressure. The organization tries to carve out an autonomous, stable existence within these constraints. The procedures and aspirations then shape what the agency does even if certain interest groups are not mobilized on a particular issue. For example, unions or public interest groups might actively lobby for a certain chemical control, and businesses may not be directly involved. However, exhaustive review procedures could by then be built into the system as standard operating procedures and thus the control would be issued, if at all, only after a long delay.

However, this analysis ignores part of the organizational perspective. What about the independent effects of leaders? Can a leader turn a regulatory organization against powerful interest groups, shattering what more timid officials consider to be constraints? This issue will be considered in the next chapter.

5.2.3. The Capitalist State View

The capitalist State view does not hold up well. OSHA's responsiveness to unions and public interest groups before business mobilized shows that it was not by nature an active, autonomous guardian of capitalism. Further, OSHA did not try to override capitalism's narrow special interests either; it bent before industry pressure. As Clause Offe noted, such responsiveness to interest groups undercuts the ability of the State to function as a capitalist State (1975: 140) (see Sections 1.1.2.2., 1.1.2.3. above).

Further, while the Council on Wage and Price Stability's intervention in OSHA's decisions is superficially the type of activity one expects from the higher levels of a capitalist State, remember that CWPS and the Council of Economic Advisors were accused of being public advocates of corporate attacks on regulations. Christopher DeMuth (1980a) argued that the regulatory review program of the Executive Office of the President was superfluous to industry's interventions because they advanced the same arguments. Even if CWPS had great marginal impact, if it functioned as an advocate of regulated firms' positions it did nothing to moderate the competitive excesses of capitalism and was simply one more tool in a game of pluralist bargaining and pressure. But judgements on this issue should be reserved until one sees how the review program developed from 1977 to 1980.

CHAPTER 6

OSHA's Regulations After 1976

6.1. THE NEW ADMINISTRATION

In 1977 the Carter administration did not reappoint Dr. Morton Corn as Assistant Secretary of Labor for Occupational Safety and Health. In April, 1977, Eula Bingham was named to replace Corn. Like Corn, Bingham had a strong background in occupational health. She had served on the standards advisory committee for the coke oven emissions standard and had been a toxicologist at the University of Cincinnati. She quickly let it be known that she would prefer to err in favor of workers' protection than in favor of industries' compliance capabilities. Her top staff included Basil Whiting, who had worked on civil rights, community development, anti-poverty programs, and occupational safety and health for the Ford Foundation; Bertram Cottine, who had worked for Ralph Nader's Health Research Group; Franklin Greer, who had worked for a public interest consulting firm; and Susan Nelson, Peggy Taylor, and Jeannie Warner, all of whom once worked for Senate and House committees overseeing OSHA.

The draft General Accounting Office report criticizing OSHA's health standards program was distributed in March, 1977. On April 28, 1977, Dr. Bingham told a subcommittee of the House Committee on Government Operations that

> in reviewing OSHA's efforts to regulate toxic substances, the General Accounting Office, among others, has pointed out that the agency has been reluctant to use section 6(c) of the Act. This allows emergency temporary standards to be issued, taking effect immediately, if employees are exposed to "grave danger" from workplace hazards and if such standard is necessary for their protection. I believe that this authority is crucial to employee protection. I intend to use this mechanism whenever needed, not only in regard to unregulated substances but also where present standards are inadequate and employees are therefore exposed to "grave" danger" (U.S. House Committee on Government Operations, 1977: 76).

Breaking with the previous policy, Bingham's administration did use the ETS provision three times between April, 1977, and January, 1978.

6.1.1. Benzene

On April 15, 1977, the National Institute for Occupational Safety and Health notified OSHA that new epidemiological data "conclusively" showed that benzene caused leukemia. On April 29, the day after Bingham's Congressional testimony, OSHA issued an emergency temporary standard for benzene of one part per million, prescribing other protective measures as well. The new administration's attitude toward emergency temporary standards prompted the ETS as much as the new data. This was not the first evidence of benzene's link to leukemia. NIOSH had "strongly recommended" that OSHA issue a benzene ETS in 1976 (U.S. General Accounting Office, 1977a: 27). In fact, about ninety percent of the studies OSHA cited in justifying the permanent standard ten months later were completed prior to 1975, although—as industry pointed out—virtually all of the data on benzene exposure involved concentrations far above the current standard of ten parts per million.

On May 10, the American Petroleum Institute, the National Petroleum Refiners Association, and ten oil companies asked the U.S. Court of Appeals for the Fifth Circuit to review the standard, arguing that they could not possibly comply with it. On May 20, the Court granted a stay of the standard. On February 10, 1978, OSHA issued a permanent standard of one part per million to replace the still suspended emergency standard. On March 13, the permanent standard was also stayed by the Fifth Circuit Court pending further review.

The American Petroleum Institute, the American Iron and Steel Institute, the Independent Petroleum Association of America, and the Manufacturing Chemists Association asked the Fifth Circuit Court to permanently strike down the standard. They argued that there was no evidence that an exposure limit of ten parts per million, the current limit adopted in 1971, was hazardous; OSHA had allegedly misinterpreted studies in concluding that exposures of 10–15 ppm could induce leukemia. Industry charged that OSHA had ignored studies showing that low level exposures were not harmful, and that, because the agency lacked evidence of benzene's danger, OSHA "retreated" to a position that there is no safe level of exposure to a carcinogen. Also, they claimed, OSHA never attempted to identify and evaluate benefits of the standard, and "such an evaluation would show that the standard will yield virtually no health benefits despite its enormous costs." Finally, the standard allegedly had too many requirements (Bureau of National Affairs, May 11, 1978: 1831-1832). On June 22, OSHA and the AFL–CIO defended the standard before the same Court.

In October, the Fifth Circuit Court permanently suspended the benzene standard. The Court argued that OSHA did not show that the standard's benefits had a "reasonable relationship" to its costs. It stated that OSHA did not have to do an elaborate cost-benefit analysis, but did have to demonstrate that the standard was "reasonably necessary" to provide a healthy workplace.

OSHA then took the case to the U.S. Supreme Court. The Fifth Circuit decision had said that OSHA must demonstrate *measurable benefits* of reducing benzene exposure. In asking for a Supreme Court hearing, OSHA argued that "If the relationship between exposure and disease is imperfectly known, so that the benefits cannot be measured, then the Secretary of Labor cannot order a reduction in exposure." In effect, OSHA would never be able to regulate a carcinogen because of the uncertainty involved. OSHA cited three earlier court decisions which upheld OSHA's policy of not conducting cost-benefit analyses (the D.C. Circuit Court upholding the asbestos standard, the Second Circuit Court for New York upholding the vinyl chloride standard, and the Third Circuit Court for Philadelphia upholding the coke oven emissions standard). These earlier decisions maintained that when the evidence established no safe level of exposure to a carcinogen, OSHA should favor workers' health. In fact, the Fifth Circuit Court had recognized that its decision clashed with these three cases, but made no attempt to reconcile them with its own ruling.

On July 2, 1980, the Supreme Court upheld the Fifth Circuit court in a 5–4 decision, striking down the benzene standard (448 U.S. 607). Justices Stevens, Burger, Stewart, and Powell concluded that the standard was invalid because OSHA had not shown it to be "reasonably necessary or appropriate to provide safe or healthful employment." While noting that OSHA ought to have some discretion in handling uncertain scientific issues, they argued that OSHA's conclusion that "significant" benefits would result from a 1 ppm as opposed to a 10 ppm limit on benzene was unreasonable given the evidence. Thus, "the written explanation of the standard fills 184 pages of the printed appendix. Much of it is devoted to a discussion of the voluminous evidence of the adverse effects of exposure to benzene at levels of concentration well above 10 ppm. The discussion demonstrates that there is ample justification for regulating occupational exposure to benzene and that the prior limit of 10 ppm, with a ceiling of 25 ppm (or a peak of 50 ppm) was reasonable. It does not, however, provide direct support for the Agency's conclusion that the limit should be reduced from 10 ppm to 1 ppm. The evidence in the administrative record of adverse effects of benzene exposure at 10 ppm is sketchy at best" (448 U.S. 631).

Voting with the majority, Justice Rehnquist argued that the section of the OSH Act telling the agency to prevent any "material impairment" of health gave no Congressional guidance on where to set exposure levels and was therefore invalid (448 U.S. 671).

Dissenting Justices Marshall, Brennan, White, and Blackmun held that the Act quite clearly told OSHA to set the most protective standard which was feasible and—also referring to the voluminous record—said that OSHA had done so in the benzene case. The four dissenters accused the majority of "ignoring the plain meaning of the Occupational Safety and Health Act of 1970 in order to bring the authority of the Secretary of Labor in line with the plurality's own views of proper regulatory policy" (448 U.S. 688).

In 1977 and 1978, OSHA also issued emergency standards for two other chemicals—DBCP and acrylonitrile.

6.1.2. Dibromochloropropane (DBCP)

In July, 1977, workers at Occidental Chemical's Lathrop, California plant sought medical help from the University of California because of an obvious pattern of infertility. Thirty-eight workers sent sperm samples and fourteen showed overly reduced sperm counts. Leaders of the Oil, Chemical, and Atomic Workers Union (OCAW) informed the State Division of Industrial Safety. One week later Occidental suspended production of dibromochloropropane (DBCP).

On August 23, the union asked OSHA to issue an emergency standard for the chemical limiting exposure to one part per billion (1 ppb). OSHA issued an emergency standard of 10 ppb. Based on evidence that DBCP was a carcinogen as well, OSHA proposed a permanent standard of 1 ppb on November 1, 1977. Neither the ETS nor the permanent standard were challenged in court. The "horror story" overtones of the sterility, the clearness of the data, and qualities of the DBCP production market (by August only Dow Chemical and Shell Oil were producing DBCP) inhibited a suit. OSHA noted that Dow and Shell were "large organizations with vast experience in the control of toxic substances" and were "able to institute 'state-of-the-art' control technology given sufficient financial incentives to do so." The value of DBCP as a pesticide provided the incentives, and "the economic considerations appear even more favorable in light of the fact that up to the promulgation of the ETS only two plants were active in the production of DBCP. Control technologies can thus be concentrated in the relatively few workplaces where exposures exist" (U.S. Department of Labor, OSHA, 1978a: 11519). In April, 1978, the permanent standard went into effect.

6.1.3. Acrylonitrile

In March and April, 1977, the Manufacturing Chemists Association submitted data to OSHA showing that laboratory rats exposed to acrylonitrile developed tumors, lesions, and other pathologies. In May, a DuPont study demonstrated an excess rate of cancer among workers exposed to acrylonitrile in a Camden, South Carolina textile plant in the 1950s. The threshold limit value list adopted by OSHA in 1971 included a 20 ppm exposure limit for acrylonitrile. On January 16, 1978, OSHA issued an emergency temporary standard limiting exposure to acrylonitrile to 2 ppm.

The Society of the Plastics Industry, Inc., immediately said that the standard was "uncalled for" because industry was already holding exposure to a level "considerably lower" than the 20 ppm standard. Its president claimed that industry might not be able to comply with the standard, and also that the evidence of acrylonitrile's carcinogenicity was not yet adequately evaluated. On February 9, four companies, led by Visitron Corporation, petitioned OSHA to hold off the standard. They maintained that it presented "impossible compliance difficulties" and that the MCA and DuPont data were still ambiguous. OSHA denied the petition.

Visitron et al. filed a similar petition in the U.S. Court of Appeals for the Sixth Circuit in Cincinnati. On February 15, the court granted a stay of the standard. OSHA asked the court on February 24 to lift the stay because the evidence supported the ETS, because the industry petitioners did not show that they would be irreparably harmed by the standard, and because of the cancer risk that the stay perpetuated. The Court agreed to lift the suspension.

OSHA announced that it was considering limits of 2 ppm, 1 ppm, and .2 ppm for the permanent standard. At hearings on the proposed standard, industry said that it could live with the 2-ppm limit and that a 2-ppm limit would be sufficiently protective. Despite earlier claims of "impossible compliance difficulties," the technology to control vinyl chloride had been modified to control acrylonitrile (U.S. Department of Labor, OSHA, 1978d: 45774-45775). DuPont affirmed that its plants were already operating at the 2-ppm level. Union Carbide said that it could meet the 2-ppm level. Visitron also said that the 2-ppm proposal was "feasible and provides adequate protection." Visitron said that it had already invested in the controls to meet the 2-ppm limit.

The Council on Wage and Price Stability raised several issues about the standard (U.S. CWPS, 1978a). First, the Council noted that the marginal protection declined and the marginal cost per life saved increased dramatically as the exposure limit was lowered from 20 ppm to 2 ppm, 1 ppm, and .2 ppm. CWPS estimated that the incremental cost per life saved at 2 ppm would be $3.5 million; at 1 ppm, $28.8 million; and at .2 ppm, $169.2 million. In the preamble to the final standard, OSHA questioned attempts "to indicate both the magnitude of the risk and hypothetical 'cost per worker protected' under the alternative sets of permissible exposure limits. When the health effectiveness of alternative approaches is extremely uncertain and likely to vary from situation to situation, OSHA believes it is appropriate to adopt the compliance strategy which provides the greatest certainty of worker protection within bounds of feasibility, even if the approach carries with it greater economic burdens for affected employers" (1978d: 45790). (Having said this, OSHA adopted the 2 ppm limit.)

Second, CWPS suggested that different levels of exposure could be set for different industry segments depending upon the costs per employee protected. OSHA dismissed the differential exposure limits as administratively infeasible for acrylonitrile processing. Finally, the Council urged that OSHA allow employers to rely more freely on personal protective devices—rather than engineering controls—to control exposure to acrylonitrile. OSHA rejected any primary reliance on respirators because they were flawed protections, tiring for workers, and safety hazards; respirators could be used only as interim measures, or in areas where engineering controls could not feasibly attain the exposure limit (1978d: 45774, 45801).

In October, 1978, OSHA issued a final acrylonitrile standard with an exposure limit of 2 ppm, calling this the lowest feasible exposure limit. Industry did not challenge the standard, since many firms were already at the 2-ppm limit and others could follow relatively easily.

6.1.4. Inorganic Arsenic

On May 3, 1978, OSHA issued a final standard for arsenic to take effect on August 1. The arsenic standard proposal issued in 1975 had an exposure limit of 4 micrograms per cubic meter of air. The final standard permitted exposure of up to 10 micrograms. The agency stated that the 10 microgram limit "minimizes, to the maximum extent feasible, excess lung cancer deaths resulting from exposure to inorganic arsenic. It is achievable generally through engineering and work practice controls. Limited respirator use will be needed to achieve the limit in some locations in some facilities, and one facility will require extensive respirator usage. . . . What is clear is this standard will provide significant protection of workers from arsenic-induced lung cancer" (U.S. Department of Labor, OSHA, 1978b: 19604).

The Council on Wage and Price Stability and OSHA had what was by then a customary exchange. CWPS criticized OSHA for not trying to systematically quantify the standard's benefits and for not permitting personal protective devices as substitutes for engineering controls (Levine, 1979). OSHA rejected the use of respirators and said that while a "systematic evaluation of costs and benefits" should be "encouraged within the limitations of the estimation techniques," OSHA was given "discretion which is essentially legislative in nature. In setting an exposure limit for a substance like inorganic arsenic OSHA has concluded that it is inappropriate to substitute cost-benefit criteria for the legislatively determined directive of protecting all exposed employees against material impairment of health or bodily function" (U.S. Department of Labor, OSHA, 1978b: 19607).

Five smelting companies immediately challenged the standard in the U.S. Court of Appeals for the Ninth Circuit in San Francisco. The vice-president of the American Smelting and Refining Corporation (ASARCO) argued that the evidence did not support a 10 microgram exposure limit because mortality studies of workers exposed to arsenic dealt with exposures in the 1930's and 1940's and "We would expect much less of an excess (number of deaths) now, if any." He also claimed that a 50 microgram limit was the lowest level attainable with current technology.

The arsenic standard was still being litigated at the end of 1980. Some provisions were in effect, and others were suspended. For example, the Ninth Circuit Court exempted ASARCO and two other companies from the engineering requirements pending the Court's decision on the entire standard. The companies agreed to use personal protective devices to control exposure until the Court's final decision.

6.1.5. Cotton Dust

President Carter's "Improving Government Regulations Program" was announced on March 23, 1978. This continued, in somewhat different form, the inflation/economic impact statement program started four years earlier by President Ford. On April 18, 1978, President Carter's special counsel on inflation, Robert Strauss, singled out "postal workers, Teamsters, and environmental regulators" as initial targets in the administration's anti-inflation program. Strauss affirmed that he had asked EPA head Douglas Costle to suggest cost-cutting regulatory changes; that "he was prepared to seek presidential intervention if the EPA is not responsive;" and that "easing environmental and other regulatory costs would make it easier to persuade business leaders to restrain their prices" (Broder, 1978).

The cotton dust case was the first occasion on which a clash between the Council on Wage and Price Stability and the Occupational Safety and Health Administration pulled in the President. One reason for the President's intervention was the particularly high cost of the cotton dust standard. The annual cost of OSHA's draft final standard for cotton dust was about $695 million, while the annual costs of the benzene, DBCP, acrylonitrile, and arsenic standards were about $200, $3.6, $24.3, and $111 million, respectively. Another possible factor was that it followed the kickoff of Carter's regulatory reform program, and—even more so than before—costly regulations were topical and freshly legitimated concerns for Presidential economists.

Certain materials in cotton dust produce a serious, in late stages irreversible, lung disease called byssinosis. In December, 1975, the Textile Workers Union (since merged with the Amalgamated Clothing Workers to form the Amalgamated Clothing and Textile Workers Union, ACTWU) and the North Carolina Public Interest Research Group sued OSHA in the U.S. District Court in the District of Columbia. They demanded that OSHA be compelled to issue a standard for employee exposure to cotton dust.

OSHA proposed a permanent standard for cotton dust in December, 1976. The standard stipulated an exposure limit of .2 milligrams of respirable cotton dust per cubic meter of air wherever workers were exposed to cotton dust. Industry objected that the majority of the epidemiological data on lung disease from cotton dust were collected in the textile industry, and that no evidence indicated that a regulation was needed for cottonseed mills, cotton ginning, and other nontextile operations. Textile representatives, on the other hand, argued that the risk of developing byssinosis diminished as raw cotton was processed in a mill; the cleaning and treatment needed to turn cotton into cloth gradually eliminated the harmful elements. If any regulation were to be issued, the textile firms maintained that it should apply only to the early stages of cotton processing.

In the preamble to the proposed standard, however, OSHA cited four studies showing lung problems from cotton dust in nontextile operations, and also initially discounted the textile industry's arguments. The agency argued that it

> ... has considered the suggestion that different standards based upon industry-specific epidemiological evidence be established for the different industries involved and perhaps even for varying processes within each particular industry. However, there is a lack of data indicating that exposure to cotton dust affects workers differently in the various affected industries. Indeed, the evidence which is available supports the view that exposure to cotton dust, regardless of the stage of processing in which the dust is encountered, results in byssinosis and other respiratory diseases. It is OSHA's view that the need to protect workers in all industries outweighs the constraints on regulatory action which might be advocated because of the fact that much of the epidemiological data has arisen from one segment of the cotton industry. OSHA invites comments and testimony regarding the scope of this cotton dust standard (Bureau of National Affairs, January 6, 1977: 1011).

Hearings were held in 1977, and industry continued to object to the breadth and cost of the standard.

OSHA's inflation impact statement estimated that the *proposed* standard would cost about $695 million annually. The Council on Wage and Price Stability suggested that this probably overstated the cost "because of the strong incentive to reduce costs through technological modifications." The long period given employers to comply with the standard fully (seven years) increased the opportunities for technical innovation. "However," CWPS added, "we emphasize that this conclusion is extremely sensitive to the design of the final standard. We will suggest certain improvements in the proposed standard that should enhance the possibilities that innovation and technical change will substantially reduce the social costs of the standard" (1977: 11-12).

The Council maintained, as had others, that both the hazards of cotton dust and the costs of redesigning equipment to control it varied by process. "Because both benefits and costs for the proposed standard vary widely by stage of processing, a standard that took these differences into account could produce major cost savings and/or greater worker protection." As evidence for this, CWPS cited a study done in 1973 by James Merchant which had been used heavily by OSHA. "Interpolating from Merchant's Figure 2, it can be seen that a standard of .2 mg/m^3 in yarn preparation is equivalent in toxicity to about a .75 mg/m^3 in weaving" (1977: 24-26).

CWPS also suggested, as an alternative to the proposal, a system of fines for each case of byssinosis in a firm. This would, the Council argued, induce firms to develop creative ways of directly preventing the disease, such as developing new types of cotton or shifting workers when they began showing some sign of the disease. Of course, "safeguards to provide job security and prevent unlawful discrimination would have to be developed" (1977: 30-36).

The *proposed* standard set a uniform exposure limit of .2 mg of respirable cotton dust per cubic meter of air wherever workers were exposed to cotton dust. In the draft *final* standard OSHA accepted the variable exposure limits suggested by industry and CWPS. The prospective final standard set a .2-mg limit for yarn manufacturing, .75 for slashing and weaving, .5 for cotton waste processing, cotton seed oil, and warehousing sectors, and no limit for cotton ginning. With respect to slashing and weaving, the draft final standard estimated that the costs of engineering changes to reduce dust to .2 mg would be $1.3 billion. "Of course," OSHA interjected,

> . . . the agency does not view the economic and technological feasibility of dust exposure in a vacuum. It is primarily concerned with the health of workers, and the record supports the conclusion that a permissible exposure limit of (.75 mg) will provide weavers as safe an environment as their co-workers in other textile operations exposed to (.2 mg). In addition, OSHA agrees with the reasoning of the North Carolina Department of Labor that optimal worker protection would be served by concentrating the textile industry's technical and economic resources on achieving (.2 mg) in yarn manufacturing as rapidly as feasible, rather than diverting substantial resources to eliminating dust exposure in weaving (1978c: 58-60).

OSHA later admitted that the price of loosening the exposure limits was about 5,260 cases of byssinosis (or "brown lung" disease). Its regulatory analysis, requested by Congress, claimed that the .2 mg uniform exposure limit would have meant that some segments of the industry paid high costs for "relatively few" cases avoided. The *proposed* standard with the uniform limit would have cost about $803 million annually (up from OSHA's earlier estimate of $695 million) and prevented 28,750 cases of an expected 84,000 cases of brown lung. The *final* standard cost $205 million and would prevent 23,490 cases, "only" 5,260 fewer (OSHA disregarded as being too costly the standard recommended by the Textile Workers' Union and the Brown Lung Association. "Assuming full compliance is even attainable," this would have cost about $1.9 billion annually, prevented 46,320 cases, and would "largely eliminate brown lung disease") (Bureau of National Affairs, May 24, 1979: 1781-1782).

The draft final standard also specified that engineering controls, rather than respirators, would be the primary way to control exposure to cotton dust.

The director of the Council on Wage and Price Stability, Barry Bosworth, said that the revised exposure limits reflected "great advances" in applying "cost effectiveness considerations." However, he alleged that, while the final standard if released in present form would result in "considerable savings" to employers, OSHA was "only willing to go half way." He recommended that OSHA could loosen the exposure limits even further before issuing the final standard, and permit employee use of respirators as a substitute for engineering controls. Finally, employers could be given a longer time to comply with the standard. These "improvements" would save another $125 million annually. The CWPS evaluation was given to President Carter.

On May 24, Secretary of Labor Ray Marshall sent the President a memo saying that "the economic considerations which are legitimately the concern of the (Council of Economic Advisors and the Council on Wage and Price Stability) have been taken into account in this standard to the maximum extent possible." He criticized the CWPS proposal that respirators be substituted for engineering controls, saying that the issue had been hammered out in earlier hearings and that "I can only consider it presumptuous for CEA/CWPS to second guess OSHA on technical issues, such as the respirator issue." He also noted that stretching out the compliance period any longer was unnecessary because the regulation permitted OSHA to be flexible in fining employers for violations if they made good faith efforts to comply with the standard. "Thus," he said, "an employer could theoretically have an unlimited period to comply. Although I will strive to bring all firms into compliance as soon as possible, the technical and economic realities of each case will be taken into consideration."

Marshall noted also that "delaying the standard will cause a major political upheaval among such groups as the textile unions, the AFL–CIO, the Brown Lung Association, public interest groups, and the Congress. These groups are very sensitive since there is documentation that the Nixon administration held out delaying this standard as an enticement to generate political contributions to the 1972 campaign. Indeed, the Department was sued by the Textile Workers' Union to force the issuance of the standard. The suit is now pending in Federal District Court and I have pledged to the judge that the final standard will be issued by May 31."

Industry and labor were actively lobbying the White House over the standard as well. In May, the National Cotton Council approached Senator James Eastland of Mississippi about a meeting with the Carter administration on the standard. Eastland spoke with Carter advisor Stuart Eizenstat, who recommended a meeting with the Labor Department. In that meeting the National Cotton Council told the Secretary of Labor and Eula Bingham that the standard was "highly inflationary."

George Taylor of the AFL–CIO and George Perkel of the Textile Workers' Union met with Charles Schultze, chairman of the Council of Economic Advisors, Barry Bosworth, and Stuart Eizenstat. Taylor remarked later that "I don't think that we got through to them," that the Council of Economic Advisors intended to make OSHA the "scapegoat for inflation," and had "decided to make their stand on this and subsequent standards." The AFL–CIO would "take whatever action Mr. Meany decides—it's at his level now." Also, A.F. Grospiron of the Oil, Chemical, and Atomic Workers wrote to Carter urging him to "reject the cynicism of those in your administration who put profits over life," and to "allow the cotton dust standard to be issued by OSHA as it was originally proposed and without further delay." Grospiron affirmed that cotton workers not protected by an effective standard "will be introduced into the health care system where costs are escalating rapidly" and that the costs "will be prorated among the American people, providing a subsidy for employers who do not control cotton dust" (Bureau of National Affairs, June 8, 1978: 27-28).

Early in June, Chairman of the CEA Charles Schultze ordered the Labor Department to further reduce the regulation's costs. Schultze's memo to Ray Marshall stated that he was acting on President Carter's instructions (Dewar, 1978a). Sixteen members of the U.S. House of Representatives protested the White House intervention in a letter, saying that it "threatened to undermine the basic procedures" set up by the Occupational Safety and Health Act. The letter pointed out that Carter had said during his campaign that workers' exposure to toxic substances "cannot be tolerated." The Labor Secretary immediately requested a meeting with Carter and Schultze.

At the meeting the President partially reversed himself. Some modifications in the draft final standard were made, but "Labor Department officials—almost ecstatic in their reaction—said 'there is no significant change . . . no reduction in worker protection.'" For example, the regulation would still require engineering controls for cotton dust (Dewar, 1978b).

On June 19, OSHA announced the final standard. It was virtually the same final standard which OSHA had defended before President Carter; employers were given a bit longer to comply with some parts of the regulation. The standard was announced at a press conference at which Ray Marshall, Charles Schultze, and Director of Health Standards Grover Wrenn participated.

Some congressmen called the regulation evidence that OSHA was now an aggressive protector of workers' health. Congressman David Obey of Wisconsin said that "it would be absolutely unconscionable to ask workers to run the risk of contracting lung disease just so the rest of us can spend a few cents less for a shirt . . . it is good to know that there are still a few people in government with a passion for justice and decency who care enough about workers' lives and health to take on the White House staff in order to reverse a bad decision" (Bureau of National Affairs, June 15, 1978: 60). Actually, the success that OSHA had in implementing the draft standard over industry, CWPS, and CEA pressures must be qualified. The proposal's exposure limits were modified much as CWPS suggested, and the only remaining issue was whether or not OSHA would go, to use Barry Bosworth's phrase, more than "half way" in altering the regulation.

According to its later regulatory analysis, OSHA traded off 5,260 cases of byssinosis to save the cotton processors about $598 million annually. Its accompanying estimate was that the cost of a single case of byssinosis disability (including reduced earnings, lost work time and early retirement, and direct medical expenses) was about $100,852 (Bureau of National Affairs, June 24, 1979: 1781-1782). Therefore, it would cost "society" about $530 million to compensate the 5,260 victims, which is considerably less than the compliance costs saved (whether such compensation would actually be made, of course, is doubtful; occupational disease victims usually absorb most of the costs). This was the first time OSHA explicitly acknowledged trading off feasible but expensive disease prevention for cost reductions, and showed—again in Barry Bosworth's words—"great advances" in applying "cost effectiveness considerations."

Nevertheless, after the standard was announced industry sued. The American Textile Institute maintained that meeting the requirements would be "technologically impossible." The Textile Workers' Union also announced that it would sue because the exposure limits were too high and employers were formally given too long to meet them. In October, 1979, the U.S. Court of Appeals for the District of Columbia upheld the standard, for the most part, over both sets of objections (Bureau of National Affairs, November 1, 1979: 515-516).

6.1.6. Lead

The lead standard was a major, expensive regulation which followed soon after the cotton dust controversy. Did OSHA—or the Executive Office of the President—treat it any differently?

The 1974 proposed lead standard would have replaced the present

200 microgram per cubic meter of air limit with a 100 microgram limit and other protective measures. The final standard was issued on November 13, 1978, four years later.

OSHA spent much of the interim considering a "rate retention" provision for the standard, which would protect workers participating in medical programs for lead exposure. As indicated in Section 5.1.5., employees frequently do not participate in medical programs because they may be transferred to cleaner but lower paying jobs, or laid off, if they show symptoms of a disease that could be aggravated by a regulated chemical. The employer thereby avoids a workers' compensation claim or lawsuit for damages. With a rate retention provision in the regulation, lead-affected workers would be transferred to other jobs with less exposure or laid off until their blood lead levels fell to a safe point, but their pay would not be reduced. Grover Wrenn pointed out in hearings on the proposed standard on November 1 that

> without protection of an employee's job, wages benefits, seniority, and other employment rights, it is obvious, and experience has demonstrated, that an employee who recognizes the possibility of adverse economic consequences from medical determinations will often be forced to place his or her family's financial security before his or her own health and will refuse to participate in the medical program or seek ways to defeat it (Bureau of National Affairs, November 3, 1977: 773).

The Steelworkers union and the Health Research Group strongly supported the rate retention provision. To prevent the possibility of blood lead levels being underestimated by company medical personnel, they urged that workers be paid for examinations by doctors not affiliated with the company.

In November, 1977, the Lead Industries Association, the Manufacturing Chemists Association, the American Iron and Steel Institute, Organization Resources Counselors, Inc., and other business groups questioned whether OSHA had the authority to require such economic protection. The Lead Industries Association said that "neither the Act, its legislative history, nor subsequent legislative developments" permitted OSHA to require economic protection which would "constitute a form of Federally-mandated workers' compensation and, in many instances, would alter and affect the employer's statutory rights and duties under existing state programs." The Labor Department responded that the OSH Act states that a standard shall prescribe "suitable protective equipment and control or technological procedures," and that OSHA considered economic protection to be a "control mechanism." It also cited section 3(8) of the Act which defines a standard as a "standard which requires conditions, or the adoption or use of one or more practices, means, methods, operations, or processes, reasonably necessary or appropriate to provide safe or healthful employment and places of employment." Rate retention was the most effective method of ensuring workers' protection in medical programs required under the lead standard and so it was a "reasonably necessary or appropriate" practice.

The American Iron and Steel Institute argued that the rate retention provision would impose an "incalculable cost" on the steel industry. Its vice-president for industrial relations, John Stenmark, said that "while the steel industry is being severely shaken by foreign imports, trying to comply with regulations by local, state, and federal governmental agencies which do not coordinate their efforts, and sorely criticized for giving their employees 'too much' at the bargaining table, it is not the time to impose upon it another substantal impact." He argued that employee hygiene, the nonwork environment, and tasks performed by the employee away from his job could increase blood lead levels so that it was not fair to impose the costs of lead control on industry (Bureau of National Affairs, November 10, 1977: 819-820). OSHA responded that the overwhelming source of lead poisoning in workers was the working environment.

Early in 1978, the Lead Industries Association changed its position from outright opposition to favoring a modification of the proposal. It maintained that rate retention should not pay for outside review of company doctor decisions, that there should be controls on outside reviewers if such reviewers were allowed, and that rate retention should not be carried on for more than ninety days lest employees not try to recover from lead poisoning. The Battery Council International, however, continued to charge that the lead standard "would put out of business the majority of firms in the battery industry" (Bureau of National Affairs, January 26, 1978: 1329). An economic impact study done for OSHA claimed that the rate retention provision would result in "substantial" but not "infeasible or destructive" costs to the lead industry (Bureau of National Affairs, December 8, 1977: 952-953).

In November, 1978, the final standard had been prepared for release. It gradually lowered the exposure limit to 50 micrograms per cubic meter of air, as opposed to the proposal's 100 and the present limit of 200. It included rate retention phased in over five years. As organized labor requested, it permitted outside review of blood lead levels, although the preamble to the standard said that most company doctors could be trusted.

However, the final review of the Council on Wage and Price Stability and the Council of Economic Advisors held up the release of the standard. On November 3, an irritated Eula Bingham told a conference of the United Steelworkers that "Ray Marshall and I have been through the palace guard to see (President Carter) once about a standard (cotton dust), and we are ready to do it again." Bingham did not specifically state that the lead standard was being held up by the CWPS and CEA, but was critical of "economists" and those who argued that health and safety regulations are inflationary. She also suggested that the Steelworkers could help her "free the lead standard." "Maybe your president knows someone in Washington. Maybe the president of the United Auto Workers knows someone in Washington."

Steelworker representatives said that the White House was being flooded by business letters saying that the standard would be destructively costly, and that steelworkers should exert the same type of pressure. University of Illinois professor Samuel Epstein told the conference that "what is happening is classic in all attempts to regulate a toxic hazard"—that industry always argues that the danger is not great and that compliance costs would bankrupt firms and fuel inflation. "The science is trivial. The politics is important. If there is not a standard, it is because you have failed politically" (Bureau of National Affairs, November 9, 1978: 827-828).

On November 13, OSHA did issue the final standard. Although Bingham had expressed concerns about the economic review of the standard, Director of Health standards Grover Wrenn affirmed that both the Council on Wage and Price Stability and the Council of Economic Advisors agreed that the standard was "well conceived and cost effective" and "made dramatically clear substantive health benefits." (Identifying benefits was less of a problem with lead than with carcinogens because more is known about the *toxic* (poisoning) effects of substances than carcinogenic effects. Also, CWPS called the standard "well conceived and cost effective" despite the fact that OSHA—once again—rejected its suggestion that personal protective devices be permitted as a substitute for engineering controls; see U.S. CWPS, 1977: 14-15). Wrenn said that the CEA and CWPS reviews did not affect the final regulation. Sidney Wolfe of the Health Research group and United Auto Workers' president Douglas Fraser said that they basically approved of the rule. Industry groups called it economically destructive (Bureau of National Affairs, November 16, 1978: 853.)

The Steelworkers, the Oil, Chemical, and Atomic Workers (OCAW), and the Lead Industries Association all sued the Labor Department. Although the standard contained most of the provisions supported by the Steelworkers, the union filed a suit in the Third Circuit

Court in Philadelphia, which had upheld the coke oven emissions standard. The Steelworkers claimed that the Labor Department had not adequately shown why it did not adopt the 40 microgram limit favored by the union, although the principal reason the union sued was in fact to establish the Philadelphia Court as the Court with jurisdiction in the case (See Section 3.1.5.). The Lead Industries Association filed their suit in the Fifth Circuit in New Orleans, which had struck down the benzene standard. After legal complications, the case was eventually turned over to the D.C. Circuit Court. There the Oil, Chemical, and Atomic Workers intervened, claiming that the standard's five year phase-in of exposure limits, the design of the rate retention provision, and an exemption of the construction industry excessively weakened the standard (Bureau of National Affairs, June 28, 1979: 84-85). In August, 1980, the D.C. Circuit Court upheld the regulation as issued.

I would argue that the final lead standard was modified less than the cotton dust standard (and that it was also tied up less in the White House review process) for three reasons. First, the unions actively backing a strong lead standard—the Steelworkers, the United Auto Workers, and the Oil, Chemical, and Atomic Workers—are relatively influential in occupational health work. These unions did support a strong cotton dust standard, but would have tolerated a weakened dust standard much more than a weakened lead standard. This is because lead exposure was a more immediate problem in their industries than cotton dust. Thus, gutting the lead standard would have alienated OSHA's strongest union supporters.

Second, OSHA would have lost an enormous amount of credibility with all groups favoring chemical regulation if it had followed up a dramatically modified cotton dust standard with a weakened lead standard. A strong lead standard, backed as it was by critical unions, was a way to regain some regulatory prestige.

Third, after the cotton dust controversy, the White House economic review process was attacked by unions, some Senators, and regulatory officials themselves (Bureau of National Affairs, February 8, 1979; March 1, 1979; Branscome, 1979). A sustained CWPS or CEA attempt to weaken the lead standard—comparable to the cotton dust case—would have been politically costly for themselves and the White House generally. In fact, CWPS and CEA officials began to stress that they also recognized the benefits of environmental regulation, and that they were simply interested in attaining environmental goals more efficiently (U.S. Senate Committee on the Environment and Public Works, 1979: 329–421).

But it may be a mistake to make too much of the White House intervention or nonintervention. True, the CWPS, officials at OSHA, and the Assistant Secretary for Policy, Evaluation, and Research in the Labor Department noted that OSHA was sensitive to CWPS's pressures (Hopkins, 1976: 69). James Miller III, a former assistant director of CWPS wrote that "because CWPS is part of the Executive Office of the President and because the interventions are highly publicized, it has considerable clout." Miller also stated that the agencies' fears of exposure of shoddy analyses by the Council induced them to consider economic issues earlier when designing regulations (Miller, 1977: 18).

But others say that the CWPS had little or marginal impact on occupational health regulations. The Occupational Safety and Health Administration *was* sensitive to CWPS, but then OSHA was sensitive to most vocal private organizations as well. The central resistance to "protective" but costly regulations comes from industry, according to this viewpoint. Even if the White House economic staff were not involved, OSHA would continue to exhaustively review the economic and technological feasibility of proposed regulations to defend against businesses' objections and lawsuits.

Christopher DeMuth, director of the Harvard University Faculty Project on Regulation, argued in 1980 that "OSHA's change of heart (on the cotton dust standard) did not result from any regulatory review or pressure from the Council on Wage and Price Stability. . . . Only at the very last stage, when OSHA was about to issue a highly modified proposal, did CWPS become involved." (Actually, the Council *was* involved in hearings on the earlier proposal, and OSHA's revisions followed its, as well as industry's, suggestions.) DeMuth added that CWPS's "institutional inability to review more than a few regulations in any depth" and its "inherent inability, as (a) mere (reviewer), to affect the rate at which regulations are generated" mean that it has little influence on the outcome of regulatory controversies. What influence the White House staff has is superfluous, maintained DeMuth, because the objections CWPS makes are made and pressed more strongly by the private parties with immediate stakes in the regulations (DeMuth, 1980a: 19-23).

It is interesting to see White House economists squabbling with "environmental" agencies, and these conflicts probably do affect some of the content and timing of the standards. But the political power of CWPS may be less important in understanding what regulatory agencies do than the political, economic, and legal power of the industries trying to avoid the regulations.

6.1.7. Chemical Labeling

In 1978, OSHA proposed a regulation requiring businesses to list the generic as well as trade names of chemicals used in the workplace.

Remember that workers have often not had information on substances they work with. The National Institute for Occupational Safety and Health, based on its National Occupational Hazard Survey, estimated in 1977 that seven million workers in the United States were exposed to trade name products containing an OSHA-regulated toxic substance, and that there might be more than 300,000 workers exposed to trade name products containing one or more of the sixteen carcinogens then regulated by OSHA. In these cases, neither the employee nor the employer may have been aware of the ingredients because they were known by trade name rather than by chemical composition. In the survey, manufacturers of the substances designated as trade secrets nearly one-third of the products containing a known carcinogen. The proposed regulation affirmed that this information could no longer be withheld.

The proposed regulation required that the manufacturer give to the employer, and the employer make available to the workers, a data sheet for each toxic substance used in the workplace. This data sheet would give the name, physical data, and specific hazards associated with the substance. Employees would have to be trained on the hazards of the chemicals, whether or not the chemical was covered by a complete OSHA standard. The proposed regulation gave employees, their representatives, OSHA, and NIOSH access to employee medical records and records of exposure to chemicals. Such records were previously made available only at mnagement's discretion. All chemicals listed in the National Institute for Occupational Safety and Health Registry of Toxic Substances were to be covered by the regulation.

OSHA maintained that employees could thus more easily identify the dangers of the chemicals they worked with and that this would sharpen the diffuse anxiety characterizing the early stages of occupational disease "horror stories" (see Section 3.2.2.). The standard, while not addressing the workers' economic security, would indicate to them what they were handling and the substances' possible effects.

Industry criticized the proposed standard on four basic grounds. First, it claimed that OSHA had no authority to pass the regulation because OSHA had no right to require employee access to records of substances for which there were no complete OSHA standards. Second, firms argued that the regulation would require them to reveal secret proprietary information about the chemical composition of products to employees who, particularly when disgruntled, could pass the information on to competitors. Third, the proposal would violate employees' privacy by allowing government access to their medical records. Fourth, industry charged that the standard would cost too much.

Organized labor, public interest groups, and some scientists and State agencies testified in support of the proposal or said that it ought to be strengthened. Steven Wodka of the Oil, Chemical, and Atomic Workers' Union called it "probably the most important regulation ever considered by OSHA." Michael Silverstein, a medical consultant for the United Auto Workers, remarked that "the proposed rule should have been one of the first OSHA regulations . . . it begins to put workers, and the government agencies charged with protecting workers' health, on an equal footing with the companies in knowledge about health and safety at the plant."

Countering the privacy objection, George Annas, a professor of law and medicine at the Boston University School of Medicine, noted that "the record of occupational medicine in protecting and promoting employee health and the doctor–patient relationship is not a good one. OSHA should look carefully at the motivations of industries that now cite 'patients' rights' and 'medical ethics' as reasons to restrict patient or OSHA access to such records. In fact, the interests of industry in continuing certain production practices may be directly opposed to the health and well being of specific workers." Supporters of the proposal argued that the potential for abuse of records could be eliminated by removing information which could identify the individual (e.g., name or social security number) when the employee had not signed for release of the records, or by stipulating restrictions on their use or distribution.

Throughout 1979, Bingham and her staff actively publicized that the Agency wanted the standard released as soon as possible (Bureau of National Affairs, July 5, 1979: 117). However, in September, the Health Research Group sued in the U.S. District Court for the District of Columbia to force OSHA to issue the standard, claiming that the Act compelled OSHA to warn workers of all hazardous substances. In January, 1980, the Court rejected the suit, saying that OSHA was not *compelled* to require such warnings for substances not covered by complete OSHA standards (as of January, 1981, there were twenty-one of these substances).

OSHA eventually split the access to medical and exposure records and chemical labeling components of the standard. The regulation giving employees, OSHA, and NIOSH access to the existing records was issued on May 21, 1980. It permitted access to records of substances on the NIOSH Registry of hazardous substances. The AFL–CIO filed for a review of the standard in the D.C. Circuit Court, but only to establish that Court's jurisdiction for the case. Several industry trade associations sued OSHA over the standard both in the D.C. and New Orleans Courts, objecting to the regulation on three grounds.

First, they said that giving employees exposure records would necessarily indicate the chemical composition of products and that this, in turn, would reveal trade secrets. Second, the regulation required access to records of many chemicals which OSHA had not yet specifically reviewed. Industry contended that OSHA had no authority to require access to such a broad list of chemicals. Third, they argued that the regulation would compromise employees' privacy because it would give government agencies access to medical records of employees. At the end of January, 1981, the standard was being enforced, although the litigation continued.

A revised labeling standard was *proposed* on January 16, 1981. The proposed standard required "employers to identify chemicals in their workplaces and to inform their employees of the identity and nature of the employees' hazardous exposures." OSHA said that the regulation would "substantially improve the ability of workers to participate actively in the promotion of health and safety in the workplace, whether their efforts be individual or combined with the efforts of physicians, unions, or agencies of government concerned with worker health" (U.S. Department of Labor, OSHA, 1981: 4412, 4414).

Shortly after taking office, President Reagan's staff suggested that there would be a one-year moratorium on new regulations. Therefore, it seemed extremely unlikely that a final strong labeling regulation would be issued in the foreseeable future.

6.1.8. Generic Policy for Carcinogens

The Occupational Safety and Health Administration has relatively few scientific, technical, and legal resources. This is one explanation for its limited accomplishments. On October 3, 1977, OSHA proposed a formal policy for the identification, classification, and regulation of carcinogens. The regulation would presumably make it easier for OSHA to regulate a carcinogen. The proposal was drafted under Morton Corn but was issued by Eula Bingham's administration.

The reasoning behind the proposal was as follows. Certain basic scientific questions had been debated every time OSHA proposed a regulation for a carcinogen. This constant debate was time consuming and costly. The proposed rule stated that, as a policy decision, OSHA would take programmed steps from stipulated types of evidence. The rule would foreclose debate on certain issues such as the applicability of animal data to humans or the existence of "safe" levels of exposure to carcinogens.

The proposal would do this by first classifying toxic substances into one of four categories. Category I, probable human carcinogen, would be for substances which, according to epidemiological evidence, caused cancer in humans, or which caused cancer in two mammalian test species, or in one test species if the results had been replicated. Category II would be for substances that were suspected carcinogens, but for which the evidence was only "suggestive," such as a test in one species which had not been replicated. Category III would be for substances which deserved further study. Category IV would be for substances not used in American workplaces which would have to be reclassified if introduced into the United States.

Once a chemical was classified, prescribed regulations would have automatically followed. For a Category I substance, an emergency temporary standard would automatically be issued. A model permanent standard for both Categories I and II were outlined in the proposal; this feature led some to call it a "fill in the blanks" regulation. The Category I permanent regulation would reduce exposure to the lowest feasible level, which Eula Bingham defined as "engineering feasibility that's actually available." Engineering controls, and not personal protective devices, would be the primary means of control. Also, the Secretary of Labor could order firms to use substitutes if they were available. The Category II permanent regulation would lower exposure to a level "low enough to prevent acute or chronic toxic effects."

The scientific questions debated in every carcinogen proceeding would be settled once and for all—for regulatory purposes—by this rule. The rule allowed that animal data *are* applicable to humans—the evidence justifying a Category I classification (probable human carcinogen) could be animal data. The rule would also formally establish a regulatory policy that there is no safe level of exposure to a carcinogen; exposure would have to be reduced to the lowest level feasible. The rule would, once and for all, rule out personal protective devices in favor of engineering changes as the main method of chemical control.

The regulation would not foreclose debate on two important issues. First, firms could appeal the classification of the chemical. The Secretary of Labor could overturn a Category I classification if he/she found that (a) an alleged carcinogenic effect did not result from the chemical but from "non-specific physical induction;" b) the route of exposure in the studies was grossly inappropriate relative to the probable routes of occupational exposure (e.g., a chemical was given by injection rather than inhalation, and this was inappropriate); c) the studies were only suggestive and not conclusive; d) the studies were totally inadequate; or e) for some scientific reason the positive results in mammals were not relevant to man. But the regulation did tilt the burden of proof toward regulation; OSHA now had to prove that the studies were *inadequate*, rather than adequate. Thus, it would be easier to regulate a chemical.

Second, even if a Category I label stood up, firms could argue that significantly lower levels of exposure were not technologically feasible. Marshall Miller, a lawyer and former deputy administrator in OSHA (who first suggested the idea of a generic policy in 1974), advised a Chamber of Commerce symposium not to make a "broadside" attack on the proposal, but to hit it "where the policy hurts you" and the evidence was weakest. He said that the policy might work to industry's advantage because "rulemaking on an individual substance would deal mostly with the issue of technological feasibility, an area in which OSHA is weak" (Bureau of National Affairs, January 12, 1978: 1241). Of course, business has always argued about the exposure levels that are feasible, and the generic policy would not foreclose this issue.

Although arguments remained open, industry felt that the procedure would make it easier for OSHA to issue regulations, and thus made a concerted effort to weaken the policy. On November 22, 1977, a group of thirty companies banded together as the "American Industrial Health Council" to "assist OSHA in developing a rational, practical, and effective policy." Associations backing the Council included the Synthetic Organic Chemical Manufacturers Association, the Society of the Plastics Industry, and the Manufacturing Chemists Association. Its cochairman, Dow Chemical president Paul Oreffice, called OSHA's proposal too "far reaching" and remarked that "reports of cancer in a couple of foreign publications" would be enough to have a chemical banned from the workplace. (This was not necessarily true. If the studies were inadequate, which Oreffice seemed to mean by "foreign," OSHA could discount them. Also, substances would not necessarily be banned—exposure to them would be reduced to the lowest level feasible.) Oreffice maintained that many smaller companies did not "realize the problem they have" with the OSHA proposal, and that the Council would help them prepare testimony against the proposal and supply information and background (Bureau of National Affairs, December 1, 1977: 915). The Society of the Plastics Industry said that the Council's role was to prepare "exhaustive documentation" of industry's position. "As large a procession as possible" of witnesses would appear on its behalf at hearings on the cancer policy, and the Society would provide "a very strong cohort" (Bureau of National Affairs, February 23, 1978: 1463).

By the end of December, the membership had expanded to sixty companies, including Burlington Industries, Georgia Pacific, Exxon, Shell Oil, and trade associations like the American Petroleum Institute, the American Textile Manufacturers Institute, the American Iron and Steel Institute, and the Western Wood Products Association. It had passed a fund-raising goal of $1 million to pay for "scientific and economic studies done as well as for support operations" (Bureau of National Affairs, January 5, 1978: 1188).

On January 10, 1978, the American Industrial Health Council (AIHC), now with 75 members, offered its own proposal "completely in a spirit of cooperation with OSHA." It said that the OSHA plan was overzealous because it tried to eliminate "all risks" of occupationally-related cancer. The AIHC was against "unnecessary risks." Its plan set up a Category I for any "Known Human Carcinogen" classified solely on the basis of epidemiological evidence or "other human data." Unlike the OSHA plan, it did not accept animal data as showing that a substance could cause cancer in humans. A Category II would be "Confirmed Animal Oncogens," that is, substances inducing tumors in animals. A third category would be for substances that required further testing.

Under the AIHC plan, the Occupational Safety and Health Administration could not order firms to use available substitutes for carcinogens. Also, OSHA's plan called for an emergency temporary standard to be issued as soon as a carcinogen was identified; OSHA said that any exposure to a carcinogen ought to be considered a grave danger to employees. The American Industrial Health Council plan used emergency standards "only when a life-threatening hazard is known to exist." The industry group argued that there were safe levels of exposure to carcinogens, and so exposure to one would not necessarily be a grave danger.

The AIHC took the initiative in preparing an economic impact statement for OSHA's plan, saying that it would have "substantial economic impact." On March 27, the AIHC released a report saying that "there is no cancer epidemic as implied by OSHA," that the agency's plan would have a capital cost of between $9 and $36 billion, and an annual operating cost of between $6 and $36 billion, depending on its enforcement. The AIHC commented that "Unlimited spending on meeting workplace anti-cancer standards is a wasteful and dangerous policy" and would particularly harm "small businesses" (*Washington Post*, March 28, 1978: A2).

The Regulatory Analysis Review Group, through the Council On Wage and Price Stability, also criticized OSHA's proposal. It argued that the policy ought to systematically rank carcinogens according to their potency and the general risk they posed. The critique granted that "Cancer risk quantification is at the frontiers of science and the results must be regarded as crude because of the great number of uncertainties involved." Nevertheless, risk assessment was used by the EPA, the FDA, and the Consumer Product Safety Commission, and the "procedures afford some measures, however imprecise, of the magnitude of the cancer risk . . . which can be an important factor in determining how to regulate a substance or what priority to assign its regulation" (U.S. CWPS, 1978b: 20).

The Regulatory Analysis Review Group's report also suggested that the cancer policy rely more on "performance standards" than mandatory engineering or work practice controls. "Although OSHA has determined that respiratory protection should not be allowed as a primary means of compliance given today's technology, OSHA should not foreclose the possibility that effective respirators that meet OSHA's requirements might be developed in the future. By ruling them out as a matter of policy, OSHA itself may be discouraging investment and innovation in this area" (U.S. CWPS, 1978b: 35).

The Occupational Safety and Health Administration's final policy for the "Identification, Classification, and Regulation of Potential Occupational Carcinogens" was announced on January 18, 1980. The final rule continued to reject personal protective devices as primary controls because of their "intrinsic limitations" (U.S. Department of Labor, OSHA, 1980: 5225). But the final policy differed from the proposed policy in two major ways.

First, the final policy was far more cautious on how quickly proven carcinogens would be regulated. The proposal intimated that OSHA would regulate substances quite quickly after the minimum number of required studies appeared. The final rule explicitly relied on risk assessment, saying that OSHA would establish "priority lists" of ten substances for possible regulation under Category I (confirmed human carcinogen) and Category II (possible human carcinogen). OSHA would select the list from the "vast quantity" of potential carcinogens based on 1) the estimated number of exposed workers; 2) the estimated levels of human exposure; 3) the levels of exposure which had been reported to cause an increased incidence of tumors in animals or humans; 4) the extent to which the substance caused diseases in addition to cancer; 5) whether the molecular structure of the substance was similar to known or suspected carcinogens; 6) whether there were substitutes available for the substance or the costs of regulation would be small; and 7) whether other government agencies were studying the same substance (U.S. Department of Labor, OSHA, 1980: 5240). However, in setting exposure limits OSHA would not treat some carcinogens as more "potent" than others because, the agency argued, there was no accepted way to differentiate strong from weak carcinogens. Thus, OSHA's regulations would continue to reduce exposure to the lowest feasible level.

President Carter's domestic policy staff praised OSHA for being "more flexible" in the final standard. OSHA's willingness "to use risk assessment" showed "cost sensitivity," they said. However, the American Industrial Health Council criticized the "limited" use of risk assessment which "would be limited to establishing agency priorities and not be considered in establishing control levels" (Bureau of National Affairs, January 24, 1980: 787).

Second, the proposal stipulated that an emergency temporary standard (ETS) would be issued automatically after a substance was found to be a human carcinogen. OSHA would not—could not legally—delay the ETS after a Category I classification. The final policy dropped the automatic ETS rule, saying only that OSHA would use discretion in issuing ETSs.

The changes in the final policy shifted it from the proposal's stress on certainty to a continued substance-by-substance negotiation—the "case-by-case" approach which the proposal had criticized. The final rule still established significant presumptions about chemical controls, such as the proper role of experimental data in regulation, the flaws of personal protective devices, and the need to reduce exposures to carcinogens to the lowest feasible levels. However, the final policy also stressed that "much of the evidence as to whether a substance will be classified and regulated will be weighed in individual rulemakings" (Bureau of National Affairs, January 17, 1980: 763).

OSHA maintained that loosening the rule permitted the agency to consider compliance difficulties in each case. Loosening the rule also took the agency out of a politically volatile commitment. The proposed automatic emergency temporary standard for carcinogens, for example, would have left no room for maneuvering in controversial situations. While OSHA had earlier praised the virtues of certainty, certainty would undercut the case-by-case hedging, deliberation, and negotiation through which the agency coped with external pressures.

The American Petroleum Institute filed for a review of the policy in the Fifth Circuit Court even before it was officially announced. The API did so after an "invitation only" briefing on the policy that OSHA gave to certain industry and labor representatives. Other businesses and trade associations followed API after the policy was released.

The American Industrial Health Council, besides criticizing the "limited" use of risk assessment, argued that the priority lists would mean "unnecessary adverse and potentially misleading publicity" for the substances on OSHA's priority lists. The AIHC also charged that, to the extent that the policy established presumptions about scientific evidence (e.g., that animal data had certain implications for humans, or that there were no safe levels of exposure to carcinogens), it would "freeze" science and deprive parties of the "right" to present "all relevant data." (In fact, the original point of the proposal was to cut short the potentially interminable presentation of "all relevant data" which had historically delayed regulations.)

The Oil, Chemical, and Atomic Workers said that the policy would expedite regulation of carcinogens and that it was a "significant improvement" over the proposed regulation, although the union later sued OSHA over the dropping of the automatic ETS provision. The Steelworkers' union representative, George Taylor, charged that dropping the ETS rule "removed the cornerstone of a cancer policy that would benefit American workers—mandatory standards setting for substances determined to pose occupational carcinogen hazards." But Dr. Sidney Wolfe of the Health Research Group affirmed that the final policy "is much closer to what we want than industry wants. It's definitely a workers' standard" (Bureau of National Affairs, January 24, 1980: 787–788).

At the end of 1980 the policy was in effect. OSHA was about to issue the first "priority list" of chemicals for possible regulation. The policy was being challenged in court, however, with the final decision likely to come in the Supreme Court months—or years—later.

6.2. SUMMARY OF OSHA'S HEALTH REGULATION AND SOME GENERALIZATIONS

The Occupational Safety and Health Act of 1970, if enforced literally, was revolutionary. Its section 6(b)5 mandated that "no employee shall suffer material impairment of health or functional capacity even if such employee has regular exposure to the hazard dealt with by (an occupational health standard) for the period of his working life." Within the broad constraints of technological feasibility (Is a control available or could it be shortly?) and economic feasibility (Will a regulation destroy a large number of firms?), the law subordinated profit to the elimination of health and safety risks.

But the radical commitment to workers' health was due to a transient state of interest group pressures, not a fundamental change of social values. At hearings on the Act organized labor and public interest groups actively argued that "one injury or fatality is too many." Businesses, not wanting to appear unconcerned about human life, went along with the rhetoric and apparently figured (correctly) that they could cope with any "excesses" of the new agency later. The Senate and House committees writing the Act felt that economic factors ought to weigh in OSHA's decisions, but feared that if "economic feasibility" were mentioned in the Act that was all that OSHA would consider when designing regulations. The committees also felt uneasy about defining the health–economic tradeoffs (Mendeloff, 1979: 20-21). The strongly worded Occupational Safety and Health Act of 1970 passed the House of Representatives 384–5 and the Senate 83–3. Senator Eagleton of Missouri, in 1979 a leading advocate of cost-benefit analysis in regulatory decision making, argued in 1970 that

> the costs that will be incurred by employers in meeting the standards of health and safety to be established under this bill are, in my view, reasonable and necessary costs of doing business. Whether we, as individuals, are motivated by simple humanity or simple economics, we can no longer permit profits to be dependent upon an unsafe or unhealthy worksite (cited in U.S. Department of Labor, OSHA, 1980: 5010).

After ten years of OSHA, what can be concluded about occupational health regulation?

First, the Occupational Safety and Health Administration reduced several major occupational health hazards. There are now 21 complete health standards (asbestos, 13 carcinogens, vinyl chloride, coke oven emissions, acrylonitrile, DBCP, arsenic, cotton dust, and lead). There are also compulsory exposure limits for about 400 substances in the Threshold Limit Value List, although, as outlined in Section 4.1.2.1., these are relatively inadequate protections. Industry intensely opposed the vinyl chloride, coke oven, arsenic, cotton dust, and lead standards, so this was a significant accomplishment by OSHA.

Second, much of this activity came in two periods. Shortly after the Act was passed, OSHA issued the asbestos and carcinogens standards relatively quickly after labor and public interest groups petitioned for them. Affected firms had not yet, I believe, tried to closely monitor and shape the agency.

The second wave of activity followed Eula Bingham's appointment as Assistant Secretary of Labor for Occupational Safety and Health in 1977. In 1977 and 1978 OSHA issued the acrylonitrile, DBCP, arsenic, cotton dust, and lead standards, and also the benzene rule which was later suspended by the Supreme Court. Organized labor's pressure had much to do with this, of course (for example, the textile workers' lawsuit helped move the cotton dust standard). Nevertheless, Bingham's leadership of the agency was important. One cannot attribute an output of six final standards in 1977-78 *vs.* one standard in 1975-76 to fluctuations in interest-group pressures, which are constant.

Third, OSHA's original ambitions declined markedly from 1974 to 1980. By 1981, the National Institute for Occupational Safety and Health had recommended complete standards for over 250 substances. In 1977, OSH Assistant Secretary Morton Corn said that fifteen to twenty standards *per year* would not adequately address the occupational disease problem. Yet, OSHA had issued 21 standards in its ten years in existence (14 of them in the first four years). It was assumed in 1971 that substances such as lead and cotton dust would be regulated relatively quickly, but by 1978 the lead and cotton dust standards were considered tough, aggressive initiatives. OSHA's cancer policy was an attempt to cope with this backlog.

Fourth, chemical controls are delayed, or never issued, because the agency now analyzes the bases for regulations far more extensively than in its early years. The OSH Act resoundingly committed the Occupational Safety and Health Administration to act on the available evidence to protect workers. Early court decisions maintained that the uncertainties in chemical control were so pervasive that decisions had to reflect policy judgements rather than purely factual analysis. However, as the General Accounting Office and others noted, the regulatory process now runs far longer than one would expect based on a literal reading of the Occupational Safety and Health Act or these early court decisions.

"Rationality" increases as alternatives and relevant data are considered. As Herbert Kaufman noted, "lack of comprehensiveness in weighing alternatives can result in a course of action inferior to available alternatives. . . . It may produce policies offensive to a segment of the community capable of strong resistance and even of overturning them" (1977: 46-47). Critics of OSHA usually focused on its "irrational" single-mindedness, insensitivity to the costs of regulations, and unwillingness to control chemicals with personal protective devices or to measure the benefits of regulations. By the end of 1980 OSHA was sticking to some of the criticized policies; for example, the agency insisted on engineering changes rather than respirators to control workers' exposures to toxic substances. However, the agency began calculating the benefits of regulations, and also exhaustively outlining the reasons for its "single-mindedness." The explanatory preamble to the cancer policy, for example, took 279 tripled-columned, single-spaced, small-typed pages of the Federal Register (January 22, 1980: Book 2).

Corporations thoroughly documented their regulatory testimony and court suits. The Occupational Safety and Health Administration maintained that it must do the same. Under Morton Corn, OSHA told the Carter transition staff that extensive economic analyses of regulations were needed to answer business' objections, whether or not the Inflation Impact Statement program was continued by the President (Bureau of National Affairs, December 16, 1980: 884). Corn's successor, Eula Bingham, noted that "Any economic analysis must show whether an industry can comply. When an industry says it cannot comply, we must know whether we are getting all the facts and see if we can assist and come up with alternative information" (Bureau of National Affairs, June 2, 1977: 3).

Similarly, in a memo to the Labor Department in 1979, Secretary of Labor Ray Marshall said that "there is no doubt in my mind that the quality of the department's regulatory activities will be one of the major issues we will have to deal with during the next two years," stressing that the Department must "develop high quality regulations that can be defended both inside the Government and in public forums." "Some members of the business community," he added, had been "exaggerating the inflationary impact of regulations" (Bureau of National Affairs, February 8, 1979: 1434). He told a March 1979 meeting of the League of Women Voters that "business pressure to reduce government regulation has forced government to set priorities, improve the management of government programs, and seek ways to measure the benefits of standards that promote worker health and safety and protect the environment." Marshall noted that government agencies were beginning to search out ways to quantify the benefits of regulations in order to justify their programs in the face of a "mounting assault" from businesses. "It has caused us to search through many of our basic assumptions, to recognize our limits, to improve management, and to set priorities." He added that some of industry's worst predictions of economic dislocations from regulations had been disproved in the process (Bureau of National Affairs, March 29, 1979: 1577).

In September, 1979, Mary Ellen Weber, the director of OSHA's Office of Regulatory Analysis, projected that it could take the Occupational Safety and Health Administration from three and one-half to four years to issue major standards as a result of the regulatory analyses required under President Carter's "Improving Government Regulations" program.She noted that there was "no doubt" that "the sophistication and level of effort" needed were greater than before the Executive Order, but "to the extent we have done our homework" OSHA expected to be "better able to survive" legal challenges to standards. She affirmed that prior to Carter's program economic analysis emphasized the costs of regulations, whereas the new program had "more stringent requirements to show the benefits of standards" (Bureau of National Affairs, September 27, 1979: 380).

The new director of OSHA's health standards program, Bailus Walker, also noted that because of new "time-consuming regulatory reform requirements" standards would be delayed. He denied that OSHA was hesitating to regulate chemicals because of court challenges, saying that the agency was not "timid," but that it would be "unwise to forge ahead to get a large number of regulations out" and better to issue "a small number of well developed, well-thought-out regulations" able to withstand "rigorous social, economic, and scientific scrutiny." Cost-benefit analysis "won't veer us off course—it will just take us longer to get to our goal." Having noted that OSHA could now regulate few toxic substances, he added, "Everybody who works should have a safe and wholesome work environment" (Bureau of National Affairs, October 18, 1979: 468).

The notion that the Occupational Safety and Health Administration would now do cost-benefit analysis of regulations because of the "new" requirements of the Carter program was shaky. President Ford's inflation/economic impact statement program required thorough attention to benefits of regulations, as CWPS kept reminding OSHA from 1974–1978. More likely, OSHA was adjusting to broader political and legal pressures. In 1979 OSHA lost the benzene decision in the Fifth Circuit Court in New Orleans because it failed to quantify the benefits of reducing exposure to benzene. Businesses and economists outside as well as inside the government (Weidenbaum and DeFina, 1978; MacAvoy, 1979) were blasting away at safety and health regulation for its alleged trivial benefits. The Ralph Nader-affiliated Corporate Accountability Research Group released "An Analysis of the Benefits of Safety and Health regulation" as a rebuttal to the conservative argument (Green and Waitzman, 1979). The debate on health and safety regulation was conducted in cost-benefit terms. OSHA had to document the benefits of regulations in order to participate.

The agency did have an incentive to attribute its cost-benefit analysis program to President Carter's executive order—organized labor opposed the program. In 1976 OSHA suggested to President-elect Carter that it would be politically easier to label its economic impact statement program as a White House mandate than as a necessary accomodation to corporate legal and political pressures (Bureau of National Affairs, December 16, 1976: 884). I suspect that the reasoning in 1979 and 1980 was the same.

A fifth, and final, generalization about OSHA's health standards is that historical circumstance has been at least as important as "rational analysis" in successful regulations. The asbestos and carcinogen standards were released relatively quickly because business had not yet intimidated the agency. The benzene, DBCP, and acrylonitrile emergency standards were issued quickly because a new administration pledged a new reliance on ETSs; permanent standards for DBCP and acrylonitrile were implemented, and the benzene standard was stopped only by a 5–4 vote of the Supreme Court. The cotton dust standard was issued not because of some culmination of "rational analysis," but because the textile workers sued OSHA.

Further, whether a standard is upheld or overturned in court has apparently depended as much on the values of the court that hears the case as the characteristics of the regulation. The District of Columbia, New York, and Philadelphia courts did not require cost-benefit analyses by OSHA, while the New Orleans court did. Had the benzene case not been heard in the New Orleans court it might well have been decided differently, and perhaps would not even have gone to the Supreme Court. Had one Supreme Court Justice voted differently, a 5–4 "stunning rebuke to government regulators" would have been a 5–4 "affirmation of national health and safety goals."

Thus, administrative impulse and external pressures prompted most successful regulations. OSHA asserted itself by issuing three emergency standards in the nine months after Eula Bingham took office and objectively came off quite well. The textile workers' lawsuit forced OSHA to issue a cotton dust standard, and the standard survived. It is therefore wrong to envision an all-powerful corporate monolith forcing OSHA to interminably analyze regulations lest they be smashed in court. The agency may in fact interminably analyze regulations and argue that they would otherwise be smashed in court. But this argument reflects organizational and political hesitance—which was suspended early in Bingham's administration—and not objective legal constraints on the agency. Undoubtedly, OSHA and NIOSH must carefully review the available data on a toxic substance to sucessfully defend a regulation. But OSHA has long reviewed the data, but not yet proposed standards by the end of 1980, for beryllium, MOCA, pesticides, nickel, silica, and numerous other substances. Periods of aggressive chemical regulation thus are far more likely to coincide with new, ambitious administrations—when they are new—and agitated "liberal" interest groups than with a cluster of "completed regulatory analyses."

6.3. OSHA'S HISTORY AND VIEWS OF REGULATION

Earlier, three different views of regulation were outlined. These emphasized 1) interest-group influence (pluralism); 2) governmental concern for the welfare of capitalism in opposition to anti-capitalist groups and businesses with only short-run and special interests (the capitalist State perspective); and 3) organizational concerns for stability and autonomy, and the effects of organizations' leaders (the organizational perspective). Pluralism, supplemented by the organizational perspective, best explains the Occupational Safety and Health Administration's health standards program. This additive perspective is useful because organizational procedures come to reflect the balance of interest-group power. (See Sections 5.2.1., 5.2.2. above).

Regulatory agencies respond to conflicting pressures. Given the resource distribution in occupational health work outlined in Chapter III, businesses generally can wear an agency like OSHA down. However, there will be sporadic bursts of effective regulation after some leadership changes or in response to labor or public interest groups' pressures. The absolute strength of interest groups varies, but so does their attentiveness and effectiveness at different times.

Consequently, an agency may well be active early in life. Groups which fought for it watch closely and prod when the agency is balky. Regulated groups have not yet felt the pinch of the agency. Thus, OSHA quickly responded to scientists, public interest groups, and unions when they petitioned and/or sued OSHA for standards for asbestos, fourteen carcinogens, and pesticides. Later, OSHA was harder to move. What had happened?

Having had some encounters with OSHA, business became more aware of how to deal with the agency. Industry persuaded OSHA to dilute the standards for asbestos, carcinogens, pesticides (standards for which were eliminated altogether), and cotton dust. Business also pressured OSHA on the vinyl chloride, coke oven emissions, arsenic, lead, and benzene standards. OSHA did issue strong standards for these substances. However, the agency had learned. The costs of defending standards inhibited OSHA from moving quickly on other chemicals. OSHA exhaustively documented the need for and feasibility of a very few regulations. Analysis not only put off the day when OSHA was taken to court, but also made its eventual action more defensible. The agency could not avoid all conflicts and pressures in a world of conflicting interests. Nevertheless, by modifying its procedures to satisfy or at least hold off very strong businesses and trade associations, OSHA did try to avoid as much conflict as possible.

Did Eula Bingham change this pattern after 1976? True, her leadership did accelerate OSHA's chemical standards activity. But critical pluralists could snicker that this spurt of activity ought to be compared to the OSH Act's mandate. The fact that OSHA issued a few more standards under new management is noteworthy. But the fact that OSHA did not issue final standards, recommended by the National Institute for Occupational Safety and Health, for hundreds of other substances underlines the limits of OSHA's regulation. Even Eula Bingham's administration slowed; all of its toxic substance standards were issued in 1977 and 1978.

Thus, OSHA's history shows how conservative pressures can diminish an agency's aspirations. Organized labor's and public interest groups' praises of the Bingham administration only demonstrated how little they had come to expect; the delays and limits of the past established very low benchmarks for measuring success (Edelman, 1977: 148-149).

The Occupational Safety and Health Administration's regulatory history does not support the capitalist State perspective on regulation. OSHA's responsiveness to pressure undercuts the view that regulatory agencies place the welfare of the capitalist system above firms with only special interests.

Consider the cotton dust standard. OSHA proposed this after a textile workers' suit; delayed the final standard; and then issued a final standard after another textile workers' suit. But the final standard was much weaker than the proposed standard. OSHA later explained that the costs of about 5,260 extra cases of byssinosis permitted by the modified standard were less than the extra costs of compliance required by the proposed standard. If OSHA diluted the standard because it only wanted to prevent disease to the point where compliance costs were offset by the costs of disease, then the capitalist State view would be supported. However, that perspective does not explain why OSHA only issued the final standard after the textile workers' sued. If the fundamental justification of the standard was that it was economically rational for the capitalist system, why was it delayed for so long and then issued only under worker pressure?

A capitalist State theorist could argue that the standard was diluted because of the intervention by the President's economic advisors; a high State organization intervened to prevent a system-threatening regulation. However, this would ignore the evidence that the Council on Wage and Price Stability and the Council of Economic Advisors were reacting to industry's complaints about the standard (see Sections 3.2.6. and 6.1.6.). Consistent CEA and CWPS sympathy with industry's short-run difficulties fits the pluralist view far better than the capitalist State view.

There are relatively few adequate occupational health standards. The Occupational Safety and Health Administration admits this; it issued the "cancer policy" to try to cope with the backlog. There are various services and information programs that the Federal government could use to reduce the risk of occupational disease. Chapter 7 discusses a few of these.

Service Activities

OSHA and NIOSH do more than research and regulation. This chapter discusses how the two agencies have handled certain service projects. These concern notification of workers exposed to dangerous chemicals, employee and employer requests for health hazard evaluations, and employee requests for workplace inspections.

7.1. EMPLOYEE NOTIFICATION

On April 25, 1977, the *New York Times* reported that the National Institute for Occupational Safety and Health studies had identified the names and addresses of at least 74,000 workers who had worked in plants handling carcinogens. The director of NIOSH, John Finklea, affirmed that about 123,000 other workers would be identified in future planned NIOSH studies. This raised the issue of whether or not NIOSH planned to pass the information on exposures on to workers. Dr. Finklea stated that the question of what to do about contacting such workers was one of the major pending national health issues. "Of côurse I'm concerned," he said, "but the problem far exceeds my personal or even NIOSH's ability to do much about it. Given the present circumstances, you try to do the best you can and hope that others will do the same" (Burnham, 1977).

At the National Advisory Committee on Occupational Safety and Health (NACOSH) meeting of May 6, 1977, Finklea remarked that "right now, I don't think that the compensation systems of the States or the regulatory programs that we have in place under health and safety standards or the health insurance programs would give us a good mechanism for counseling such people or assuring that they had adequate medical follow-up. I think that this is the gap issue that will have to be dealt with." He added that workers might not get medical follow-up with their companies because they would be afraid of being labeled as a health risk and possibly losing a job, pay, or seniority. He did not mention the possibility that the employee, given the information in confidence, could pass it on to a family physician.

Eula Bingham, who had just taken over as OSH Assistant Secretary, remarked that

> I guess that I think this situation exemplifies better a rather poor attitude. I am talking about the poor attitude throughout all of this, the professional area, having to do with workers, people exposed to chemical agents. I feel very strongly, and I don't know whether it is NIOSH's jurisdiction or whether OSHA can do it or not, but even if immediate remedies are not available, that workers have a right to know that they have been exposed to benzidine for five years, and this is a carcinogen. . . . I would like to point out that if a person came through who had some very contagious disease, let's say smallpox, the Public Health Service would do everything within its means to track down the people who had contacted that individual, and some of the people at the (Center for Disease Control) are masters at doing this. But we won't do it for workers who have been exposed, let's say, to benzidine, and I think it is—reflects the state of the maturity of the medical profession, of all of us, in terms of being willing to face up to this. . . . If we can do it for smallpox, why can't we do it for benzidine?

Dr. Finklea responded that notification ought to be made, but that "it is a very large social issue that is going to require a lot of discussion." John Sheehan, legislative director of the United Steelworkers, told Finklea that

> I would hope that the enormity of the consequences of disclosure would not unduly influence (agencies) not to want to disclose itself, because I do feel too that the gaps in the delivery system might be more—we might close them or try to close them if we were under pressure to realize that the gaps were there. We don't have this disclosure of information, then I think that we don't know that we have such a problem with the delivery system. As I was listening to you this morning I think that I was very impressed by the comments that you were making as to what happens to these workers once you tell them. What is the responsibility of the union? Sitting here this morning I really don't know. But I think that we will—but we better get on the stick of knowing, but we won't unless that disclosure faces us, and if plants in the country and unions, if you wish, on Monday morning, all of a sudden get a delegation of diseased workers, saying "What are you going to do about me?" I think that we might have more of a confrontation with the gap but I would hope that that kind of consequence would not suppress the development of a mechanism to search out, as we were doing in the Legionnaires' Disease, where these people are.

Finklea said that notification should not be made until a "counseling" program could be arranged. Some people would "react well," some "are organized," a number of people "who don't have their peers around may just seek to deny it" and not get help, and others "may become very, very disturbed." Sheehan asked, "Isn't that more of a larger social issue as to whether agencies of government have a right to withhold information because they don't think that the constituencies are able to adjust to it?" A coffeebreak was called for at that point. Subsequently the meeting turned to another subject.

NIOSH had identified a large group of people at risk. NIOSH, OSHA, and others had recognized the value of notifying workers who could have been exposed to carcinogens. They had notified workers exposed to asbestos, vinyl chloride, and Leptophos. However, these were efforts to pick up the pieces of situations. They involved undeniable health emergencies. No one could deny the necessity for, or lose anything from, government efforts to notify workers whom everyone— including the firms involved—admitted were ill because of workplace chemicals. Also, these were small projects. For these reasons the projects involving asbestos, vinyl chloride, and Leptophos were remedial, noncontroversial, and well within the bounds of current plans, procedures, and resources.

Notifying thousands of workers that they might be at greater risk of developing cancer because of possible exposure to specific employers' chemicals was very different. This would have been a preventive public health program, and thus there were uncertainties as to which of the workers would become ill. As Sheehan said, notification would have stimulated much conflict. Industry would castigate NIOSH and OSHA for "unnecessarily alarming" employees and prompting "inflationary" lawsuits and compensation demands. Notification would also have been a major project, disrupting current plans and programs. These consequences would strain the security, plans, and managerial capabilities of OSHA and NIOSH. No one, including OSHA, in the months ahead followed through on Bingham's frustrated observation that public health leads of lesser importance had been followed in the past.

The agencies reconciled the contradiction between the importance of the lead and the failure to follow it by labeling the situation as a "major social issue." "Major social issues" are not matters one works into this year's plans. They are matters Congress, employers, employees, agencies, and other responsible persons ought to be concerned about, study, and formulate "long range policy options" for. Conducting small follow-up projects for acknowledged "horror stories" was one thing. Telling about 74,000 probably unsuspecting workers that they had worked with carcinogens was another.

On May 9, 1977, the subcommittee on Labor of the Senate Committee on Human Resources held a hearing on "Monitoring of Industrial

Workers Exposed to Carcinogens" (U.S. Senate Committee on Human Resources, 1978). At the session John Finklea remarked that "a vital part of our research program is getting information to those who can put it to good use." The information program he outlined consisted largely of the availability of NIOSH publications. He also declared that, after NIOSH studied plants, "we discuss the results of our research with management and labor at plants where the studies were conducted. Although we do not notify workers individually, unless we have examined them, we expect that those still employed at the plant would generally be informed about our study results by their union or by management. We would not expect that workers in other similar plants would be directly informed about the results of our studies. An even bigger problem involves workers who once worked in such plants but no longer do so. These workers who may have changed jobs or retired are less likely to know of health risks attributable to past workplace exposures" (9). Dr. Finklea's sensitivity about the consequences of a notification program suggests that many of these workers were not getting the information; in particular, separated employees had no chance of being notified.

Finklea indicated that NIOSH did not have the necessary funds or legal authority to notify workers, and that "notification without an effective follow-up system might do more harm than good" (12). He did not request funds to carry out the program. Rather, he emphasized the legal restraints and the likely problems from lack of "counseling" for workers. Senator Schweiker of Pennsylvania cited a section of the OSH Act saying that NIOSH's information would be "disseminated . . . to employers and employees and organizations thereof," and then asked "why does that section not apply?" Dr. Finklea responded that "I do not mean to imply that it would not be possible to write letters telling people they had been at risk. But I think if we are to assure that they have adequate medical counseling and adequate medical follow-up, that is where we run into the problem." Therefore, the legal restraints were, after all, not a problem; the problem was the possible reactions to the information. Schweiker, recognizing this, pointed out that

> It says nothing about that, doctor, in here. It addresses only the information obtained. It does not say whether they have had adequate medical counseling or inadequate follow-up. It does not put any responsibility on you in that regard. I admit that. But the question at issue, as I see it, is if we at least inform the people at risk, they can seek their own medical help. That is the first thing I or you would do, if we were at risk, regardless of whether the Government had resources to follow it up. There is absolutely nothing regarding your capacity to follow it up, but it does seem to place primary responsibility on NIOSH to inform employees and organizations thereof.

Where am I missing the boat (U.S. Senate Committee on Human Resources, 1978: 20)?

Finklea responded tht "I think that we are coming at it in slightly different ways." He said that NIOSH would "inform" employee groups and individual employees through criteria documents and work practice documents," routine NIOSH publications. Very few employees— particularly in nonunion shops—ever write to NIOSH for these, even if they know that they are available. For that matter, workers may not know that they work, or worked, with carcinogens unless they are informed of it. The difference between the availability of government publications and actively notifying workers that they may have been exposed to carcinogens was enormous; indeed, note that the NIOSH director did not cite any "counseling" or "follow-up" problems with the number of workers requesting criteria or work practice documents. NIOSH—and by its silence, OSHA—would not try to directly notify workers.

What further action would NIOSH take? "We wanted to work with the National Advisory Committee on Occupational Safety and Health to discuss the best way of taking care of this problem. . . . I think that it is a very large area." Judging from the previous NACOSH meeting, such a discussion might air some issues, but it definitely would not produce any substantive notification program.

The subcommittee asked NIOSH to report on the size of the notification problem. I will discuss this report below.

The subcommittee took other witnesses. One, Dr. Guy Newell, Jr., Acting Director of the National Cancer Institute, was asked by Senator Javits "You feel, Dr. Newell, that the state of the art just does not allow us to make any broad-scale exams in the field of industrial health?" Newell responded

Let me put it this way, Senator. I think that the state of the art does not allow us to launch any demonstration programs other than those that we have going on now. On the other hand, I think, as a physician, if I were in practice, and I had a patient, and I were taking an occupational history, which all physicians do, it would be very important for me to know that an individual has worked in an industry or a plant where he has been exposed to some occupational hazard. I would follow him more closely, first of all, probably more frequently. I would pay more attention to the history of cancer and other diseases in his family. I would follow his family more closely. I would do all these things. *That would be very positive and could be very beneficial. That could be done, as you were alluding to earlier, by letting the individual worker know that he has been in some kind of unhealthy environment. That information can be translated, given to his physician. That is important* (my emphasis) (U.S. Senate Committee on Human Resources, 1978: 89).

In July, 1977, NIOSH submitted a paper to the subcommittee on "the social responsibility of biomedical research for occupational health and the need for employers with knowledge to take affirmative action to notify and provide fair health protection from exposure to health-related environmental risks." It called the issue of notification "one of the most difficult long range problems facing the Executive Branch." "Clearly, workers have the right to know" whether they had been exposed to hazardous substances, said the paper. "However, this right is linked to a complex series of problems which must be faced and resolved if any worker notification program is to be successful" (U.S. Department of Health, Education, and Welfare, NIOSH, 1977).

There were questions about "how accurately past exposure measurements" had been taken. NIOSH had analyzed exposure patterns within the firms. NIOSH had expressed no major reservation about its technical methods in the health hazard survey before the notification issue faced it, and has expressed few reservations since. It is extremely doubtful that such technical uncertainties were sufficient reason for NIOSH to avoid the project. Other "complex . . . problems" were then listed.

It was difficult to identify the workers who had been exposed because the chemical composition of substances were often hidden by trade names (however, and the paper did not mention this, thousands of workers who were identified could have been notified, and workers in the future could have been notified as a matter of policy). Counseling of workers would have to be available. Why? Because some might not take the situation calmly. Some would organize; some would deny a possible problem. Many would demand treatment if necessary, but "there is currently no effective mechanism . . . for arranging and paying for medical examinations." NIOSH noted that States' workers' compensation systems do not adequately recognize occupational diseases and do not adequately compensate diseases when they do recognize them. Also, "most existing health insurance plans do not pay for medical procedures or follow-up examinations made necessary by exposure to toxic substances in the workplace or in the general environment." NIOSH may not have cited this gap in the health care system to deflect any pressure for notification. It is undeniable, however, that NIOSH did not even mention the possibility that what it called "the right to know" justified forcing the confrontation on the health care system. As John Sheehan had mentioned in the NACOSH meeting of May 6, such a confrontation might have helped close the health care "gap." Also, as Dr. Newell noted in the Senate hearing, the information on exposure would have been valuable to the employees' personal physicians. These benefits were ignored by NIOSH, which merely compiled a list of possible social, political, and economic disruptions that the program would entail.

Also, "unprotected workers may hesitate to seek desirable medical follow-up because their current employment may be jeopardized or future job opportunities limited." But NIOSH was aware that the worker alone—and not his employer—could be notified; it ignored this possibility. Also, NIOSH's statement was inconsistent with its earlier warning that the medical care system would be swamped by the demands of the affected workers.

The agency stated that the program would shift the costs of industrial diseases from workers to employers or government. "Inflationary impact statements required for occupational safety and health standards consider only direct outlays by industry. They do not consider the costs of workplace exposures including counseling and medical follow-up which are now hidden or borne by others." Further, the costs of research would go up because no provisions now existed to pay for follow-up examinations.

"Questions about the relationship of workplace exposures to personal habits and about legal liability and compensation" would be forced into view before the system was ready to handle them voluntarily. "Notification without counseling and adequate medical examination may prove socially disruptive and lead to an undermining of confidence in government and perhaps also in private industry and even labor unions."

This "complex series of policy issues" had to be "considered together" before "responsible" policy makers could—or would—tell a large number of workers that they may have been exposed to particular carcinogens in the workplace.

It is reasonable to assume that the National Institute for Occupational Safety and Health and, by its silence, OSHA, did not want to be saddled with the program. The Institute's director at the earlier NACOSH meeting and in the Congressional hearing, and NIOSH in this policy paper, took great pains to compile an exhaustive list of possible "problems" with the project, never mentioning the benefits of notification. The "Right to Know" position paper basically said to Congress "Here's what you're getting into if we do this. Now do you REALLY want us to go ahead?"

Nor did the Senate follow up on the matter. The earlier Congressional reaction signalled concern with a morally visible issue. Senators, such as Senator Schweiker, had for a moment pointed out the fragility of NIOSH's reasons for not directly notifying workers about their past exposures to toxic substances. But the indignation did not extend beyond the immediate debate. Nor, in fact, did the indignation expressed earlier by union representatives at the May 6 NACOSH meeting reappear. No doubt the Senate, the AFL-CIO, and agencies had other problems with more immediate benefits or, if slighted, costs. Also, much of the political heat generated by a "hasty" notification program would have fallen on any Senator who put a great deal of political weight into the project, or the agency that implemented it. There were simply more routine, certain, and immediate issues to worry about. Any early inclination to "stir up" the issue by notifying the workers was not reinforced by the day-to-day operations of the organizations involved. Notification would have caused administrative and political problems. The issue faded.

However, in January, 1981, the National Institute for Occupational Safety and Health was about to start a small, cautious pilot notification project, comparable to those for asbestos, Kepone, and Leptophos. The Institute would notify workers in Augusta, Georgia, who had been exposed to beta-Naphthylamine, one of the thirteen carcinogens regulated by OSHA in 1974. By limiting the project to one substance in one local area the Institute did not risk the "socially disruptive" consequences of a larger notification effort, but could see how the community responded. An Augusta newspaper announced the program with the headline "Government to Notify Cancer Victims."

7.2. THE HEALTH HAZARD EVALUATION PROGRAM

The U.S. General Accounting Office issued a report on May 18, 1978, which analyzed the National Institute for Occupational Safety and Health's Health Hazard Evaluation Program (U.S. General Accounting Office, 1978b). Section 20 of the OSH Act requires NIOSH, upon request from an employer or employee, to determine if a substance normally found in a workplace has toxic effects in concentrations found in the workplace. NIOSH must submit the findings of the investigations to employers and employees as soon as possible. According to the GAO, only 892 requests for health hazard evaluations had been received in six years.

The GAO's report noted that "NIOSH has done little to publicize and promote the program. Institute officials believe that most employees and employers are not aware of either NIOSH or its health hazard evaluation program. Because of its potential for helping protect workers from hazardous substances, we believe NIOSH should aggressively promote the health hazard evaluation program."

The Institute's officials told the GAO that, although NIOSH "encouraged" promotion of the program, there were neither written policies nor guidelines as to how to promote it. Regional NIOSH officials, the Institute claimed, promoted the program through meetings and speaking engagements with industrial hygienists, process design engineers, labor union representatives, safety and health officers, and others with a "professional" interest in safety. A NIOSH official admitted that this approach would not reach small businesses or the approximately three-fourths of the workforce that is not unionized.

In comments on the draft report, NIOSH stated that "We do not concur that the program should be publicized to the point of creating a potential demand that would exceed our capability to perform. . . . The program has been made known to unions, industry groups, and professional groups. Regulations were published in the Federal Register (November 17, 1972) prescribing the conditions and procedures for persons to request and NIOSH to conduct" health hazard evaluations. The GAO commented that "We doubt if most workers or employers are aware of the Federal Register," let alone read it (let alone read a copy six years old). Thus, NIOSH consciously endorsed restricting employees' demands for a program to which they had a right under the OSH Act; it resisted publicizing the Health Hazard Evaluation Program.

NIOSH was reluctant both to notify workers exposed to toxic chemicals and to publicize the Health Hazard Evaluation Program. Director John Finklea's testimonies, the NIOSH position paper "The Right To Know," and NIOSH's statements about the workload from the health hazard evaluation program emphasized the disruptions from the efforts and did not consider their likely benefits. The Institute seemed to be avoiding two large, potentially controversial programs which did not mesh with its plans or priorities.

Note the qualifier "which do not mesh with its plans or priorities." NIOSH did not avoid all controversies. In 1977 the Institute, which actively researches industrial health issues, took DuPont and General Motors to court over the issue of access to health records of employees. These records could be used in future research by NIOSH. An organization's willingness to tolerate controversy is often influenced by the potential profit to its cherished activities. Health records would be valuable to NIOSH's research program. The notification and Health Hazard Evaluation programs promised no such research payoff. Thus, they were slighted.

John Finklea left NIOSH in 1978. He was replaced in early 1979 by Anthony Robbins. Robbins, in a speech to the American Industrial Hygiene Conference in May, stated that "People who ought to know don't even know what NIOSH is," noting, as the GAO had, that the Health Hazard Evaluation Program was little known. Robbins claimed that the failure of NIOSH scientists to "take sides" on occupational health issues made them "lose touch with the NIOSH function of protecting workers." "NIOSH," he added, was not supposed to be "neutral" (Bureau of National Affairs, June 7, 1979: 6).

In a letter to the September, 1979 *American Journal of Public Health*, Robbins and NIOSH Deputy Director John Froines wrote that NIOSH's field functions had "almost been kept a secret for fear that the nation's demand for assistance in exploring occupational health problems would outstrip the Institute's ability to respond." NIOSH research would now, they announced, "always be reported to all at risk, including the general public." The response "indeed . . . would, and should overtax our resources," providing "a true reflection of the state of occupational health in our country" (Robbins and Froines, 1979).

On September 20, 1979, Robbins told the National Advisory Committee on Occupational Safety and Health that the Institute would transfer 30 positions from its technical services and manpower divisions into the Division of Surveillance, Hazard Evaluations, and Field Studies. This would permit NIOSH to conduct 500 health hazard evaluations in 1980 compared to a projected 150 in 1979.

NIOSH did in fact try to publicize the Health Hazard Evaluation Program more extensively under Robbins. It increased contacts with unions, circulated summaries of its evaluations to physicians nationally, and actively published findings of its studies, if any. The number of requests, the number of evaluations completed and reported by NIOSH, and the backlog of active requests all increased substantially after Robbins' appointment, although the number of evaluations fell short of his earlier projections (Table 7.A.; some requests were withdrawn because of the length of time required to conduct and report an evaluation—11 months in 1980, down from 12 months earlier).

About two-thirds of the requests for evaluations came from labor, and 90 percent of these were from unionized firms. Preliminary data for 1980 showed that smaller firms were requesting evaluations somewhat more frequently than before. NIOSH officials speculated that word of the program was filtering down to the smaller firms, which were more likely to be nonunionized (Bainbridge, 1981).

The program apparently had some impact on working conditions. Urban Systems, Inc., analyzed 200 health hazard evaluations conducted in 1978 and 1979. The firm found that about 60 percent of the evaluations uncovered serious hazards. One-third of the firms complied totally with NIOSH's recommendations, about 60 percent complied partially, and

Table 7.A.
Health Hazard Evaluations, 1972-1981

	Requests received	Investigations completed and reported	Active request backlog
1972	150	25	60
1973	152	80	100
1974	190	60	110
1975	170	90	160
1976	200	160	195
1977	190	160	140
1978	210	140	160
1979	230	140	205
1980	429	192	330
1981 (est.)	600	330	—

SOURCE: J. Bainbridge, NIOSH-Cincinnati, telephone interview, February 4, 1981.

8 percent ignored the recommendations. Both employers and employees questioned in the survey said that less costly changes—cleaning and maintenance, protective equipment, ventilation, and the like—were more likely to be made than expensive changes such as engineering controls or environmental monitoring and sampling. Anthony Robbins suggested that firms would be more likely to comply with recommendations after 1979 because OSHA would follow up an evaluation with an inspection (Bureau of National Affairs, April 10, 1980: 1053; it is unclear how employees and employers will react to the program if a request for a health hazard evaluation also becomes, in effect, a request for an OSHA inspection).

7.3. THE INSPECTION PROGRAM

OSHA performs four types of inspections. *General schedule* inspections are divided randomly among firms in industries, although industries with high injury rates or suspected health problems have more inspections allocated to them. *Accident* inspections investigate incidents involving fatalities or multiple hospitalizations. *Follow-up* investigations check for abatement of violations cited in previous inspections. Also, under the OSH Act workers can request an inspection of their firm by filing a *complaint*. They remain anonymous, and if their identity is discovered the employer cannot legally retaliate.

In 1976, the AFL–CIO began to inform workers about their rights to complaint inspections. OSHA did the same. OSHA's compliance force soon became burdened by the large number of ensuing complaints. In

1977, OSHA expressed doubts about its information program. An official in the Office of Field Coordination, Zoltan Bagdy, had the following exchange with the AFL-CIO's George Taylor, Burlington Industries' Harold Imbus, and General Electric's Ed Deck at the National Advisory Committee on Occupational Safety and Health meeting of April 15, 1977:

> Mr. Taylor: What would be the desirability of holding off public information? It would be desirable to have public information and training programs as you go along, rather than wait until such a time (as the compliance force is increased) and have to make such a determination as to when you begin. . . . It seems to me that (education and compliance force growth) should go along contemporaneously.
>
> Mr. Bagdy: . . . (I)f we start more serious training in the public information program, then concurrent with that the complaints would be increasing further. So, whether it is advisable to do that now, while we are facing the backlog, I am not sure. . . .
>
> Mr. Taylor: Well, I can't help but think it is, but that is my own opinion, that I think as far as people in the unions are concerned, a great many of them don't know a damned thing about that and don't know how to assert their rights once they have it. Employers don't know (that they cannot retaliate against workers who file complaints) and maybe will take action against an employee without knowing the consequences. It just seems to me that it ought to move.
>
> Mr. Deck: . . . You are holding out expectations to the employee that you are not able to meet, and I think that that was one of the reasons that—once he filed a complaint, he is not going to hear about it because of the backlog. So you don't build a bigger backlog until you have the staff to expeditiously handle the complaints.
>
> Mr. Imbus: I think that the program, the educational, is necessary. It is just a matter of timing and priorities, and I, you know, I agree, I think it should be here now. On the other hand, I would hate to see (OSHA) create a flood, through the educational thing, a creative flood of complaints that . . . couldn't be handled expeditiously. I think that would be worse than not having the program at all. . . . I think that creating a demand before we can take care of it is not a good thing.

Thus, there was here also a concern that if workers became generally aware of their options under the Occupational Safety and Health Act the response would overwhelm an agency mandated to protect their rights. This concern was, as it turned out, accurate.

After her appointment Eula Bingham said that she was surprised by the small amounts of money allocated for employee and employer information. Her first budget increased funds for employee and employer training from $2.95 million to $7.95 million. The Fiscal Year 1981 budget request would have increased the training budget to $13.9 million.

Word of OSHA did circulate. The percentage of inspections due to complaints increased steadily until Fiscal Year 1979 (Table 7.B.). Nearly

Table 7.B.
OSHA Inspection Activity by Type of Inspection, 1973-1979

Fiscal year	General schedule	Accident	Follow-up	Complaint	TOTAL
1973	32,223	2,456	7,135	6,623	48,437
Percent	(66.5)	(5.1)	(14.7)	(13.7)	(100.0)
1974	56,350	2,216	12,114	6,409	77,089
Percent	(73.1)	(2.9)	(15.7)	(8.3)	(100.0)
1975	56,547	1,884	15,375	7,139	80,945
Percent	(69.9)	(2.3)	(19.0)	(8.8)	(100.0)
1976	63,381	1,914	15,866	9,160	90,321
Percent	(70.2)	(2.1)	(17.6)	(10.1)	(100.0)
TQ*	9,828	489	3,395	4,689	18,401
Percent	(53.4)	(2.7)	(18.4)	(25.5)	(100.0)
1977	24,847	1,777	13,942	19,270	59,836
Percent	(41.5)	(3.0)	(23.3)	(32.2)	(100.0)
1978	20,220	2,064	13,424	21,485	57,193
Percent	(35.3)	(3.6)	(23.5)	(37.6)	(100.0)
1979	23,755	2,301	11,696	20,158	57,910
Percent	(41.0)	(4.0)	(20.2)	(34.8)	(100.0)

*Transition quarter required by change in fiscal year.
SOURCE: Bureau of National Affairs, *Occupational Safety and Health Reporter.* March 27, 1980: 1013.

all workers' complaints were investigated; the Philadelphia, St. Louis, and Pittsburgh area offices told the U.S. General Accounting Office that virtually all of their inspections dealt with complaints (U.S. General Accounting Office, 1979). In July, 1978, Eula Bingham told the House Education and Labor subcommittee on Compensation and Safety that OSHA had a backlog of 2000 complaints, some of which possibly involved serious violations (Bureau of National Affairs, July 20, 1978: 238).

One might expect complaints to draw inspections to serious problems (Diver, 1980: 275–276). The General Accounting Office analyzed data on 2,807 complaint inspections at five OSHA regional offices and concluded otherwise. Most complaints had been lodged for nuisance conditions like dirty restrooms, rodents, wet floors, poor lighting, and no hot water in employee factory showers. These were objectionable conditions, but they were not compelling health or safety hazards. A complete review of 196 complaint case files found that 113 involved "nonserious" conditions. The report commented that "Since a small percentage of workplaces can be inspected each year, programmed (General Schedule) inspections are directed toward what OSHA considers high risk industries. However, complaints have affected the inspection program by taking away resources from programmed inspections" (U.S. General Accounting Office, 1979: 7).

The GAO had criticized the inspection program a year earlier on other, probably related, grounds. In April, 1978, a report called inspections for toxic substances "inadequate and sporadic." Many workplaces known to be using high risk substances like lead, mercury, and MOCA had not been inspected by OSHA, while its industrial hygienists were too often inspecting workplaces with low risk or no health hazards (U.S. General Accounting Office, 1978a). Many of these "needless" inspections could well have been prompted by workers' complaints about conditions involving no violations of standards or low risk hazards.

But even when OSHA's hygienists did visit a "high hazard establishment," the inspection could be deficient. A third GAO study of the inspection program found that inspectors often failed to measure the airborne concentrations of hazards like absestos or lead, that follow-up inspections to check compliance with prior orders were untimely and sometimes not even made, and that employers' requests for extra time to abate hazards were often approved without evaluation (U.S. General Accounting Office, 1978c).

OSHA answered these reports as it usually answers GAO studies— by suggesting that the problems existed when the reports were being researched, but that they had been or were being remedied. The regional and State offices were now resolving many of the complaints by

Table 7.C.
Types of Violations Cited, 1973-1979

Fiscal year	Nonserious	Serious	Willful or repeat	TOTAL
1973	153,670	1,973	117	155,760
Percent	(98.7)	(1.3)	(.0)	(100.0)
1974	282,211	3,087	1,107	286,405
Percent	(98.5)	(1.1)	(.4)	(100.0)
1975	307,893	4,068	2,556	314,517
Percent	(97.9)	(1.3)	(.8)	(100.0)
1976	365,752	8,031	4,787	378,570
Percent	(96.6)	(2.1)	(1.3)	(100.0)
TQ*	63,826	2,261	1,314	67,401
Percent	(94.7)	(3.3)	(2.0)	(100.0)
1977	153,106	21,547	4,655	179,308
Percent	(85.4)	(12.0)	(2.6)	(100.0)
1978	96,176	33,578	4,904	134,658
Percent	(71.5)	(24.9)	(3.6)	(100.0)
1979	85,907	38,104	5,034	129,045
Percent	(66.6)	(29.5)	(3.9)	(100.0)

*Transition quarter required by change in fiscal year.
SOURCE: Bureau of National Affairs, *Occupational Safety and Health reporter*, March 27, 1980: 1014.

letters or phone calls, and then checking with complaining workers to see if any violations had abated or if another inspection were now necessary. OSHA also claimed to be targeting health inspections more carefully and tightening the rules for monitoring and citing violations.

Some data do indeed suggest that OSHA targeted and conducted inspections more systematically after 1977. As noted in Table 7.B., the proportion of inspections due to complaints leveled off. The number of total inspections actually declined; the agency argued that more careful inspections were time-consuming.

Table 7.C. shows that the proportion of violations involving "serious" hazards increased. Some of that increase was due to a change in the minimum penalties for "serious" violations. Morton Corn lowered the minimum so that inspectors would be more willing to cite "serious" violations (Nichols and Zeckhauser, 1978: 208). This dropped the average penalty for a "serious" violation from about $534 in 1976 to about $373 in Fiscal Year 1977 (Table 7.D.). But the classification change alone cannot explain the tremendous increase in violations cited as "serious," nor the fact that penalties increased substantially even as the number of inspections declined and then stabilized.

7.4. THE IMPACT OF OCCUPATIONAL HEALTH ASSISTANCE

Many occupational diseases have long latency periods. Cancer, for example, may take 10–30 years to develop after exposure to a toxic substance. Any increase in the incidence of chemically-related cancer in the last decade was determined years before OSHA existed. Therefore, rates of disease do not show whether or not OSHA has improved occu-

Table 7.D.
Average Penalties, Serious and Nonserious Violations

Fiscal year	Serious	Nonserious
1973	$742	$44
1974	634	41
1975	593	42
1976	534	42
TQ*	560	43
1977	373	60
1978	429	82
1979	$406	$81

*Transition quarter required by change in fiscal year.
SOURCE: Occupational Safety and Health Administration, Office of Management Data Systems, March 1980.

pational health conditions (there are also some difficulties in measuring the agency's impact on occupational *safety*; see McCaffrey, 1980). We can, however, ask whether or not government information and enforcement programs have made workers more aware of occupational disease and more capable of avoiding it.

(The increases in employee requests for inspections and health hazard evaluations show that a large number of workers are now willing to call on OSHA or NIOSH to handle health problems. Also, labor–management relations apparently focus more on health and safety now than several years ago. After studying plants unionized by the International Association of Machinists, Kochan, Dyer, and Lipsky wrote that since OSHA's establishment, "management has assigned a higher priority to plant safety, the ability of the union to influence management decision making on safety issues has increased, and the role of union management safety committees has been bolstered." They found that 69 percent of the workers, and 48 percent of the managers, reported that OSHA had a "strong" or "very strong" impact on safety consciousness and responsiveness in the plant (1977: 5, 36, 76–77). A survey of chemical workers by Cambridge Research Reports for the Shell Oil Company reported that 64 percent of the workers said that safety conditions had improved in their plants in the 1972–78 period (1978: 110), and that OSHA was a contributing factor.)

Granting these improvements, occupational health problems persist, and workers still receive only fragmented information about hazards. The Quality of Working Life Survey found that, overall, a stable proportion of workers reported unpleasant physical conditions from 1969 to 1977 (Quinn and Staines, 1978: 99). The Cambridge Research Reports' study also found that 48 percent of the chemical workers reported health hazards in their workplaces (1978: 92-94). The 1979 INFORM report on copper smelting noted that union safety committees paid little attention to health, as opposed to safety, problems (Bureau of National Affairs, April 12, 1979: 1649-1650).

In the 1978–79 hearings on OSHA's chemical labeling standard, John Mroczkowski of the Steelworkers testified that "Approximately 150 new chemicals come into that plant every day, many of them with just trade names, many with just a code number. As I have been investigating, every company uses a different code number. Many times our people are exposed for a month, six weeks or two months before we find out (the chemical identity) . . . then, after we have it evaluated, (the company) will remove it; but the damage is already done." Victor Horvath of the International Association of Machinists said "The thing that we are asking for is a labeling, a chemical labeling of what really is contained in that lubricant or coolant. And I think we can take it from there. We are not asking for a hell of a lot. But if the men don't know what they are being exposed to on a daily basis, there is nothing they can do about it until years later. And then it is too darned late." Michael Gaffney of the United Autoworkers testified that "Without some kind of very efficient labeling data we are absolutely in the dark about many chemicals that are used in our shop" (U.S. Department of Labor, OSHA, 1981: 4413).

If employees were as familiar with chemical exposures as with visible nuisances like rodents or poor lighting they would be more likely to actively participate in occupational health work. They could describe exposures to physicians if they suspected an occupational disease, help design hazard controls and, if necessary, knowledgeably request OSHA or NIOSH intervention. The information would also improve the fairness of labor–management negotiations because the health conditions of the workplace would be better known. There is a precedent for such an information program in the public warnings about cigarettes. When the information was advertised, the rate of cigarette consumption declined (Agran, 1977: 133-134). Since 1960 there has also been a tremendous shift to less toxic—though by no means "safe"—cigarettes (Cohn, 1978; Cohn, 1981).

OSHA's "access to exposure and medical records" regulation, the *proposed* chemical labeling standard, and OSHA's support of employee training were designed to pass such information along to workers. Because the agency has, as we have seen, relatively few resources for standards development and enforcement, worker involvement is, in principle, valuable.

Both OSHA and NIOSH hope that more "informed" employees can monitor and "regulate" their firms, taking much of the occupational health enforcement load off the Federal government (Hilts, 1980: A10). However, the information programs may have an opposite effect. To the extent that workers' consciousness of occupational health problems is raised they will be more likely to use all the resources at their disposal to combat the problems. This would include demanding inspections or health hazard evaluations or, at least, using the agencies as "clubs" in disputes. Originally intended to ease the burden on the agencies, the information may simply stimulate new demands for health assistance and increase the backlogged work. Either OSHA and NIOSH would have to be expanded—which seems unlikely in the Reagan administration—or labor, tired of waiting for governmental responses, will have to cope with the problems internally.

7.5. SERVICE ISSUES AND THE PERSPECTIVES ON REGULATION

OSHA was unable to issue and enforce standards for most industrial health hazards. Therefore, Eula Bingham argued, the agency had to involve workers in occupational health regulation. In the last half of the seventies OSHA greatly increased the number of its complaint inspections and worker training programs, and tried to issue "information oriented" regulations. Also, as the new director of NIOSH, Anthony Robbins affirmed that NIOSH had to provide more technical assistance to employees. NIOSH thus increased substantially the scope of the health hazard evaluation program.

The new emphases were rooted in past limits to regulation. These regulatory "failures" can be attributed largely to interest groups' objections to and pressures on OSHA. Thus, the cases of services show the agencies, limited by interest-group pressure from businesses and trade associations, trying to cope with a problem by strengthening the knowledge and bargaining power of another interest group (labor). Pluralism's focus on interest groups' influence on public agencies, and the organizational perspective's focus on how agencies try to shape interest-group demand, are both relevant.

But OSHA and NIOSH would strengthen labor's role in occupational health work only through "normal" channels—inspections, health hazard evaluations, training, "access to records," and the labeling standard, all of which the agencies had been doing since the OSH Act was passed. On the other hand, the notification issue had no precedent. Therefore, they pushed it aside.

One might argue that the case of the notification issue supports the capitalist State perspective. The government's information and research programs had begun to threaten the stability of capitalist operations. It had been suggested that OSHA and NIOSH ought to tell workers about their chemical exposures. OSHA and NIOSH, sensing that this program would be an economically unnecessary burden on business, slighted it.

This raises the difficult question of whether the agencies were operating under the general assumption that such programs "just cannot be done" because of their effect on business stability, or whether the agencies were pursuing their own interests (as in the organizational perspective), independent of serious concern for business stability.

I lean toward the latter explanation. The threat to business from the notification program was the likely pressure from an informed workforce. The capitalist State position would predict that OSHA and NIOSH, out of concern for business stability, would have consistently and autonomously suppressed information programs. They have not done so. OSHA issued the final "access to medical and exposure record" regulation and proposed, with NIOSH support, a regulation that would require businesses to label all hazardous chemicals. These regulations would give workers the information about their exposures to toxic chemicals. Workers would then cause businesses the same types of problems as those which would have been prompted by the notification program.

True, in 1981 OSHA had still not released the *final* labeling regulation. Like other standards, it had been exhaustively analyzed and delayed because of the legal and political pressure that will surely follow its release. But this delay was because of interest group and organizational factors, not OSHA's autonomous concern for business stability.

In contrast, the agencies willingly slighted the notification program because it was organizationally disruptive. It is not that OSHA and NIOSH inherenty oppose giving workers information, but rather that they wish to give the information through normal channels.

Of course, we could turn to the NIOSH paper "The Right to Know" and recite the references to the notification program's likely disruptive effect on the capitalist system. How could we seriously construe that paper as suggesting that NIOSH and OSHA were avoiding the notification program out of concern for *their* own stability?

I would reply that NIOSH was floating the specter of agitated workers simply because it was compiling a shopping list of objections to a program it was desperately trying to avoid for organizational reasons. On this occasion, concern for business's stability was organizationally convenient. On the other hand, to issue the "access to records" regulation and propose the chemical labeling rule this self-imposed "constraint" had to be discarded by the agencies. Organizational theory predicts that ideological consistency is not a compelling constraint when agency interests are at stake (Section 1.1.3).

CHAPTER 8

Regulatory Balance

8.1. THE CURRENT ARGUMENT: EXCESSIVE REGULATION

8.1.1. The "Three Faces of the Problem"

The American Bar Association Commission on Law and the Economy compiled a report in 1979 called *Federal Regulation: Roads to Reform.* A highly influential definition of the "problem" of regulation, it said that

> Our government has adopted a wide variety of national goals. Many of these goals—checking inflation, spurring economic growth, reducing unemployment, protecting our national security, assuring equal opportunity, cleaning up the environment, improving energy sufficiency—conflict with one another, and all of them compete for the same resources. One of the central tasks of modern democratic government is to make wise balancing choices among courses of action that pursue one or more of these conflicting and competing objectives (1979: 68).

The Commission identified "three faces of the problem" of regulation. First, agencies tend to be independent of elected officials. Legislation, to some extent, insulates *commissions* such as the Federal Trade Commission and the Consumer Product Safety Commission from Presidential or Congressional intervention. *Executive agencies* such as the Environmental Protection Agency or Occupational Safety and Health Administration are arguably somewhat politically independent because Congress and the President pressure them only at some political cost.

Second, regulatory agencies are "singleminded." "We have only lately begun to appreciate that the goals of one agency could conflict with those of another, and that the cumulative impact of pursuing all of the goals of all the regulatory agencies to the fullest measure can materially affect costs, prices, employment, and economic growth." Several of the regulatory statutes are silent or ambiguous on whether or how agencies are to balance competing considerations, and the proregulation "single interest" groups prodding the agencies resist such balancing (American Bar Association, 1979: 70).

Third, there is a "multiplicity of agencies," often with overlapping duties. As each "new" problem appeared, "even though the new problem was only an extension of an older problem already confided to an existing agency, we sometimes decided to create a new agency anyway, perhaps on the theory that two (or four) could do better than one" (American Bar Association, 1979: 70).

Thus, a principal theme of the regulatory reform movement is the need to balance consumer, worker, and environmental protection with "neglected" economic considerations.

8.1.2. Reforms

8.1.2.1. Internal Balancing

One type of reform requires agencies themselves to balance conflicting objectives. President Ford's inflation–economic impact statement program and President Carter's "Improving Government Regulations Program" required that executive agencies consider the costs and benefits of regulatory proposals and alternatives. Several unsuccessful legislative proposals introduced in the 96th Congress would have tightened these requirements and extended them to independent agencies (U.S. Senate Committee on Governmental Affairs, 1979).

Also, the Reagan administration tried to quiet regulatory agencies by appointing only persons of "balanced" judgement to head them. A "balanced" view clearly meant a view primarily sensitive to business's complaints about regulation. David Stockman, his director of the Office of Management and Budget, said that "You need a whole new mindset down at EPA or you're not going to do anything about regulation." The deputy director of OMB, James Miller III, argued that the EPA officials were "mission-oriented" toward environmental protection and that they had to be replaced by those who would not advocate "aggressive regulation" over what fit into "important national policy considerations." President Reagan would change this and appoint regulatory officials who were neither "business-oriented" nor "ideological fanatics" (Behr and Brown, 1980).

Certainly President Reagan's early appointments were as "business-oriented" as President Carter's appointments of Michael Pertschuck to head the Federal Trade Commission and Eula Bingham to head OSHA were consumer and worker-oriented. James Watt, the new Secretary of the Interior, was a conservative, development-oriented lawyer. Thorne Auchter, a Florida construction contractor, replaced Eula

Bingham as the head of OSHA. Murray Weidenbaum, the new chairman of the Council of Economic Advisors, was a long-time critic of Federal regulation who urged a one-year moratorium on any new regulations. Dr. Weidenbaum suggested that emergency regulations—controls for extreme hazards like vinyl chloride or asbestos—ought to be permitted during the moratorium, but only if their costs were offset by a loosening of other occupational health standards (Behr and Brown, 1980).

8.1.2.2. External Balancing

Other reforms would increase the external controls over agencies. The American Bar Association endorsed a plan which would give the President formal power to overrule agencies' actions, a power which is now legally ambiguous and controversial (1979: 79-84). A variety of legislative veto plans—in which a regulation could be overruled by one or both houses of Congress, a committee, or even a committee chairman—have been proposed (Breyer and Stewart, 1979: 95-96).

Another current proposal involves establishment of a "regulatory budget." A regulatory budget would limit the annual economic impact of a particular agency on the economy. Just as the fiscal budget allocates funds among competing programs, a national regulatory budget would set a total regulatory burden which would be "parceled out" to the agencies. This would force the President and Congress to favor and limit particular regulatory programs (DeMuth, 1980b). Finally, Senator Dale Bumpers of Arkansas proposed that the Administrative Procedure Act of 1946 be amended to eliminate any judicial presumption in favor of an agency's actions. Under the amendment courts would *independently* review the validity of regulations (see Section 3.1.5.).

Agencies' independence, singlemindedness, and multiplicity allegedly produced imbalanced regulation. The reforms outlined above would ultimately increase elected officials' controls over agencies. They would also require that regulatory organizations worry less about worker, environmental, and consumer protection, and more about the effects of regulation on industrial productivity, inflation, and so forth.

Some reforms would be more powerful than others. For example, cost-benefit analysis is very sensitive to the assumptions of the analyst. Agencies forced to use it could, if they wanted, defensibly justify a preferred conclusion on a given issue (Baram, 1980; Ashford, 1979). On the other hand, President Reagan's appointments of industry consultants to key regulatory positions would effectively damage any lingering "sense of mission" in the agencies.

But if the "three faces of the problem" are self-evident, what were the original justifications for agency independence and "singleminded" mandates? Are they at all relevant today?

8.2. THE PROBLEM OF BALANCE: ANOTHER VIEW

8.2.1. Agencies as Technicians

According to the traditional model of administrative regulation, independent agencies were to be specialized and technically efficient. Elected officials had neither the time, the training, nor the inclination to regulate industrial practices—often controversially—as various laws required. The political pressures to which elected officials respond could subvert sound controls. Thus, it was left to "technicians," guided by professional norms and "zeal for the public interest," to work out and enforce the details of regulatory laws. Judicial review of agency action, and agency facilitation of judicial review, were considered sufficient to prevent oppressive and unfair regulations (Stewart, 1975: 1669-1681).

But this view was shaken by the "revelation" that regulatory officials often depended on regulated industries for information, cooperation, and subsequent jobs, and thus excessively favored them when making decisions (Stewart, 1975: 1681-1687; see also Section 1.1.1.2. above). This was a central critique of regulation in the late 1960s and early 1970s.

A "Nader report" on the Federal Trade Commission argued that the FTC was miserably passive and key officials incompetent or uncaring about the FTC's mission. A critical American Bar Association report followed. Although the FTC was substantially reorganized under new management in 1970 (Breyer and Stewart, 1979: 770-794), even in the mid-1970s Congress accused the Commission of moving too slowly on critical anti-trust or consumer issues. "By 1975 a Democratic Congress and Republican President had joined to give the agency additional powers to protect consumer rights." Michael Pertschuck, a former Nader associate and Senate Counsel, was named chairman in 1977 amid high hopes that he would revitalize the FTC (Gellhorn, 1980).

Drafters of the 1970 Clean Air Act and the 1972 Federal Water Pollution Control Act subscribed to Marver Bernstein's views that political pressures gradually wore agencies down. The laws mandated specific timetables for pollution reduction to try to assure that political considerations would not deter environmental improvements. Both laws passed the House and Senate overwhelmingly (Marcus, 1980). We have already discussed the ambitious wording of the OSH Act; OSHA would regulate all occupational health problems on the basis of the best available evidence (Section 6.2.)

In the early 1970's Congress would criticize a passive FTC and argue that occupational and environmental health problems were compelling. Congress and the President encouraged the FTC, EPA, and OSHA to vigorously and "independently" enforce the laws. Ostensibly, independence meant that agency scientists and administrators could competently, "professionally" attack these problems within the general procedural guides of their statutes and normal external reviews, without further interference with their judgment.

8.2.2 The Backlash against Independence

By the late 1970s the "solution" of agency independence had become the "problem of regulation." Independence meant that safety engineers and industrial hygienists staffing OSHA would try to shape its policies. Their professions historically regarded personal protective devices as inferior substitutes for engineering changes to control exposure to chemicals, and also advocated very protective exposure limits. Remember, for example, that the American Conference of Governmental Industrial Hygienists, a private organization, had recommended zero exposure levels for carcinogens (Section 4.1.2.1.). OSHA's policies developed along these lines (Kelman, 1980). In the cotton dust case Secretary of Labor Ray Marshall remarked that it was "presumptuous" of the economists at the Council on Wage and Price Stability and the Council of Economic Advisors to "second guess OSHA on technical issues, such as the respirator issue."

But business's pressures consistently intruded on OSHA. By 1981, no reasonable definition could characterize OSHA as an "aggressive" regulator. Yet the new Reagan administration planned to cut it back even further. James Miller III, deputy administrator of the Office of Management and Budget, urged that OSHA's new head permit personal protective devices as substitutes for engineering controls, asserting that "in many cases, the result will be an increase in worker protection." This argument, rejected repeatedly by the safety engineers and industrial hygienists at OSHA, would probably be accepted by the new conservative administration. An industry lobbyist commented that "I certainly don't think that the climate is favorable for new engineering controls" (*Business Week*, January 26, 1981: 31).

From 1977 to 1979 the Federal Trade Commission under Michael Pertschuk aggressively tried to prohibit certain "unfair practices" in a group of industries that included advertising, funeral homes, eyeglasses, and used cars. The targeted industries intensely and successfully lobbied the Congress to cut back the FTC's powers. While even the FTC's supporters had criticized the proposed restriction on children's advertising, the industry campaign lashed out even at more cautious and flexible proposals (Gellhorn, 1980).

In 1980, Congress passed a rule permitting legislative vetoes of the Commission's regulations. Further, the campaign intimidated the agency. In March, 1980, the FTC's general counsel, Michael Sohn, commented that "You can sue five funeral directors or five used car dealers and not get much political heat. But when you take on the whole industry, you hear about it. I'd hope that the Commission would think more carefully about which ones it picks" (Behr, 1980a). In May, 1980, the director of the FTC's Bureau of Competition, Alfred Dougherty, Jr., resigned, protesting that the agency had begun giving in to its political opponents. He claimed that "an air of calculating caution has spread within the Commission." Dougherty told Pertschuck that he was "increasingly doubtful" that the Commission could achieve "the goals to which you and I have committed ourselves" (Behr, 1980b).

As noted above, the Reagan administration singled out the EPA as a prime target for regulatory cutbacks. The Office of Management and Budget director David Stockman said that "They've got rules that would practically shut down the economy if they were put into effect. This is the critical agency. You need a whole new mindset down at EPA or you're not going to do anything about regulation" (Behr and Brown, 1980). (A 1981 report by the National Commission on Air Quality said that, despite industry complaints to the contrary, the Clean Air Act was broad enough to allow construction of all energy development projects that the country had considered, although certain parts of the Act could be streamlined or eliminated as useless; Omang, 1981.)

Thus, the most influential criticisms of regulatory agencies no longer focused on their passivity. That "problem" had allegedly been solved. Now the "problem" was the "solution" of the earlier period— the independent and "mission-oriented" pursuit of worker, consumer, and environmental protection. The American Bar Association report argued that "the cumulative impact of pursuing all of the goals of all the regulatory agencies to the fullest measure can materially affect cost, prices, employment, and economic growth" (1979: 70). The OSHA, FTC, and EPA experiences show that there is little danger of regulatory agencies being so successfully aggressive.

8.2.3. Agency Independence and Policy Debates

As Aaron Wildavsky has argued, a government in which agencies vigorously pursue "singleminded" ends may in fact coordinate and balance policies quite well. It is extremely costly and practically impossible for an agency to rationally weigh all competing means and ends. A system where many agencies defend their preferred policies is more likely to adequately air the range of options than a system where a single agency is relied on to consider all alternatives. Competing agencies defending preferred options—for example, OSHA defending a protective standard versus the Council on Wage and Price Stability arguing for a looser but less costly alternative—will try to construct the best cases that can be made for different approaches. Certainly OSHA will initially argue for, or be a conduit of arguments advocating, protective regulations; the working principle of the Occupational Safety and Health Act was that worker health would be vigorously defended by somebody. But OSHA is a relatively weak agency negotiating and compromising with relatively strong industries and others. "When one thinks of all the participants who are continuously engaged in interpreting the wishes of others, who try to feel the pulse of Congress, the President, interest groups, and special publics, it is clear that a great many adjustments are made in anticipation of what the other participants are likely to do. This, it seems to me, is just another term for coordination" (Wildavsky, 1974: 155). OSHA has bargained and compromised—to the point where its regulatory aspirations are a fraction of those mandated by the OSH Act—in order to accommodate and evade complaints about economic costs. Interest groups and government economists will not let regulatory agencies ignore economic considerations; in turn, we should not have to depend on industry and the President's economists to defend occupational health or environmental protection.

Certainly the regulations coming out of agencies have not been the workings only of "ideological fanatics." The EPA developed new approaches to pollution control such as the pollution offset program and the "bubble" technique, which set limits on emissions but allowed areas or companies to meet them as they saw fit. Corporations praised these methods of regulation (U.S. Environmental Protection Agency, 1981).

As we have seen, OSHA designed toxic substance controls within quite tight political and economic constraints. And specifically, what final standards were excessively costly? Businesses called the vinyl chloride standard infeasible, but then adjusted to it relatively easily. B.F. Goodrich, Inc. subsequently praised the case as a "study in prevention" (B.F. Goodrich, 1977). Industry did not challenge the final DBCP and acrylonitrile standards. OSHA drastically modified the cotton dust standard because of objections from business and the Council on Wage and Price Stability. In 1976, the steel industry and CWPS castigated the coke oven emissions standard, but in 1981 a *Business Week* article noted that

"OSHA observers" called the coke oven rule "the agency's most reasonable and effective standard" (Cahan, 1981: 89). Perhaps after the controversy settles the arsenic and lead standards will seem "reasonable" as well.

But through its appointments, the Reagan administration tried to eliminate any annoying residual inclination of OSHA to argue strongly on behalf of workers' health. Certainly as a result labor and public interest groups will increase their legal pressure on OSHA, and liberal Congressional staffers and the General Accounting Office will continue to criticize regulatory passivity. But while Eula Bingham was sympathetic to arguments favoring strong health regulations, a conservative OSHA administrator in a conservative administration—already sympathetic to relatively powerful industries—will drastically diminish standards development activities. Since OSHA's history shows that the balance of interest group pressures already opposes occupational health controls, calling the Reagan appointments a "balancing" of the regulatory system is nonsense.

8.3. CONSEQUENCES OF DIMINISHED REGULATION

8.3.1. Costs of Controls and Innovation

Firms do spend a significant amount to reduce health and safety hazards. Relatively new hazard control firms, and new environmental control divisions of established companies, have also shown above average growth rates, although only average or lower than average profitability (Kramer, 1978b; Hornblower, 1978). This spending is very sensitive to regulatory requirements and deadlines (Segel and Dreiling, 1978; Arthur Andersen, Inc., 1979).

The expenses involved in these efforts have undoubtedly increased prices and retarded measured economic growth (Data Resources, Inc., 1979; see Section 3.1.6.). However, increased prices may simply show that the costs of production previously imposed on third parties—e.g., on workers as occupational disease—are now being internalized by manufacturers and consumers; this would indicate that the regulatory system is working properly.

The costs of hazard controls tend to diminish as firms learn more efficient techniques; in fact, regulations may be a necessary spur to innovation. Hayes and Abernathy argued in the *Harvard Business Review* that American managers have become preoccupied with short-term profits, neglected the need to innovate, and "effectively foresworn long-term technological superiority as a competitive weapon" (1980: 70). Three out of four corporate executives in a recent poll criticized corporate incentive plans for rewarding short-term performance at the expense of long-term projects. One out of three said that senior managers did not know enough about technology and underemphasized innovation (Vogel, 1981).

Regulation, like foreign auto and steel competition, may be an unwelcome but necessary pressure for technological innovation. A report of MIT's Center for Policy Alternatives done for the Senate Committee on Governmental Affairs noted in 1980 that

> regulation may bring about both product and process innovation. Most product innovation results from forces outside the firm, such as new market demand or changes in the regulatory climate. Process innovation, which is usually motivated by the need to reduce costs, can be stimulated by regulation as well as by market factors. A new process may spread throughout an industry or to other industries, providing benefits to many parties. The need to comply with new regulations, especially those with stringent requirements, can produce a flurry of innovative activity and even change the pattern or role of innovation in an industry. Government regulation that specifies performance requirements for products may assist product innovation by reducing the risk of market failure. Regulation may also accelerate the pace of innovative activity that might eventually have occurred anyway. Process improvements may even exceed those necessary for compliance (1980: 14).

For example, in 1978 Bell Telephone Laboratories announced that its engineers had developed a new system for electroplating materials—a major source of industrial fumes—that was "cheaper, cleaner, and more productive than current methods" (Washington Post, May 18, 1978: D14). Nicholas Ashford noted in the National Advisory Committee on Occupational Safety and Health meeting on April 6, 1977 that

> Let me remind the group . . . that the plastics industry calculated that its industry would be absolutely collapsed by the adoption of a vinyl chloride standard, and that 2 million people would be put out of work; and I invite the examination of that document from the Congressional Research Services which indicates no such impact was ever observed. In fact, the truth of the matter is that a new process which was energy-conserving, safer, and more profitable emerged in terms of technology "pull" than before the regulation. And it was directly attributable, the acceleration of that technology, was attributable to that regulation.

As noted in Section 6.1.3., industry used the new technology described above, with some modifications, to control acrylonitrile. It will probably be used for other materials as well.

A new secondary lead smelting process developed by Paul Bergsoe and Son Company of Denmark, now being marketed internationally, both improves company productivity and substantially cuts exposure to airborne lead (U.S. Department of Labor, OSHA, 1978e: 54483). Michael

Royston in the *Harvard Business Review* surveyed numerous cases where new technologies had both reduced hazardous emissions and paid for themselves in materials recycling in surprisingly short periods (1980).

The fact that regulation stimulates innovation helps explain why standards that firms call "technologically impossible" eventually become "reasonable." It also means that drastically reducing regulatory development will retard technological improvement, something to be weighed against the short-term economic savings.

8.3.2. Benefits

Safety and health regulations also have some benefits not adequately included in standard measures of economic welfare such as the Gross National Product. Disability costs, medical expenses, and damages to property values and the environment are avoided. Several analysts argue that these savings offset or exceed the cost of controls. In a case such as Love Canal, an initial investment of $4 million would have prevented a $27 million cleanup. Early controls on asbestos would have prevented a monumental occupational disease epidemic (Green and Waitzman, 1979; Center for Policy Alternatives, 1980). Certainly there is no consensus on the benefit–cost balance of health and safety regulation, or even on how to measure the balance (Baram, 1980). But to the extent that there are significant net benefits, regulatory costs are valuable investments and not dead-weight burdens. Concurrently, cutting back regulations will permit avoidable damages to workers, consumers, and the environment.

8.3.3. Product Liability Suits

Disease and other damages may also result in more product liability suits against manufacturers and suppliers of hazardous materials and products.

In the late 19th and early 20th centuries, injured workers were beginning to successfully sue employers for negligence. This encouraged firms to support workers' compensation laws (Posner, 1972; Weinstein, 1968). Under these laws, labor gave up the remedy of suing employers—which was slowly becoming more effective—for quicker, assured, and very limited compensation for industrial injuries.

Although workers gave up the right to sue their employers, they may still sue third parties, such as the suppliers of materials or technology. Workers can usually obtain legal help because of the contingency fee system whereby the plaintiff's lawyer collects a large minority of the award if the client wins and nothing if the client loses. Awards in such cases can be—and frequently have been—very large, and lawyers are attracted to them.

For example, in 1978, a $1.84 million settlement was made in Ohio between construction workers and seventeen producers of asbestos. The suit charged that the defendant companies had not adequately warned the workers about the hazards of asbestos. The workers' lawyer, Robert Sweeney, said that "As knowledge of hazardous substances increases, manufacturers' liability is likely to increase," and that manufacturers who fail to respond by protecting workers handling their products "will lose their place in the marketplace as a result of the high costs of litigation" (Bureau of National Affairs, February 2, 1978: 1343). The draft report of a Department of Labor Task Force on Occupational Disease pointed out in 1979 that there were currently 2,000 claims filed against a single manufacturer of asbestos, that the number of new awards or settlements against this firm was 155 in 1978 compared to 14 in 1975, and that the average award was now up to $30,000 (U.S. Department of Labor, ASPER, 1979: Chapter II, 37-42). The report suggested that "Some likely future candiates for product liability suits are manufacturers of textile equipment, producers and distributors of chemicals, and manufacturers of mining equipment" (Chapter II, 37; see for example, Taylor, 1976).

The "access to medical and exposure records" regulation and the chemial labeling regulation—if it is ever issued—inform employees of their exposures to chemicals on the job. Workers will therefore be more likely to link symptoms of diseases with specific substances and file either workers' compensation claims or these third-party lawsuits. The product liability bar is extremely aggressive (O'Connell, 1979), and many of these suits would be filed even if OSHA were free to issue and enforce standards at will. But discarding occupational illness prevention as a national policy goal will permit avoidable diseases to occur and will enlarge the pool of cases from which lawsuits can be drawn.

8.3.4. Mobilized Liberal Pressures

Labor and public interest groups largely tolerated OSHA's inactivity under Eula Bingham. They could arguably trust the agency to resist business's attempts to gut health regulation. Still, corporate pressures continued to wear OSHA down from 1976 to 1980. With the appointment of a construction firm owner to head OSHA in the conservative Republican Reagan administration, any hope that OSHA would aggressively protect workers' health—always shaky—was shattered.

Labor and public interest groups will certainly be more likely to sue the agency for stalling controls on hazardous substances. Contributions to public interest law groups and liberal political action committees did increase after the Republican Presidential and Senate victories in 1980. A lawyer at the Center for Law and Social Policy, a public interest law group in Washington, noted in 1981 that "Things become clearer when it looks like a 'we-they' thing. Like the Ford Foundation— they had a vice-president, Basil Whiting, who got a job in (OSHA) under Carter. And then for four years it was, you know, 'Why sue them? Basil's there.' Now he won't be there and they will see it more clearly" (Reid, 1981).

The Reagan administration anticipated some legal difficulties in cutting back OSHA. James Miller of the Office of Management and Budget said that when OSHA's new leadership, as expected, went along with OMB's suggestion that personal protective devices be substituted for engineering controls to control chemicals, he was sure it "would precipitate a few lawsuits" (Behr, 1981).

The Bingham administration sympathized with labor's and public interest groups' arguments for strong controls on hazardous chemicals. However, these groups restrained their activities partly because of that reputation. The Reagan administration's OSHA will get no such sympathy, and pro-regulation groups will concurrently be more willing and able to sue OSHA as its leaders discard occupational health goals. Since a sizable occupational disease problem remains (Section 2.1.), one would hope that their mobilized pressures could offset the new effort to cripple OSHA's occupational disease controls. But given labor's and public interest groups' early disadvantages in occupational health work (Chapter 3) that hope would be unjustified.

CHAPTER 9

Postscript

9.1. THE REGULATORY IMPACT ANALYSIS PROGRAM

Chapters 1 through 8 of this book were completed in February, 1981. As was to be expected, in the following nine months the Republican administration substantially reduced environmental, health, and safety regulation.

In January, President Reagan established a "Task Force on Regulatory Relief." Chaired by Vice-President George Bush, the Task Force was to review major regulatory proposals and current regulations, and plan regulatory reform legislation.

On February 17, Reagan issued Executive Order 12291, which replaced President Carter's "Improving Government Regulations" program. The order told agencies to make sure that their regulations were legally sound and supported by the evidence, and to publish semi-annual regulatory agendas. The agencies—"to the extent permitted by law"—had to select regulatory alternatives entailing "the least net cost to society." They had to prepare "Regulatory Impact Analyses" (RIA) for both proposed and final regulations. The RIA would describe and compare the benefits and costs of regulations, and describe "alternative approaches that could substantially achieve the same regulatory goal at lower cost, together with an analysis of their potential benefit and costs and a brief explanation of the legal reasons why such alternatives, if proposed, could not be adopted."

In principal, a complete Regulatory Impact Analysis would do no more than a *complete* Inflation/Economic Impact Statement, or a complete Regulatory Analysis (the Ford and Carter programs, respectively). But just as the Regulatory Analysis program tried to shift working control of the analysis from the program offices to agency heads, the Reagan program shifted oversight from agency heads to the Office of Management and Budget. Before proposing a major regulation, an agency *had* to submit its Regulatory Impact Analysis to OMB and give OMB a maximum of sixty days to comment on it. Before issuing a final regulation the agency had to submit it along with a final RIA to the Office of Management and Budget and give OMB thirty days to comment.

The Associate Director of OMB, James Miller III, stressed the power that the Executive Order gave to OMB, although he noted that OMB had no formal power to change either the Regulatory Impact Analyses or the regulations. But,

> . . . the executive order establishes things quite clearly. Among the people whose behavior we're trying to influence are the GS-13's and -14's who draft the rules. The executive order says to them: even if you get a nonconforming proposal past your agency heads, even if you've captured them or just plain fooled them, that proposal is likely to be caught at OMB—and there's not a chance in Hades of you're capturing those people. So if you want to get ahead, you're going to have to write new rules and review existing rules in conformance with the principles set forth by the President in the Executive Order. I believe that as internal agency procedures and the mechanism for central review settle into place, agency personnel will voluntarily comply (*Regulation*, March/April 1981: 22).

Murray Weidenbaum added that the Task Force on Regulatory Relief and the OMB had no "interest group constituency to defend. Its only constituency is the President and the President's program for rationalizing regulation." (Consistent with the President's program for "rationalizing regulation," on March 25 Task Force leader George Bush invited businesses—as well as labor—to suggest regulations that they wanted deleted or modified. He did not invite any suggestions for strengthened or new regulations.) Miller noted that most of the Reagan appointees in the agencies were willing to go along with OMB's requests. If a political appointee disagreed with the Task Force and OMB and insisted that a rule be issued (an unlikely prospect considering the corporate background of most Reagan appointees), "he or she still has the legal authority to issue the regulation, but that action could be risky—meaning that the President of the United States might decide to remove such a person from office" (*Regulation*, March/April 1981: 14-23).

The Reagan program did in effect substantially cut back regulatory activity in 1981. On June 13, the White House reported that since January 20 more than 180 regulations had been either withdrawn, modified, or reviewed. All measures of the volume of rule making dropped to from 30 to 50 percent below the 1980 levels (U.S. Office of Management and Budget, 1981: 1-6).

9.2. STOPPING OSHA

The Occupational Safety and Health Administration has been a major target for the Reagan reformers.

A Supreme Court decision gave labor a victory in the Summer of 1981, but it was largely a symbolic victory. On June 17, the Supreme Court affirmed that OSHA did not have to balance costs and benefits of standards, upholding (5–3) OSHA's standard lowering employees' permissible exposures to cotton dust. OSHA had issued the standard in 1978 and successfully defended it before the U.S. Court of Appeals for the District of Columbia (see 6.1.5. above). On January 21, 1981—carrying the case over from the Carter administration—OSHA defended the cotton dust standard before the Supreme Court. The Court's June decision noted that a standard had to be economically "feasible" and that OSHA had to demonstrate that a standard had *significant* benefits. However,

> Congress itself defined the basic relationship between costs and benefits, by placing the "benefit" of worker health above all other considerations save those making attainment of the "benefit" unachievable. Any standard based on balancing of costs and benefits by (OSHA) that strikes a different balance than that struck by Congress would be inconsistent with the command set forth in (Section) 6(b)(5). Thus, cost-benefit analysis by OSHA is not required by the statute because feasibility analysis is (ATMI v. Donovan, No. 79-1429 (slip copy)).

The decision came down as heads of OSHA—appointed by President Reagan—argued that OSHA *should* compare the costs and benefits of regulations (in fact, they had asked the court to remand the standard to the agency so that it could do the cost–benefit analysis that the industry had requested; the court rejected OSHA's request in a footnote (slip copy. p. 13)).

In July, Thorne Auchter, the new Assistant Secretary of Labor for Occupational Safety and Health, affirmed that OSHA would not use cost-benefit analysis in designing standards because of the Supreme Court's decision. Instead, OSHA would analyze a proposal's economic feasibility and then determine "the most efficient way to protect employees." Exposure levels would be set based on "scientific data," and then OSHA would select the least costly way to meet the desired protective exposure levels. Auchter stated that this system of cost-effectiveness analysis differed from cost-benefit analysis because cost-benefit analysis would "not necessarily mandate comparison of equal levels of protection;" that is, cost-benefit analysis would let OSHA opt for a less protective standard if the marginal costs of the more protective rule outweighed its marginal benefits (Bureau of National Affairs, July 16, 1981: 131). In using cost-effectiveness analysis OSHA would presumably set very protective exposure levels and then let firms use the least costly controls to meet them.

Certainly, OSHA would now permit firms to meet exposure limits through personal protective devices rather than through more expensive and, industrial hygienists argued, more effective, engineering controls. But in truth there was no chance that the new leaders of OSHA would issue standards with exposure levels as protective as those issued under earlier administrations. In 1981 OSHA withdrew the labeling standard (Bureau of National Affairs, February 19, 1981: 1265-1266). It also suspended a regulation for occupational exposure to noise, and was reviewing—probably in order to substantially weaken—the lead and cotton dust standards. The agency was effectively ignoring the carcinogen policy. OSHA also withdrew a regulation which required that firms pay workers who accompanied OSHA officials on plant inspections.

Firms were no longer criticizing the agency. Although OSHA had issued no new health regulations under Auchter, the first year of his administration strongly suggested that OSHA would now accept industries' arguments that more lenient exposure limits sufficiently protected workers (if, indeed, OSHA issued any regulations at all). Auchter's disavowal of cost-benefit analysis would not affect this cutback; his administration would simply package eased standards as being "cost-effective" rather than as having "benefits exceeding costs."

Grover Wrenn Affidavit on
Health Standards Process (Summary)

1. After OSHA receives a criteria document from NIOSH, a project officer is assigned responsibility for "collecting and evaluating all research which the criteria document does not include." An advance notice of the proposed rulemaking is then published in the Federal Register and indicates that OSHA is considering a particular standard and requesting information from interested parties. "Comments to this advance notice," Wrenn said, "may be and frequently have been so significant as to cause our office and NIOSH substantially to reexamine the type of standard needed." The period from the receipt of the criteria document to the completion of the first technical draft ideally takes two to three man-months, and "has often required much longer."

2. An advisory committee may be appointed to assist in the standard's development. "This course is chosen when direct formal participation by employers and employees, as well as representatives of concerned Federal and State agencies, professional organizations, and academics, will be beneficial and/or such participation is mandated by the controversial nature of the proceedings." Advisory committees have up to 270 days to formulate recommendations.

3. The project officer reviews the committee's recommendations and records. "Since advisory committee recommendations are generally not in the form of a standard, do not consider the compliance aspects of rulemaking, need reworking of technical language, and incorporate other technical tests and recommendations which must be substantially rewritten by the project officer, preparation of a technically sufficient standard begins at this point. Such preparation usually takes one to two man-months."

4. Full initiation of the standard's development project. A project

officer is "finally assigned to thoroughly evaluate the hazard, its conse-quences, and relevant data." An advance notice of proposed rulemaking may be published, "not(ing) OSHA's receipt of a criteria document and/or intent to consider rulemaking and (soliciting) comments on the hazard."

5. Completion of literature search, review, and analysis by the project officer. "During this stage the project officer's focus is on docu-mentation of the need for the standard." All the available literature must be reviewed, as well as relevant enforcement data, consensus standards, and comments submitted in response to the advanced notice of pro-posed rulemaking. The officer then develops recommendations for the standard.

6. Decision on initiation of rulemaking. All the gathered output is presented to the Assistant Secretary for OSH or designee. "If it is found prudent to initiate rulemaking, this decision will be forwarded to the Office of Standards Development along with a decision on the pro-spective standard's relative priority. The program area responsible for conducting assessments of inflationary and environmental impact is alerted so that necessary supplemental efforts may be initiated. NIOSH is advised."

7. Assignment of the project to an OSHA/SOL (Solicitor of Labor) team. A plan of development is formulated and sent to the OSH and SOL managements for review. The plan "includes target dates by which major activities are to be accomplished," as well as "scheduled evalua-tion" and "consultations." The team also develops a list of issues "for which data is inconclusive and additional research is required." The list may be sent to NIOSH as a request for technical assistance.

8. Initial draft of a standard. The project officer must prepare the initial document as well as the "underlying issue paper and fact sheet . . . the drafts must be sufficient of technical quality to permit meaning-ful review by other program areas within OSHA." These documents are "doublechecked by concurrent field evaluations and consultations with outside experts to insure familiarity with extant industry practices on all new developments."

9. Review for technical adequacy. This review is done to "insure the proposal's technical integrity, effective utilization of expert advice, and consideration of pertinent criteria, utilizing experts in and out of government to evaluate the proposal's technical sufficiency, the ade-quacy of the data base, and the connections between its premise and conclusions."

10. Decision briefing with the Assistant Secretary for OSH. This stage consists of a "full panel discussion of all issues surfaced during previous reviews and the regulatory options available," based on the

draft proposal, fact sheet, issue paper, and all recommendations and comments accumulated. The results of the briefing are forwarded to the Office of Standards Development in a formal "decision memorandum from the Assistant Secretary providing the project officer specific guidance on all major issues." A copy is sent to the OSHA "feasibility group" for possible inflationary and environmental impact statements. Where further research is necessary, requests to NIOSH are prepared outlining specific areas in which technical assistance remains needed.

11. The initial regulatory proposal is drafted.

12. Formal review. Formal review is done by the Standards' offices and Solicitor's Office to "ensure the proposal is technically and legally adequate." The final proposal is published in the Federal Register. "It should be noted that here, as at all other stages requiring direct approval by the Assistant Secretary . . . or staff, new developments or the full expert interdisciplinary scrutiny of top-level panel examinations may, and frequently do, reveal significant deficiencies or require altered regulatory choices necessitating further drafts before a proposal is approved for publication. Several of the above steps may accordingly be repeated several times before the next milestone is needed."

13. Publication of the proposal on Notice of Availability of the Inflationary Impact Statement or notification of No Impact in the Federal Register.

14. Public participation in actual rulemaking. "Participation in the standards development process by interested members of the public . . . is mandated following publication of a proposal, and where controversial safety standards or all health standards are concerned will at a minimum result in several hundred pages of comments supporting and opposing the proposal and advancing complex data, factual theories, and legal arguments in an attempt to establish competing positions." The hearings involve "huge" amounts of OSHA staff time to evaluate prehearing comments, compile responses to crucial factual and scientific issues raised, prepare Departmental testimony in support of the proposal, and assist the Solicitor's Office in preparing its cross-examination of witnesses. Wrenn cited the occupational noise standard's hearings, which generated 1,000 prehearing comments, a transcript of 3,700 pages, and a similar number of posthearing comments. The first half of the coke oven emissions hearings ran for 20 days and produced 4,000 pages of transcript.

15. The project officer with the assistance of the project attorney(s) prepares a summary and analysis of the record generated, with the major issues, options available, and officer's recommendations. The analysis is reviewed by OSHA and the Solicitor's Office.

16. Presentation to the Assistant Secretary for final decision. The

Assistant Secretary's recommendations are transmitted to the Standards Development Office and the Solicitor.

17. The final standard is drafted on the basis of the complete hearing record, including the inflationary and environmental impact statements. It is reviewed for technical and legal adequacy.

18. The Assistant Secretary reviews the draft final rule and if it is approved transmits it to the Federal Register.

19. Publication of the final rule in the Federal Register. "This milestone of course consumes no OSHA resources, but the inevitable pre-enforcement court challenge under section 6(f) of the Act will consume at least a man-month of a project office and other OSHA personnel time, since the Office of Standards plays a substantial and necessary role in assisting the Solicitor's defense against such suits."

References

Agran, L. *The Cancer Connection.* Boston: Houghton Mifflin Company, 1977.

Allison, G. *Essence of Decision.* Boston: Little, Brown and Company, 1971.

American Bar Association Commission on Law and the Economy. *Federal Regulation: Roads to Reform.* Washington: American Bar Association, 1979.

Aronson, E. "The Theory of Cognitive Dissonance: A Current Perspective." In: L. Berkowitz (Ed.), *Cognitive Theories in Social Psychology.* New York: Academic Press, 1978.

Arthur Andersen and Company. *Cost of Government Regulation: Study for the Business Roundtable* (Summary). March, 1979.

Ashford, N. "Presentation on the scope of the occupational disease problem." In: Interdepartmental Workers' Compensation Task Force *Conference on Occupational Disease: Proceedings.* Washington: U.S. Government Printing Office, 1976(a).

Ashford, N. *Crisis in the Workplace: Occupational Disease and Injury.* Cambridge: MIT Press, 1976(b).

Ashford, N. "Testimony in U.S. Senate Committee on Governmental Affairs," *Regulatory Reform Legislation* (Part 1). Washington: U.S. Government Printing Office, 1979.

Auerbach, S. "Top Firms Woo Graduates of Leading Schools." *Washington Post,* November 25, 1977, A4.

B.F. Goodrich Company. "Vinyl Chloride and Cancer—A Study in Prevention." *Job Safety and Health,* February, 1977, 20-28.

Bainbridge, J. Telephone interview with the author, February 4, 1981.

Baram, Michael. "Cost-Benefit Analysis: An Inadequate Basis for Health, Safety, and Environmental Regulatory Decisionmaking." *Ecology Law Quarterly* **8** (1980): 473-531.

Bardach, E. *The Implementation Game.* Cambridge: MIT Press, 1977.

Barnard, C. *The Functions of the Executive.* Cambridge: Harvard University Press, 1938.

Behr, P. "FTC Surfacing After Business Attack." *Washington Post,* March 23, 1980(a), E1.

Behr, P. "Top FTC Official Quits, Charges Agency Giving In." *Washington Post,* May 28, 1980(b), D7.

Behr, P. "Reagan Team Takes Stock of Prospects for Reshaping Regulation." *Washington Post,* February 6, 1981, A2.

Behr, P., and Brown, M. "1-Year Moratorium Recommended on New Regulations." *Washington Post,* November 9, 1980, G1.

Bell, D. *The Coming of Post-Industrial Society.* New York: Basic Books, 1973.

Bell, D. *The Cultural Contradictions of Capitalism.* New York: Basic Books, 1976 (Harper Colophon Edition).

179

Bendix, R. *Work and Authority in Industry*. New York: John Wiley and Sons, 1956 (University of California Press Edition).

Benson, J. "Organizations: A Dialectical View." *Administrative Science Quarterly* **22** (1977): 1-21.

Berman, D. *Death on the Job*. New York: Monthly Review Press, 1978.

Bernstein, M. *Regulating Business By Independent Commission*. Princeton: Princeton University Press, 1955.

Berry, J. *Lobbying for the People*. Princeton: Princeton University Press, 1977.

Blot, W., Brinton, L., Fraumeni, J., and Stone, B. "Cancer Mortality in U.S. Counties with Petroleum Industries." *Science* **198** (1977): 51-53.

Bowles, S., and Gintis, H. *Schooling in Capitalist America*. New York: Basic Books, 1976 (Harper Colophon Edition).

Branscome, J. "White House Acts to Affirm TVA Air Clean-up Agreement." *Washington Post*, March 16, 1979, A2.

Breyer, S., and Stewart, R. *Administrative Law and Regulatory Policy*. Boston: Little, Brown, and Company, 1979.

Bridbord, K. Decoufle, P., Fraumeni, J., Hoel, D., Hoover, R., Rall, D., Saffiotti, U., Schneiderman, M., Upton, A. *Estimates of the Fraction of Cancer in the United States Related to Occupational Factors*. September 15, 1978 (Mimeo).

Brittan, S. "Inflation and Democracy." In: F. Hirsch and J. Goldthorpe (Eds.), *The Political Economy of Inflation*. Cambridge: Harvard University Press, 1978.

Broder, D. "3 Targets Set as Inflation Fight Opens." *Washington Post*, April 20, 1978, A1.

Brodeur, P. *Expendable Americans*. New York: Viking Press, 1974.

Bureau of National Affairs. *Occupational Safety and Health Reporter*. Washington: Bureau of National Affairs, 1972–1981.

Burnham, D. "Agency Lists But Does not Notify Workers Exposed to Carinogens." *New York Times*, April 25, 1977.

Business Week. "Government Intervention." April 4, 1977, 42-95.

Cahan, V. "The overhaul that could give OSHA Life under Reagan." *Business Week*, January 19, 1981, 88-89.

Cambridge Reports, Inc. *Public and Worker Attitudes Toward Carcinogens and Cancer Risks*. Cambridge: Cambridge Reports, Inc., 1978.

Center for Policy Alternatives. *Benefits of Environmental, Health, and Safety Regulation*. Washington: U.S. Government Printing Office, 1980.

Cohn, V. "The Cigarette Revolution: Health Officials Press for More." *Washington Post*, August 14, 1978, A9.

Cohn, V. "Switching to Low-Tar Cigarettes is Endorsed." *Washington Post*, January 13, 1981, A4.

Collins, R. *Conflict Sociology*. New York: Academic Press, 1975.

Corn, M. *Status Report on OSHA*. January 12, 1977 (Mimeo).

Crozier, M., Huntington, S., and Watanuki, J. *The Crisis of Democracy*. New York: New York University Press, 1975.

Culliton, B. "Government Says Cancer Rate is Increasing." *Science* **209** (1980): 998-1003.

Curry, B. "Consumer Agency to Take Up Options on Asbestos Products." *Washington Post*, April 28, 1977(a), A2.

Curry, B. "3 Products Called Hazardous." *Washington Post*, April 29, 1977(b), A5.

Curry, B. "Products Safety Commission: An Agency Tied Up in Knots." *Washington Post*, May 16, 1977(c), A1.

Cyert, R., and March, J. *A Behavioral Theory of the Firm*. Englewood Cliffs: Prentice-Hall, 1963.

Dahl, R. *Who Governs?* New Haven: Yale University Press, 1961.

Dahrendorf, R. *Class and Class Conflict in Industrial Society.* Stanford: Stanford University Press, 1959.

Data Resources, Inc. *The Macroeconomic Impact of Federal Pollution Control Programs: 1978 Assessment.* January 29, 1979 (Mimeo).

Davis, K. *Administrative Law and Government,* 2d ed. St. Paul: West Publishing Company, 1975.

DeMuth, C. "The White House Review Programs." *Regulation,* January-February, 1980(a), 13-26.

DeMuth, C. "The Regulatory Budget." *Regulation,* March-April, 1980(b), 29-44.

Denison, E. *Accounting For Slower Economic Growth.* Washington: The Brookings Institution, 1979.

Dewar, H. "Brown-Lung Curb Faces Cost Cutback." *Washington Post,* June 7, 1978(a), A1.

Dewar, H. "Carter Clears Way for Issuance of Cotton Dust Standard." *Washington Post,* June 8, 1978(b), A9.

Discher, D., Kleinman, G., and Foster, F. *Pilot Study for Development of an Occupational Disease Surveillance Method.* Rockville, Maryland: U.S. Department of Health, Education, and Welfare, 1975.

Diver, C. "A Theory of Regulatory Enforcement." *Public Policy,* **28** (1980): 257-299.

Edelman, M. *The Symbolic Use of Politics.* Urbana: University of Illinois Press, 1964.

Edelman, M. *Political Language.* New York: Academic Press, 1977.

Edsall, J. "Scientific Freedom and Responsibility." *Science* **188** (1975): 687-693.

Epstein, S. *The Politics of Cancer.* San Francisco: Sierra Club Books, 1978.

Fox, H., and Hammond, S. *Congressional Staffs.* New York: The Free Press, 1977.

Geber, A. "Safety Reps—Which Way Will the Cat Jump?" *Occupational Safety and Health,* October, 1978, 13-14.

Gellhorn, E. "The Wages of Zealotry: The FTC Under Siege." *Regulation,* January-February, 1980, 33-40.

Green, M., and Waitzman, N. *Business War on the Law: An Analysis of the Benefits of Safety and Health Regulation.* Washington: Corporate Accountability Research Group, 1979.

Habermas, J. *Legitimation Crisis.* Boston: Beacon Press, 1975.

Hayes, R., and Abernathy, W. "Managing Our Way to Economic Decline." *Harvard Business Review,* July-August, 1980, 67-77.

Health Research Group. *Survey of Occupational Health Efforts of Fifteen Major Labor Unions.* September, 1976 (Mimeo).

Heclo, H. *Modern Social Politics in Britain and Sweden.* New Haven: Yale University Press, 1974.

Heclo, H. *A Government of Strangers.* Washington: The Brookings Institution, 1977.

Hilts, P. "OSHA Head Fears Successor Will Kill Rules." *Washington Post,* November 23, 1980, A10.

Hirsch, F. *Social Limits to Growth.* Cambridge: Harvard University Press, 1977.

Hoover, R., and Fraumeni, J. "Cancer Mortality in U.S. Counties with Chemical Industries." *Environmental Research* **9** (1975): 196-207.

Hopkins, T. *An Evaluation of the Inflation Impact Statement Program Prepared for the Economic Policy Board.* Washington: U.S. Council on Wage and Price Stability, 1976.

Hornblower, M. "Major U.S. Industries Discover Profits Fighting Pollution." *Washington Post,* April 3, 1978, A2.

House, J. "The Effects of Occupational Stress on Physical Health." In: J. O'Toole (Ed.), *Work and the Quality of Life.* Cambridge: MIT Press, 1974.

Jaffe, L. "Federal Regulatory Agencies: Administrative Limitations in a Political Setting." *B.C. Industrial and Commercial Law Review* **11** (1970): 565-570.

Kasl, S. "Work and Mental Illness." In J. O'Toole (Ed.), *Work and the Quality of Life.* Cambridge: MIT Press, 1974.

Kasl, S., and Cobb, S. "Health Behavior, Illness Behavior, and Sick Role Behavior." *Archives of Environmental Health* **12** (1966): 246-266.

Katz, D., and Kahn, R. *The Social Psychology of Organizations,* 2d ed. New York: John Wiley and Sons, 1978.

Kaufman, H. *Red Tape: Its Origins, Uses, and Abuses.* Washington: The Brookings Institution, 1977.

Kelman, S. "Occupational Safety and Health Administration." In: J. Wilson (Ed.), *The Politics of Regulation.* New York: Basic Books, 1980.

Kochan, T., Dyer, L., and Lipsky, D. *The Effectiveness of Union-Management Safety Committees.* Kalamazoo: W.E. Upjohn Institute for Employment Research, 1977.

Kolata, G. "Love Canal: False Alarm Caused by Botched Study." *Science* **208** (1980): 1239-1242.

Kolko, G. *The Triumph of Conservatism.* New York: The Free Press, 1963 (Paperback Edition).

Kramer, L. "Paying the Price of Regulation." *Washington Post,* December 1, 1977, F9.

Kramer, L. "Consumer Movement Hits Mid-Stride." *Washington Post,* January 13, 1978(a), C9.

Kramer, L. "Pollution-Control Industry is Cleaning Up." *Washington Post,* October 15, 1978(b), F5.

Krause, E. Power and Illness. *The Political Sociology of Health and Medical Care.* New York: Elsevier, 1977.

Landis, J. *Report on Regulatory Agencies to the President-Elect.* Washington: U.S. Government Printing Office, 1960.

Larson, A. *The Law of Workmen's Compensation, Volume 1A.* New York: Mathew Bender, 1973.

Lenin, V. *State and Revolution.* New York: International Publishers, 1932.

Leone, R. "The Real Costs of Regulation." *Harvard Business Review,* November-December, 1977, 57-66.

Levine, D. "Exposure to Inorganic Arsenic in the Workplace." In: J. Miller III and B. Yandle (Eds.), *Benefit-Cost Analyses of Social Regulation: Case Studies from the Council on Wage and Price Stability.* Washington: American Enterprise Institute, 1979.

Liem, R., and Liem, J. "Social Class and Mental Illness Reconsidered: The Role of Economic Stress and Social Support." *Journal of Health and Social Behavior* **19** (1978): 139-156.

Lindblom, C. "The Science of 'Muddling Through.'" *Public Administration Review* **19** (1959): 79-88.

Lindblom, C. *Politics and Markets.* New York: Basic Books, 1977.

Lubar, R. "Making Democracy Less Inflation Prone." *Fortune,* September 22, 1980, 78-86.

Lukes, S. *Power: A Radical View.* London: The British Sociological Association, 1974.

MacAvoy, P. *The Regulated Industries and the Economy.* New York: W.W. Norton, 1979.

Malbin, M. "Congressional Committee Staffs: Who's In Charge Here?" *The Public Interest,* #47 (1976): 16-40.

Mancuso, T. "Occupational Cancer and Medical Causality." Paper delivered to the National Meeting of the International Association of Industrial Accident Boards and Commissions, New York, New York, September 10, 1979 (Mimeo).

March, J., and Simon, H. *Organizations.* New York: Wiley, 1958.

Marcus, A. "Environmental Protection Agency." In: J. Wilson (Ed.), *The Politics of Regulation.* New York: Basic Books, 1980.

Maugh II, T. "Cancer and the Environment: Higgenson Speaks Out." *Science* **205** (1979): 1363-1366.

McCaffrey, D. "A Test of OSHA's Recent Impacts on Injury Rates and Hazard Prevention Work." Proposal to the National Science Foundation, December 10, 1980.

McCarthy, J., and Zald, M. *The Trend of Social Movements in America: Professionalization and Resource Mobilization.* Morristown: General Learning Press, 1973.

McGarity, T. "Substantive and Procedural Discretion in Administrative Resolution of Science Policy Questions: Regulating Carcinogens in EPA and OSHA." *Georgetown Law Journal* **67** (1979): 729-810.

McNeil, P. "1975 Study at Hooker Plant Found Dangerous Emissions." *New York Times,* April 17, 1979: A1.

Mechanic, D. "Correlates of Physician Utilization: Why Do Major Multivariate Studies of Physician Utilization Find Trivial Psychosocial and Organizational Effects?" *Journal of Health and Social Behavior* 20 (1979): 387-396.

Mendeloff, J. *Regulating Safety.* Cambridge: MIT Press, 1979.

Miliband, R. *The State in Capitalist Society.* New York: Basic Books, 1969 (Harper Colophon Edition).

Miller III, J. "Lessons of the Economic Impact Statement Program." *Regulation,* July-August, 1977, 14-21.

Miller III, J., and Walton, T. "Protecting Workers' Hearing: An Economic Test for OSHA Initiatives." *Regulation,* September-October, 1980, 31-37.

Miller III, J., and Yandle, B. *Benefit-Cost Analyses of Social Regulation: Case Studies from the Council on Wage and Price Stability.* Washington: American Enterprise Institute, 1979.

Morrall III, J. "Exposure to Occupational Noise." In: J. Miller and B. Yandle (Eds.), *Benefit-Cost Analyses of Social Regulation: Case Studies from the Council on Wage and Price Stability.* Washington: American Enterprise Institute, 1979.

Morton, W. The Responsibility to Report Occupational Health Risks. *Journal of Occupational Medicine* **19** (1977): 258-260.

Mosher, F. *The GAO.* Boulder: Westview Press, 1979.

Moynihan, D. *Maximum Feasible Misunderstanding.* New York: The Free Press, 1970 (Paperback Edition).

Müller, W., and Neüsuss, C. 'The "Welfare State" Illusion and the Contradiction between Wage Labor and Capital.' In: J. Holloway and S. Picciotti (Eds.), *State and Capital: A Marxist Debate.* Austin: University of Texas Press, 1979.

Nichols, A., and Zeckhauser, R. "Government Comes to the Workplace: An Assessment of OSHA." *The Public Interest,* #49 (1977): 39-69.

Nichols, A., and Zeckhauser, R. "The Occupational Safety and Health Administration— An Overview." In: *Appendix to Volume VI,* U.S. Senate Committee on Governmental Affairs, *Study on Federal Regulation.* Washington: U.S. Government Printing Office, 1978.

O'Connell, J. *The Lawsuit Lottery.* New York: The Free Press, 1979.

O'Conner, J. *The Fiscal Crisis of the State.* New York: St. Martin's Press, 1973 (Paperback Edition).

Offe, C. "Structural Problems of the Capitalist State." In: K. von Beyme (Ed.), *German Political Studies, I.* Beverly Hills: Sage Publishing Co., 1974.

Offe, C. "The Theory of the Capitalist State and the Problem of Policy Formation." In L. Lindberg, R. Alford, and C. Offe (Eds.), *Stress and Contradiction in Modern Capitalism.* Lexington: D.C. Heath, 1975.

Offe, C. 'Crisis of "Crisis Management:" Elements of a Political Crisis Theory.' *International Journal of Politics* **6** (1976): 29-67.

Omang, J. "Bill Seeks Less Friendly Forum for Environmental Suits." *Washington Post,* March 27, 1980(a), A14.

Omang, J. "Love Canal Residents Get Joyless Ride." *Washington Post,* July 26, 1980(b), A1.

Omang, J. "EPA Chief's Farewell." *Washington Post,* December 14, 1980(c), A2.

Omang, J. "Report Says Clean Air Act Won't Hinder Nation's Energy Development Program." *Washington Post,* January 21, 1981, A2.

Pearlin, L., and Schooler, C. "The Structure of Coping." *Journal of Health and Social Behavior* **19** (1978): 2-21.

Perrow, C. *Complex Organizations: A Critical Essay.* Glenview: Scott, Foresman, and Company, 1972.

Perry, C. "Vinyl Chloride Protection: Less Costly than Predicted." *Monthly Labor Review,* August, 1980, 22-24.

Peterson, B., and Shinoff, P. "Firms Had Sterility Data on Pesticide," *Washington Post,* August 23, 1977, **A1.**

Piven, F., and Cloward, R. *Regulating the Poor.* New York: Random House, 1971 (Vintage Books Edition).

Piven, F., and Cloward, R. *Poor People's Movements.* New York: Random House, 1977 (Vintage Books Edition).

Pollack, E., and Horm, J. "Trends in Cancer Incidence and Mortality." *Journal of the National Cancer Institute* **64** (1980): 1091-1103.

Polsby, N. *Community Power and Political Theory.* New Haven: Yale University Press, 1963.

Posner, R. "A Theory of Negligence." *Journal of Legal Studies* **1** (1972): 29-96.

Poulantzas, N. *Political Power and Social Classes.* London: New Left Books, 1973 (Verso Edition).

Poulantzas, N. *State, Power, and Socialism.* London: New Left Books, 1978.

President's Toxic Substances Strategy Committee. *Toxic Chemicals and Public Protection.* Washington: U.S. Government Printing Office, 1980.

Price, D. Workers' Compensation Programs in the 1970's. *Social Security Bulletin,* May, 1979, 3-24.

Quarles, J. *Cleaning Up America.* Boston: Houghton Mifflin Co., 1976.

Quinn, R., and Staines, G. *The 1977 Quality of Employment Survey.* Ann Arbor: Univ. of Michigan Survey Research Center, 1978.

Reddig, W. "Industry's Preemptive Strike Against Cancer." *Fortune,* February 13, 1978, 116-119.

Reich, R. "Toward a New Consumer Protection." *University of Pennsylvania Law Review.* **128** (1979): 1-40.

Reid, T.R. "Liberal Leaders, Foot Soldiers Gird for Battles in the Reagan Era." *Washington Post,* February 6, 1981, A2.

Richards, B. 'Arsenic: A Dark Cloud Over "Big Sky Country."' *Washington Post,* February 3, 1976, A1.

Richards, B. "Pesticide Act Enforcement Bogged Down." *Washington Post,* September 12, 1977, A1.

Richards, B. "New Data on Asbestos Indicate Cover-Up of Effects on Workers." *Washington Post,* November 12, 1978, A1.

Robbins, A., and Froines, J. "On the Mission of NIOSH." *American Journal of Public Health* **69** (1979): 957.

Rosenstock, J. "Prevention of Illness and Maintenance of Health." In: J. Kosa and K. Zola (Eds.), *Poverty and Health.* Cambridge: Harvard University Press, 1975.

Rourke, F. *Bureaucracy, Politics, and Public Policy.* Boston: Little, Brown, and Company, 1976.

Royston, M. "Making Pollution Prevention Pay." *Harvard Business Review*, November-December, 1980, 6-22.

Rubenstein, M. "Norway's New Worker Safety Law Sets Pace in Western Europe." *World of Work Report*, June, 1977, 69-71.

Sabatier, P. "Social Movements and Regulatory Agencies: Toward a More Adequate—and Less Pessimistic—Theory of "Clientele Capture."' *Policy Sciences* **6** (1975): 301-342.

Sakolsky, R. "The Capitalist State and the Origins and Development of Public Administration." *Dialogue* **2** (1980): 2-16.

Schnaiberg, A. "Obstacles to Environmental Research by Scientists and Technologists." *Social Problems* **24** (1977): 500-520.

Schumpeter, J. *Capitalism, Socialism, and Democracy*. New York: Harper and Row, 1942 (Harper Torchbook Edition).

Scott, R. "Danger of Low-Level Benzene Reported." *Washington Post*, June 11, 1978, A1.

Segel, F., and Dreiling, J. "Pollution Abatement and Control Expenditures, 1972-1976." *Survey of Current Business*, February, 1978, 12-16.

Selznick, P. "Leadership in Administration." In: A. Etzioni (Ed.), *Reader in Complex Organizations*. Englewood Cliffs: Prentice-Hall, 1969.

Shabecoff, P. "Some in EPA Assail White House Moves." *New York Times*, February 22, 1979.

Shapley, D. "Occupational Cancer: Government Challenged in Beryllium Proceeding." *Science* **198** (1977): 898-901.

Shinoff, P. "University Pesticide Data Went to Firms." *Washington Post*, October 19, 1977, A17.

Smith, R.J. "Toxic Substances: EPA and OSHA are Reluctant Regulators." *Science* **203** (1979): 28-32.

Smith, R.S. *The Occupational Safety and Health Act*. Washington: American Enterprise Institute, 1976.

Sommers, P. *The Economic Costs of Regulation: Report for the American Bar Association Commission on Law and the Economy*. Department of Economics, Yale University, January, 1978.

Stallones, R., and Downs, T. *A Critical Overview of: Estimates of the Fraction of Cancer in the United States Related to Occupational Factors*. Undated, provided by American Industrial Health Council, Washington, D.C.

Steinbruner, J. *The Cybernetic Theory of Decision*. Princeton: Princeton University Press, 1974.

Stewart, R. "The Reformation of American Administrative Law." *Harvard Law Review* **88** (1975): 1669–1813.

Stone, A. *Economic Regulation and the Public Interest*. Ithaca: Cornell University Press, 1977.

Systemedics, Inc. *Development of Policy Options for Requiring Monitoring and Medical Examinations for Workers Exposed to Toxic Substances*. U.S. Department of Labor Contract #J-9-F-6-0218, 1977.

Taylor, E. 'Echoes of "Silent Spring."' *Trial*, November, 1976, 38-40.

Thaler, R., and Rosen, S. "The Value of Saving a Life: Evidence from the Labor Market." In: Nestor Terleckyj (Ed.), *Household Production and Consumption*. New York: National Bureau of Economic Research, 1975.

Throdahl, M. "Increasing Government Involvement in the Chemical Industry." *Vital Speeches*, March 1, 1978, 294-296.

Thurow, L. *The Zero-Sum Society*. New York: Basic Books, 1980.

U.S. Council on Wage and Price Stability. *Exposure to Coke Oven Emissions Proposed Standard*. May 11, 1976 (Mimeo).

U.S. Council on Wage and Price Stability. *Comments on Proposed Standard for Exposure to Cotton Dust.* June 20, 1977 (Mimeo).

U.S. Council on Wage and Price Stability. *Report on Proposed Standard for Occupational Exposure to Acrylonitrile.* May 22, 1978(a) (Mimeo).

U.S. Council on Wage and Price Stability. *Occupational Safety and Health Administration's Proposal for the Identification, Classification, and Regulation of Toxic Substances Posing a Potential Occupational Carcinogenic Risk: Report of the Regulatory Analysis Review Group.* October 24, 1978(b) (Mimeo).

U.S. Department of Health, Education, and Welfare: National Cancer Institute. *Atlas of Cancer Mortality for U.S. Counties.* Washington: U.S. Government Printing Office, 1975.

U.S. Department of Health, Education, and Welfare: NIOSH (National Institute for Occupational Safety and Health). *The Right to Know.* July, 1977 (Mimeo).

U.S. Department of Labor: ASPER (Assistant Secretary for Policy, Evaluation, and Research). *Report to the Congress on Occupational Disease* (Draft). September, 1979 (Mimeo).

U.S. Department of Labor: Bureau of Labor Statistics. *Occupational Injuries and Illnesses in the United States by Industry, 1976.* Bulletin 2019, 1979.

U.S. Department of Labor: OSHA (Occupational Safety and Health Administration). "Carcinogens." *Federal Register,* January 29, 1974, 3756-3797.

U.S. Department of Labor: OSHA (Occupational Safety and Health Administration). "Exposure to Coke Oven Emissions." *Federal Register,* October 22, 1976, 46742–46790.

U.S. Department of Labor: OSHA (Occupational Safety and Health Administration). "Occupational Exposure to 1,2-Dibromo-3-chloropropane (DBCP)." *Federal Register,* March 17, 1978(a), 11514-11533.

U.S. Department of Labor: OSHA (Occupational Safety and Health Administration). "Occupational Exposure to Inorganic Arsenic." *Federal Register,* May 5, 1978(b), 19584-19631.

U.S. Department of Labor: OSHA (Occupational Safety and Health Administration). "Occupational Exposure to Cotton Dust." June 19, 1978(c) (Mimeo).

U.S. Department of Labor: OSHA (Occupational Safety and Health Administration). "Occupational Exposure to Acrylonitrile (Vinyl Cyanide) Final Standard." *Federal Register,* October 3, 1978(d), 45762-45819.

U.S. Department of Labor: OSHA (Occupational Safety and Health Administration). "Occupational Exposure to Lead: Attachments to the Preamble for the Final Standard." *Federal Register,* November 21, 1978(e), 54354-54509.

U.S. Department of Labor: OSHA (Occupational Safety and Health Administration). "Identification, Classification, and Regulation of Potential Occupational Carcinogens." *Federal Register,* January 22, 1980, 5002-5296.

U.S. Department of Labor: OSHA (Occupational Safety and Health Administration). "Hazards Identification; Notice of Proposed Rulemaking and Public Hearings." *Federal Register,* January 16, 1981, 4412-4453.

U.S. Environmental Protection Agency. *Smarter Regulation.* Washington: Environmental Protection Agency, January, 1981.

U.S. General Accounting Office. *Slow Progress Likely in the Development of Standards for Toxic Substances and Harmful Physical Agents Found in Workplaces.* September 28, 1973, #B-163375.

U.S. General Accounting Office. *Answers to Questions on the Issuance of An Emergency Temporary Standard for Certain Chemicals Considered to be Carcinogens.* January 6, 1975(a), #B-179768.

U.S. General Accounting Office. *Emergency Temporary Standards on Organophosphorous Pesticides.* February 24, 1975(b), #MWD-75-55.

U.S. General Accounting Office. *Federal Efforts to Protect the Public from Cancer-Causing Chemicals Are Not Very Effective.* June 16, 1976(a), #MWD-76-59.

U.S. General Accounting Office. *Better Data on Severity and Causes of Worker Safety and Health Problems Should be Obtained from Workplaces.* August 12, 1976(b), #HRD-76-118.

U.S. General Accounting Office. *Delays in Setting Workplace Standards for Cancer Causing and Other Dangerous Substances.* May 10, 1977(a), #HRD-77-71.

U.S. General Accounting Office. *Government Regulatory Activity: Justifications, Processes, Impacts, and Alternatives.* June 3, 1977(b), #PAD-77-34.

U.S. General Accounting Office. *Sporadic Workplace Inspections for Lethal and Other Serious Health Hazards.* April 5, 1978(a), #HRD-77-143.

U.S. General Accounting Office. *Health Hazard Evaluation Program Needs Improvement.* May 18, 1978(b), #HRD-78-13.

U.S. General Accounting Office. *Workplace Inspection Program Weak in Detecting and Correcting Serious Hazards.* May 19, 1978(c), #HRD-78-34.

U.S. General Accounting Office. *How Effective are OSHA's Complaint Procedures?* April 9, 1979, #HRD-79-48.

U.S. House Committee on Education and Labor. *Occupational Safety and Health Act of 1970 (Oversight and Proposed Amendments).* Washington: U.S. Government Printing Office, 1974.

U.S. House Committee on Education and Labor. *Oversight Hearings on the Occupational Safety and Health Act—Part 2.* Washington: U.S. Government Printing Office, 1976.

U.S. House Committee on Government Operations. *Performance of the Occupational Safety and Health Administration.* Washington: U.S. Government Printing Office, 1977.

U.S. Office of Management and Budget. *Materials on President Reagan's Program of Regulatory Relief,* June 13, 1981.

U.S. Senate Committee on Commerce. *Toxic Substance Control Act.* Washington: U.S. Government Printing Office, 1975.

U.S. Senate Committee on Environment and Public Works. *Executive Branch Review of Environmental Regulations.* Washington: U.S. Government Printing Office, 1979.

U.S. Senate Committee on Governmental Affairs. *Study on Federal Regulation, Volumes I-VI.* Washington: U.S. Government Printing Office, 1977-1978.

U.S. Senate Committee on Governmental Affairs. *Regulatory Reform Legislation, Parts 1 and 2.* Washington: U.S. Government Printing Office, 1979.

U.S. Senate Committee on Human Resources. *Monitoring of Industrial Workers Exposed to Carcinogens, 1977.* Washington: U.S. Government Printing Office, 1978.

U.S. Senate Committee on the Judiciary. *The Environmental Protection Agency and the Regulation of Pesticides.* Washington: U.S. Government Printing Office, 1976.

U.S. Supreme Court. *Industrial Union Department, AFL-CIO and Ray Marshall, Secretary of Labor, vs. American Petroleum Institute et al., July 2, 1980.*

Vogel, D. "America's Management Crisis." *The New Republic,* February 7, 1981, 21-23.

Weaver, P. "Regulation, Social Policy, and Class Conflict." *The Public Interest,* #50 (1978): 45-63.

Weaver, S. *Decision to Prosecute.* Cambridge: MIT Press, 1977.

Wehrwein, A. "Court Backs Minnesota Firm on Dumping Site." *Washington Post,* April 9, 1977, A4.

Weidenbaum, M., and DeFina, R. *The Cost of Federal Regulation of Economic Activity.* American Enterprise Institute Reprint #88, May, 1978.

Weinstein, J. *The Corporate Ideal in the Liberal State, 1900-1918.* Boston: Beacon Press, 1968.

Weisbrod, B., Handler, J., and Komesar, N. *Public Interest Law: An Economic and Institutional Analysis.* Berkeley: University of California Press, 1978.

Whitt, J.A. "Toward a Class-Dialectical Model of Power." *American Sociological Review* **44** (1979): 81-99.

Wildavsky, A. *The Politics of the Budgetary Process,* 2d ed. Boston: Little, Brown, 1974.

Wrenn, G. Testimony before the National Advisory Committee on Occupational Safety and Health. April 6, 1977 (Transcript).

Wright, D. "Intergovernmental Relations: An Analytical Overview." *Annals of the American Academy of Political and Social Science,* #416, 1974.

Wright, E. *Class, Crisis, and the State.* London: New Left Books, 1978 (Verso Edition).

Wright, J., and Hamilton, R. 'Work Satisfaction and Age: Some Evidence for the "Job Change" Hypothesis.' *Social Forces* **56** (1978): 1140-1158.

Index